Magic Is All Around You

The natural world is not a place apart from the world of magic—they are one and the same. When you know the magical reality behind the physical form of the stars, rocks, trees, and animals, you are on your way to mastering natural magic.

This major new work reunites the diverse elements of the ancient tradition of Western natural magic. Acclaimed occultist John Michael Greer gives you all you need to know to master the magical world. For example, *Natural Magic* contains:

- An encyclopedia detailing the magical uses of the world's resources
- Complete instructions for making potions, amulets, and more
- Directions for making a Natural Magic Kit
- A guide to magical gardens, from boxes to backyards
- The philosophy, framework, and ethics of natural magic
- Connections to alchemy and ritual magic

Just as we all share the world, anyone can share in the treasure-trove of magic that exists everywhere—from the sky to the deep caverns of the Earth.

Natural Magic

Potions and Powers
from the Magical Garden

John Michael Greer

2000
Llewellyn Publications
St. Paul, Minnesota 55164-0383, U.S.A.

First Edition
First Printing, 2000

Book design and editing by Rebecca Zins
Cover design by William Merlin Cannon
Interior illustrations by Nyease Somersett

Library of Congress Cataloging-in-Publication Data
Greer, John Michael.
    Natural magic: potions and powers from the magical garden / John Michael Greer.—1st ed.
        p.   cm.
    Includes bibliographical references and index.
    ISBN 1-56718-295-X
    1. Magic.   2. Nature—Miscellanea.   I. Title.

BF1621.G745 2000
133.4'3 2 21

00-021538

Llewellyn Worldwide does not participate in, endorse, or have any authority or responsibility concerning private business transactions between our authors and the public.
    All mail addressed to the author is forwarded but the publisher cannot, unless specifically instructed by the author, give out an address or phone number.

Llewellyn Publications
A Division of Llewellyn Worldwide, Ltd.
P.O. Box 64383, Dept. K295-X
St. Paul, MN 55164-0383, U.S.A.
www.llewellyn.com

 Printed in the United States of America on recycled paper

Other Books by John Michael Greer

Circles of Power:
Ritual Magic in the Western Tradition

Earth Divination, Earth Magic:
A Practical Guide to Geomancy

Inside a Magical Lodge:
Group Ritual in the Western Tradition

Paths of Wisdom:
Principles and Practice of the Magical Cabala
in the Western Tradition

For Sara,
la migliora fabbra

Contents

Acknowledgments

In the course of my explorations of natural magic, many people have provided help and advice, not to mention access to materials, documents, and resources. Special thanks are owed to my wife Sara, herself an accomplished magician, herbalist, and gardener, whose help and support in this (as in all my projects) has been essential; to Carl Hood, Jr., friend and fellow student of the Mysteries, for help in unraveling the fine points of medieval theories of natural magic; to the Interlibrary Loan department of the Seattle Public Library, who time and again managed to find me the books I needed, no matter how long out of print or obscure they were; and to Kachi and Richard of Dandelion Botanical Company, the best herb store in Seattle, who provided not only the raw materials for my magical experiments but an always-pleasant place to chat about herbs and the progress of this project.

PART 1

THE
NATURAL
MAGIC
TRADITION

The Philosophy of Natural Magic

What is natural magic? If you ask students and scholars of the occult this fairly simple question, you'll get a good many answers.

One you're likely to get quite often, at least among people who practice magic, is that it's the branch of magic dealing with the subtle powers of herbs, stones, and other material substances. This is true as far as it goes but—as we'll see a little later on—it doesn't go far enough.

Another common answer, this time among people within the academic community, is that natural magic is an early, primitive, and ineffective attempt at the sort of thinking that led to modern technology: that is, natural magicians sought to discover and use the less obvious properties of matter, but didn't know the right way to go about it. Common though this notion is in some circles, it's almost completely off base. While it's true that the natural magician and the scientist both study the material world, they do so on the basis of completely different perspectives and approaches—and neither one of these approaches, as we'll show, is "better" or "more advanced" than the other.

Another answer one hears very often is that natural magic is the kind of magic practiced by folk magicians and wise women of the peasantry in earlier times, while magicians from the educated classes devoted themselves to ceremonial magic, alchemy, and the like. Again, though this latter notion is very common, it's actually the most incorrect of the three. While it's indeed true that an enormous amount of Western natural magic has roots in folk tradition and peasant lore, there is an equally large amount of natural magic connected to the more scholarly Hermetic and Cabalistic magical traditions as well.

For centuries, in fact, natural magic was the way most people approached *all* their dealings with the physical world. It was universally practiced and completely accepted throughout every level of society in the Western world. Even in the years when practicing ritual magic could bring a visit from the Inquisition, most kinds of natural magic wouldn't get you a raised eyebrow, even from the Church. Men and women of every station in life, from peasants to kings and queens, used herbs in natural magic as readily as they used them in cooking and medicine, wore different kinds of jewelry as much for their magical effects as for their esthetic qualities, and paid attention to the phases of the moon and the direction of the wind as much to gauge their magical messages as for any purpose that a more modern perspective would consider "practical."

Yet "practical" is one of the words that best describes natural magic. Most of the traditions of natural magic that have come down to us from the past are aimed at helping us deal with the events and situations of everyday life. People in earlier times relied constantly on natural magic to heal illnesses and protect crops, hunt game and seek lovers, bring success and banish misfortune. Along with these purposes went other subtler or stranger ones: ways of using natural magic to invite the presence of nature spirits, banish hostile entities, lay ghosts to rest, and commune with deities. Those who practiced ritual magic of various kinds also made use of natural magic as a source of additional power; when a modern Hermetic magician burns frankincense in a solar ritual, or a Wiccan priestess wears a moon crown made of silver, both are following in the footsteps of much older magical practitioners by making use of natural magic.

The Worldview of Natural Magic

To try to understand natural magic is to enter into territory that is at once very familiar and very strange to most modern people—even to most modern magicians, for that matter. It is familiar because much of natural magic has remained a living part of folktales, country lore, common habit, and traditions of magic that have survived to the present or been reconstructed in recent times. It is strange because those practices are based on an ancient way of thinking about the universe, and very little of that way of thinking is easily accessible to most people in our present culture.

The loss of contact with these ancient, magical ways of thinking has given rise to any number of attempts to explain magic in modern terms—that is, of accepting the way of looking at the world that is demanded by modern scientific ideas of reality, and then trying to find some way to fit magic into the cracks and corners of that worldview. There's a certain value to such projects, but this is not the approach that will be taken here. Instead, as in my other books, I hope to present not only magical techniques but also *the magical way of looking at the world*.

This way is just as useful, in its own terms, as the modern scientific one, and it allows the magician not only to learn the *how* of magic but to understand the *why* of it as well. It differs from the more common ways of thinking about the universe in our present culture, but that does not necessarily count as a mark against it! It's important to remember that worldviews are never "true" in any kind of ultimate sense; they are simply mental models, created by human beings in the hope of making some sense of an infinitely complex universe.

When we think about our experience from within a particular worldview, we are using that worldview the way a traveler uses a map. Metaphorically, we are trying to draw connections between the roads and towns we encounter and the lines and marks the map shows us, and then using those connections to help us find our way to the places we want to go. One of the things this metaphor points out is that different journeys and different regions of human experience require different maps—if you want to travel in the Rocky Mountains, for example, a map of New York City isn't going to do you much good. In the same way, if you want to understand the subtle and nonmaterial forces behind magic, a worldview created to explain the more predictable events of the purely material side of the cosmos (which is what the "map" of science does) isn't going to do you much good either.

Let's take this metaphor a little further. Imagine someone who has a map of New York City, and insists that it's the only "true" map. To give him credit, his map is quite a good map of New York City, and he seems to be able to find his way around Manhattan and the Bronx very well. Still, he insists that all other maps are completely false; not only that, but every place that doesn't appear on his map is imaginary, as far as he is concerned, and doesn't exist anywhere at all. He speaks scornfully of the "superstitious" people who believe in Philadelphia and Boston, not to mention those who talk about Tokyo or Tel Aviv, and when people tell him that they have been to these places, he is sure that they are either lying or insane.

Sounds bizarre, doesn't it? Yet this is precisely the sort of thinking used by those people who insist that one worldview (for example, the modern scientific one) is "true" and all others are "false." To return to the metaphor, such people mix up the map with the territory, and the result is almost unlimited confusion.

Fortunately, the scientific map isn't the only one we have. Back before the Scientific Revolution, in the heady days of the Renaissance—the last time in Western history, until the present, when magical philosophy could be taught and discussed openly on a large scale—people thought deeply about the nature of magic, and asked themselves what the universe must be like in order for magical workings to have the effects they do. They drew on raw material from more ancient traditions and teachings—from ancient Greece and Rome, from the Arabic world, and from the thought and magical practice of the Middle Ages—and hammered it together into a coherent, consistent, and meaningful worldview, one that made sense of magic and of the way magic relates to the individual and the universe alike. The "map" they created is the one we'll be using in this book.

Natural Magic is intended as a practical manual rather than a textbook of occult philosophy, so only a small part of the magical worldview—the part that's needed to understand and practice natural magic effectively—will be covered here. Still, it's important to remember that the material included in this book isn't simply a random collection of superstitions, as some people might think. Rather, it's the practical side of a deeply meaningful philosophy of life. It's also one part of a way of living harmoniously in the world—a way that most modern people have utterly forgotten, and that our age desperately needs to relearn.

The Philosophy of Natural Magic

The core insight of the traditional philosophy of magic is that all the different things we experience—whether we classify these as thoughts, emotions, dream images, energies, material objects, or what have you—are simply different forms or manifestations of the same essential, indescribable "stuff," and that this "stuff" is ultimately identical with consciousness itself. Just as the spectrum of light runs from red through all the colors of the rainbow to violet, the spectrum of consciousness runs from the densest kinds of matter through many different levels up to the most subtle and abstract forms of spirit. Everything exists on all these levels at once; thus, when we experience a material object, what we're perceiving is simply one end of a pattern that reaches all the way up to the heights of spirit.

This last concept is not just an abstract notion; it has practical consequences. To the magician, the visible part of a material object is only the most obvious part of a complex reality that exists simultaneously on all levels of being, and the other parts of that reality can be put to use for magical purposes by working with their material manifestation.

Consider, for instance, a piece of quartz crystal. (If you have one available, you may want to get it out and put it in the palm of your hand before reading further.) The crystal you're holding has a physical dimension, obviously enough; you can see the crystal, touch it, tap it on a hard surface and make a noise you can hear, and experience it in the same ways as you would any other material object.

Scientists will tell you that this material aspect of the crystal consists of silicon dioxide molecules bound together according to a particular geometrical structure—and in a physical sense, they're quite correct. This is not the whole of the quartz crystal, however. It also exists in several other ways—or, as magicians often say, on several other levels.

To start with, it also has an *etheric* existence—that is, it exists as a lattice of subtle energies, a structure of forces, which holds the material crystal together. These subtle energies are of great importance, and not just in magic. They are deeply linked with life and breath, and play a central role in many Eastern spiritual disciplines, martial arts, and healing practices. These days, many people in the West have heard of *ch'i, ki,* or *prana,* which are respectively the Chinese, Japanese, and Sanskrit words for subtle energy. Quite a few people have even practiced one or another of the Eastern martial arts, meditative practices, or healing disciplines that rely on subtle energy.

Despite the aura of Oriental mystery that sometimes surrounds such practices, etheric energies themselves aren't exotic—they surround us at every moment—or particularly hard to experience. If you pick up your crystal in one hand and move the point in the air a quarter inch or so from the palm of your other hand, you're likely to feel something like a faint breeze or a tingling against your skin. This is one manifestation of the etheric side of the crystal—a vortex of flowing etheric energy that streams out from the crystal lattice at either end. There are many other ways to experience the etheric level; in fact, it's only because our culture ignores them so systematically, and teaches us as children to do the same, that they aren't a matter of everyday awareness.

The crystal also exists on other levels besides the physical and etheric. We can speak of the *astral* aspect of the crystal, which represents another mode of subtle energy—an energy that can best be described as "concrete consciousness" or "consciousness of form." As the word "astral" implies, this level is strongly affected by the astrological tides of force that sweep through our solar system. In particular, the astral manifestation of quartz crystal resonates most strongly with the patterns of energy set in motion by the cycles of the Moon.

There is also what magicians call the *mental* aspect of the crystal, the abstract pattern of quartz crystal, beyond space and time, in the mental realm of "abstract consciousness" or "consciousness of essence." Finally, there is the *spiritual* aspect of the crystal, the root essence of quartz crystal itself at the highest level of being. In the Cabala, the traditional philosophy of Western high magic, the mental aspect of quartz crystal relates to *Yesod,* the ninth Sphere of the Tree of Life, called the Treasure House of Images; the spiritual aspect, in turn, relates to *Shaddai El Chai,* the ninth manifestation of the unknowable Unity and the Divine Name attributed to Yesod.

All this may seem a long way from the simple experience of a piece of quartz crystal resting in the palm of your hand. The crucial teaching of the magical philosophy, though, is that this sense of distance is an illusion. *All the different levels of being are present in every object at every moment.* The crystal you hold is all of these things, all at once: a collection of molecules, a lattice of etheric forces, a swirl of lunar energy, a ray from the Tree of Life, an emanation of the Absolute. As the poet-mystic William Blake wrote, "If the doors of perception were cleansed, everything would appear to man as it is, infinite." This is the essential viewpoint of natural magic.

Currents of Magical Power

The connection between these different aspects of the quartz crystal, or of anything else, needs to be clearly understood; the current magical revival has seen a certain amount of sloppy thinking on such points, and the result has been a good deal of unnecessary confusion. To say that the crystal is a complex unity existing on all these different levels is not the same thing as saying that all these levels are identical, or even that they follow the same rules. For example, even though on the other four levels, things can pass through one another without difficulty, trying the same thing on the physical level is a bad idea; if you try to walk through a solid wall, you'll get nothing but a bruised nose—unless you have a bulldozer go through first!

The physical level, according to magical teaching, is the realm of maximum manifestation; the spiritual level, that of maximum potential. Between these two extremes, patterns of what we can call magical energy flow from potentiality into manifestation; the spiritual level is the source of these patterns, and the physical level is where they "ground out" in concrete forms of matter and energy. In magical parlance, the flowing patterns of energy are sometimes called "currents," and although this is a metaphor at best—just like the red ink lines that indicate highways on a map—it communicates much about how these patterns actually function in a magical context.

To the natural magician, the crucial point about the currents of power is that different currents come into manifestation by way of different physical forms. The current of power associated with the Sun, for example, has its manifestations in various material substances—metallic gold, plants such as St. John's Wort and bay laurel, resins such as frankincense, and so on. Most of these things, by contrast, have very little to do with the currents associated with the other planetary forces of astrology, although there are exceptions: rosemary, for instance, has a significant link to the Moon as well as to the Sun. Since different energies ground out in different substances, then, it follows that by selecting and using the right substances, it's possible to bring any desired energy into focus in a given place and time.

According to magical philosophy, this is what natural magic actually is. The natural magician works with physical things—herbs and stones, oils and resins, gems and woods, winds and water—because he or she knows that these things, even the most humble, reach all the way up the spectrum of being to the highest realms of spirit and link into the currents of force that surge from spirit down to matter. Working with the forces of the other levels through their material manifestations, the natural magician weaves a web of power to reshape the universe of his or her experience in accordance with will.

This approach is somewhat different from the way of ritual magic, though both derive from the same magical philosophy. The ritual magician works, not with the manifestation of the currents of magical power in matter, but rather with the currents themselves as they take shape on other levels. Using ceremony, symbolism, and an array of intensively practiced disciplines of consciousness, the ritual magician becomes directly aware of the mental, astral, and etheric levels of being, and shapes the forces of these realms to his or her will.

Often, however, ritual magicians use some of the tools of natural magic, such as burning incense that corresponds to the forces they seek to invoke, wearing robes or lighting candles of an appropriate color, and so on. Equally, many natural magicians use some of the tools of ritual—for example, reciting invocations or charms to help attune themselves to the powers they weave. Both of these, in turn, can be brought together with the tools of the spiritual realm—meditation, contemplation, and prayer—in order to perform magical workings that reach from end to end of the universe of our experience.

The Universe of Natural Magic

It's important to remember that, as pointed out above, all these different levels are part of the universe we experience every day. There's a tendency nowadays, fostered by the fantasy novels that often spark people's first interest in magic, to think of magic as something that really belongs to the realms of faraway and long ago, not to the prosaic world of our ordinary lives. The truth is quite different. Since all the different levels of being are present here and now, in everything around us, the world we experience every day is a magical world, pulsing with hidden powers and connections. It's simply the blindness fostered by our culture that makes most of us unable to see the magic all around us.

It's possible for a skilled magician to learn to sense the currents and patterns of power directly—in fact, this is an important part of magical training—but in the elementary and intermediate levels of training, some help to the intuition is usually needed. Even if you're naturally intuitive and have an innate sense of astral patterns, it's a good idea to have some way to check your perceptions and make sure they are coming through clearly. In traditional natural magic, this is done by the use of correspondences.

What are correspondences? In the terms we've used above, a system of correspondences is a set of categories used to understand the currents of magical power. To say, for example, that an herb, a tree, or a stone corresponds to the Sun is to say that the magical energies within the material substance are part of the same current as those that stream through the Sun. Different things that share the same correspondences usually have energies that resonate well together, and so they can be used to strengthen and reinforce each others' magical effects. By contrast, things with different correspondences may not work well together, and in some cases will counteract one another.

It would probably take any one person more than a lifetime to work out the relationships among the most commonly used magical substances, to say nothing of the rare materials sometimes discussed in the old lore. Fortunately, the vast majority of this basic work was done many centuries ago, and forms the basis of the traditional correspondences used in natural magic. One result is that these correspondences contain, in compressed form, thousands of years of knowledge about the magical effects of different substances. It's for this reason that learning to understand and work with correspondences is such an important part of training in the art of natural magic.

The most important set of correspondences in natural magic is based on the system of seven planets, twelve zodiacal signs, and four elements used in astrology; these represent a selection of major currents of magical force large enough for general use but small enough to be easily learned and memorized. It may seem strange that natural magic, so solidly rooted in the Earth, would depend on the movements of stars and planets in the heavens. There is an important lesson here, though. In natural magic, everything is connected to everything else by subtle links; the flowers that grow on curbside weeds, seen with a magician's vision, are one with the splendor of the midnight sky. Ultimately, as the traditional lore of magic teaches, everything is part of a single gesture of the Infinite. It's from this fact that natural magic takes its power.

The Magical Microcosm

The patterns of astrological symbolism mentioned above are not limited to the universe outside the surface of our skins. They also exist within us. Central to traditional magical philosophy is a concept called the Principle of Macrocosm and Microcosm, which holds that each human being is a complete reflection of the entire universe, and vice versa. (The word *macrocosm* means "great universe" and refers to the cosmos around us, while *microcosm* means "little universe" and refers to the individual human being.)

This principle has sometimes been understood in a naively literal way but, as Plato pointed out a long time ago, this doesn't work very well; the universe, after all, doesn't have feet. Understood in a more useful way, what the Principle of Macrocosm and Microcosm implies is that every magical energy in the universe has its exact equivalent inside every human being.

The natural magicians and occult philosophers of the past worked these equivalences out in great detail, mapping them onto every level of the human microcosm. The relationship between astrological factors and patterns of personality is well known, and forms much of the basis of astrological interpretation. The correspondences in the traditional lore don't stop here, though. Each region of the physical body, for example, corresponds to a sign of the zodiac:

Aries—head

Taurus—neck

Gemini—arms, lungs

Cancer—stomach, upper abdomen

Leo—heart

Virgo—belly, intestines

Scorpio—genitals

Libra—hips

Sagittarius—thighs

Capricorn—knees

Aquarius—ankles

Pisces—feet

Each of the planets, in the same way, relates to part of the body, and also to one of the seven sensory openings of the head:

Saturn—right foot, right ear

Jupiter—head, left ear

Mars—right hand, right nostril

Sun—chest, right eye

Venus—belly and genitals, left nostril

Mercury—left hand, mouth

Moon—left foot, left eye

Correspondences like these formed the foundation for systems of astrological and magical diagnosis and healing, among many other things. They also have a place in natural magic; for example, an amulet of Jupiter will prove to be somewhat more effective if it's worn on a headband, fashioned into an earring for the left ear, or—since the thighs are ruled by Sagittarius, one of Jupiter's rulerships—fastened to a garter.

These physical correspondences don't exhaust the ways in which the symbolism of signs and planets relate to the human microcosm. Each sign and each planet relates to different parts of the individual human being on all of the different levels known to the traditional magical lore. The physical correspondences have a special importance in natural magic, though, since as we've already seen it's precisely the place of natural magic to trace out, and use, the reflections of magical energies in matter.

The Four Humors

The relationships of the four elements to the microcosm are more complex and even less well known nowadays. In the traditional lore, the elements were associated with four *humors* or subtle fluids within the body. (The word *humor* comes from the same root as *humid*, and simply means "moisture.") Just as the elements carry the names of physical substances—fire, water, air, and earth—the humors carry the Latin names of various biological fluids. Just as the elements are not simply material fire, water and so on, though, the humors are not substances so much as patterns of response associated with the elements. Since the balance of humors in any given person has a good deal to say to how they will respond to elemental workings, some of the basics of the humoral system will be covered here.

The four humors are the choleric humor, corresponding to yellow bile and the element of Fire; the sanguine humor, corresponding to blood and the element of Air; the phlegmatic humor, corresponding to phlegm and the element of Water, and the melancholic humor, corresponding to black bile and the element of Earth. (All these terms survive in modern English; an angry person is still sometimes called "choleric," depression is often called "melancholy," and so on.) Just as the elements are present within everything in the universe, so the humors are present within every living being. Their imbalance brings physical and emotional illness, while their proper balance brings health and happiness; in fact, when people have what the ancients would have called a proper emotional balance, we still refer to them as "good-humored."

Each of the four humors corresponds to a personality and body type that, in the traditional language of natural magic, is called a temperament—that is, a tempering or mixing together of humoral influences. The four temperaments have the same names as their ruling humors.

The choleric temperament is therefore warm and dry, ruled by the element of Fire. Its body type is muscular and tall, and its personality type is active, energetic, hasty, and clever, but prone to foolishness through not taking the time to think. Its great virtue is courage, and its vice is anger. According to the old handbooks, choleric people "have wine of the lion"—that is, they become angry and violent when drunk—and they prefer dressing in dark colors.

The sanguine temperament is warm and moist, ruled by the element of Air. Its body type is lean and agile, and its personality type is friendly, outgoing, talkative, and generous, but prone to dishonesty. Its great virtue is justice, and its vice is indecisiveness. According to the handbooks, sanguine people "have wine of the ape"—that is, they become merry and lustful when drunk—and they prefer to wear bright colors.

The phlegmatic temperament is cold and moist, ruled by the element of Water. Its body type is soft and delicate, and its personality type is dreamy, artistic, sensitive, and moody. Its great virtue is temperance, and its vice is laziness. In the handbooks, phlegmatic people are said to "have wine of the sheep"—in other words, they become gullible and easily convinced of anything when drunk—and they prefer to wear pale, pastel colors.

The melancholic temperament is cold and dry, ruled by the element of Earth. Its body type is heavy and solid, and its personality type is stable, practical, capable, and orderly, but prone to depression. Its great virtue is prudence, and its vice is greed. The medieval handbooks say that melancholic people "have wine of the pig"—that is, when they get drunk they simply fall asleep—and they prefer to dress in black, brown, or other earth tones.

These temperaments, of course, are ideals; very few people fit any one of them exactly, and in particular it's not unusual to have one body type and a different personality type. Still, it's useful to have a sense of what temperament you have, for this will have a strong effect on your relationships with the magical elements. Most people find it easiest to work with the element corresponding to their own temperament, and hardest to work with the element that shares none of the qualities with their own element. This doesn't mean that, say, a melancholic person should stick to Earth magic, or that a phlegmatic person should neglect the element of Fire—quite the contrary! It simply means that a magician of any temperament will have to work harder at some skills than others. The competent natural magician can work with any or all of the elements at will.

The Practice of Natural Magic

The universe of magic, as we've just seen, is a realm of many different powers, levels, and beings—a world where the visible is simply the outermost expression of a deeper reality, and where currents of magical power surge through even those things that seem most insignificant. Much of this seems strange to those raised in a materialistic society such as ours. Still, this magical universe is the one we inhabit here and now. The potentials for magical power are always all around us, like doors we have forgotten—but those doors can still be unlocked by the right keys.

Learning how to use those keys takes practice, time, and effort. Magicians of every kind are made, not born, and talent—while it does play a role in certain magical disciplines—counts for very little compared to the lessons of steady practice and the ordinary gifts of patience, perseverance, and common sense.

Some people who take up magic find this frustrating, but in magic, as in the rest of life, there is no such thing as a free lunch; what you get out of magic is measured precisely by what you put into it. Magic is not a way to get something for nothing, but rather it is a set of tools that allows the magician to work through subtle channels to achieve his or her goals. Work, in one form or another, is still always involved.

Given that natural magic must be learned and practiced in order to be mastered, how does one learn and practice it? Here we encounter one of the major differences between natural magic and ritual magic.

Becoming an effective ritual magician involves systematic work with exercises that teach the student how to shape magical energies, but that don't accomplish practical goals on their own. For example, a magician studying the Golden Dawn tradition of ritual magic will normally start out by learning the Lesser Ritual of the Pentagram and the Middle Pillar exercise, and practicing them every day. A little later on, the Greater Ritual of the Pentagram, the Lesser and Greater Rituals of the Hexagram, the Ritual of the Rose Cross, and a basic ceremonial opening and closing such as the Neophyte Formula or the Watchtower Ritual become part of the curriculum. All of these teach the novice magician how to summon, direct, and banish energies, and all of them have their own special effects on the magician, but none of them actually allows the student to carry out operations of practical magic. It's only after these things have been mastered that the Golden Dawn magician-in-training goes on to the formulae of practical magic and learns to consecrate talismans, summon spirits, and so on, in order to accomplish personal goals.

The Golden Dawn tradition is toward the high end of the complexity scale, granted, but this long process of training is anything but make-work. The practice of ritual magic demands the mastery of some highly unfamiliar and rather difficult skills, and without these skills the rituals simply won't get results. Most systems of ritual magic accordingly include a series of training exercises or fundamental ritual forms that have to be mastered before the practical techniques can be done effectively.

With natural magic, by contrast, this isn't true at all. There are very few training exercises in natural magic, and most of those I know have been borrowed from traditions of ritual magic or from pagan religious sources. Learning natural magic is almost entirely a matter of doing it, and it's perfectly appropriate to start doing it with practical goals in mind: to learn to make an amulet, for example, the student starts out by choosing a purpose for the amulet, working out the correspondences, and putting the amulet itself together, just as the experienced natural magician does. (The experienced natural magician is likely to get better results because of greater skill and knowledge, of course, but the process is the same.)

Another metaphor may be useful here. Learning ritual magic is much like learning to play classical music—the student starts with scales, exercises, and etudes, and has to master these before working up to real musical scores. Learning natural magic, on the other hand, is much like learning to make pottery by hand—the student may spend some time at exercises, but most of his or her training comes from picking up a lump of clay, shaping it, firing it in a kiln, and learning from the experience and its results.

Does this make one kind of magic better than the other? That depends, of course, on what "better" means to the person who is asking! Both have their advantages and their disadvantages. While the personal equation has a major effect, it's still true that for most people, natural magic can be learned more easily and more quickly than ritual magic. On the other hand, it's also true that a fully trained ritual magician can easily accomplish things that natural magic simply won't do, or won't do reliably. In many cultures, natural magic is practiced by almost everyone; ritual magic, by contrast, is quite often reserved for occult specialists, who are called in to help when the commonly used methods of natural magic are not strong enough to do the job. There is still something to be said for this traditional division of labor, although a case can also be made—especially at the present time, when only a small minority of people study any kind of magic at all—for learning both branches of magic, and using either or both as circumstances require.

Four Steps to Natural Magic

Actual magical practice is thus the heart of any kind of training in natural magic. This doesn't mean, though, that you should simply run down to the nearest herb store or rock shop and start putting together amulets according to a recipe, as though you were baking a cake. There are actually four steps to the process of carrying out a natural magic working, and assembling the material substances into an amulet or some other magical device is the last of them.

The four steps are:

1. Choosing the purpose for the working;

2. Choosing the correspondences for the working;

3. Selecting the specific materials to be used; and

4. Combining purpose, correspondences, and materials into the actual work of natural magic.

We'll cover these four steps in detail, one at a time.

Step One: Choosing the Purpose

The first and most important step is choosing the purpose for the working. As with any kind of magic, this has to be done with some care. The old joke about the man who told the genie, "Make me a milkshake," and was turned into a milkshake, has its equivalents all through magical lore. It is essential to remember, whenever you are considering magic, that when a magical working succeeds, you get what you ask for—whether or not what you ask for is what you actually want.

Before going on, then, take your time deciding exactly what you intend your magical working to do. It's a good idea to work at it until you can phrase the purpose as a single clear sentence with no ambiguities or mixed meanings. The purpose you settle on may be very specific or very general, but you should always know exactly what you want to accomplish.

The Ethical Dimension

You should also think long and hard about the ethical implications of what you are trying to do. A vast amount of confusion about magical ethics has grown up over the last few centuries, with some people insisting that any practical use of magic at all is an utter fall from grace, while others claim that the whole point of magic is being able to do whatever one wants regardless of anyone else's rights or needs. Both of these unbalanced extremes can be set aside, but there's a wide area in between that needs to be explored and understood if an ethical approach to natural magic is to be found and followed.

To some extent, every magician has to think through the basic questions of magical ethics himself or herself, and finding a personal stance here is an important part of becoming a fully trained magician. Perhaps the best place to begin in such matters, though, is the much-maligned Golden Rule. If you're considering some sort of magical working that will affect other people—and most magic will—ask yourself how you would feel if someone else did the same sort of working, and it affected *you*.

This is not simply an abstract exercise. Magical tradition warns against trying to harm, exploit, or control people by magic, and it does so for the most practical of reasons: if you do such things, the energies you summon will enter your own life at least as much as they will focus on your target. In magic, as in the rest of life, what goes around comes around, and the reality you shape for other people is the reality you'll shape for yourself sooner or later. Keep this in mind, and your experience of natural magic is likely to be a good deal less difficult.

The Possibilities of Natural Magic

In settling on a purpose for your working, you should also keep in mind what natural magic can and can't do. It does no good for you to define a purpose as clearly as you like if the purpose is something that cannot be attained by natural magic at all. The actual limits of the power of magic are complex and not entirely clear, but some pointers can certainly be given.

First of all, natural magic is exactly that—natural—and so it cannot be used to break (or even bend) the ordinary laws of nature. No matter how hard you try, for example, you won't be able use natural magic to float heavy objects in midair or make apple trees bear tomatoes. When natural magic works, in turn, the effects will come about in a natural way, not with a flash and a puff of smoke.

Second, natural magic functions within fairly strict limits of energy, since it shapes energies that have already descended into material form. In ritual magic, it's possible to call on additional sources of power from the less material levels of experience, but natural magic doesn't work that way; the powers it uses are already linked up fully with the material level. As a result, the effects of natural magic are typically very subtle and gradual in their effects. If you want the magical equivalent of fireworks, you'll need to look elsewhere.

Third, natural magic is highly sensitive to issues of scale—even more so than most other branches of magic. The larger an area you intend to affect or the more drastic a change you intend to make, the more work it's going to require, and really large-scale workings are generally not within the range of natural magic unless you have access to the sort of resources and labor force that built Stonehenge. In natural magic, as in most things, it's generally wise to start small and move to larger things as you go.

Step Two: Choosing Correspondences

The second step in working natural magic involves figuring out the symbolism and correspondences you will be using to bring your purpose into reality. Here the traditional zodiacal, planetary, and elemental symbolism can be used as a starting place, but it should always be supplemented with the lessons of your own experience.

As you work with herbs, stones, and other materials associated with the various currents of energy, you'll develop a clearer and more personal sense of what these correspondences mean, and learn to sense the energy and subtle "flavor" of each one. An amulet of success based on a Jupiter symbolism has a different quality than one based on a solar symbolism, and the two will have different practical uses and effects as well; the more attention you pay to the differences, the sooner you'll learn to use them to your advantage.

You'll also find that it's not always necessary, or even useful, to stick to a single symbolic framework for a given working. While it's sometimes useful to make an amulet using only solar correspondences, for example, or a potion or incense of a single element, it can be equally useful at other times to combine different planets or elements into a harmonious blend of forces. Here again, practice and personal experience will teach you what works and what doesn't.

Even so, the traditional symbolism is the best place to begin, and you can work effective natural magic by following its lead while your own personal grasp of symbolic patterns is still developing. The following outlines will serve as a starting place for this aspect of the work.

The Signs of the Zodiac

The first set of correspondences we'll examine are the twelve signs of the zodiac. The word *zodiac* comes from the ancient Greek phrase *kyklos zodiakos,* "circle of animals." Many thousands of years ago, those who watched the sky realized that the Sun's journey through the heavens always took it through the same set of twelve groups of stars. Each of these star groups, or constellations, was given a name based partly on its shape, partly on the season of the year that it marked when it rose just before or set just after the Sun, and partly on lore drawn from ancient mythology. Most of the clusters were named after animals: the Ram, the Bull, the Lion, the Scorpio, the Fishes, and more. Others were named after human figures, and one after a tool, the Scales. Millennia later, these same names in their Latin form mark our own skies: Aries, Taurus, Gemini, and the other signs of the zodiac.

In the same way that the stars form the background against which planetary movements can be tracked, the energies of the zodiac form the background to all the other forces, elemental as well as planetary, that move through the universe of natural magic. While it's rarely useful to do a working specifically directed to one of the signs, it's almost always wise to pay attention to the way the signs color the planetary and elemental forces that interact with them.

Each sign of the zodiac has been given a key phrase, which sums up its character in a brief and memorable way. It attunes most strongly with one of the four elements, and it also interacts with the planets in a series of different ways. The four most important of these latter interactions are rulership, in which a sign amplifies a planet's energy; triplicity, which is a milder form of rulership; exaltation, in which the sign balances and harmonizes a planet's force, raising it to its best potential; detriment, in which it weakens a planet's force; and fall, in which it unbalances and degrades a planet's energy, lowering it to its worst potential. When two of these happen at the same time, as sometimes happens, the result is a combination of the two interactions, so that (for example) a planet in its triplicity and its fall in a given sign is strong but unbalanced, while one in its triplicity and rulership at the same time is at the zenith of its power.

♈ **Aries, the Ram:** "I am"

Aries, energetic and straightforward, is attuned to the element of Fire, and its ruler is Mars. In Aries, the Sun is in his exaltation, Jupiter and the Sun are in their triplicity, Venus is in her detriment, and Saturn is in his fall.

Substances ruled by Aries include cinnamon, magnetite, and rosemary.

♉ **Taurus, the Bull:** "I have"

Solid, stubborn, and determined Taurus is an Earth sign, ruled by Venus. In Taurus, Venus and the Moon are in their triplicity, the Moon is exalted, and Mars is in his detriment; none of the planets are in their fall.

Substances ruled by Taurus include coltsfoot, diamond, and sage.

♊ **Gemini, the Twins:** "I think"

Gemini is an Air sign, as changeable and versatile as its planetary ruler Mercury. In Gemini, Saturn and Mercury are in their triplicity, and Jupiter is in his detriment; none of the planets are in exaltation or fall.

Substances ruled by Gemini include agate, oregano, and vervain.

♋ **Cancer, the Crab:** "I feel"

Sensitive and subtle, hidden in armor like the crab, Cancer is a Water sign, and its ruler is the ever-changing Moon. In Cancer, Mars is in his triplicity, Jupiter is in his exaltation, Saturn is in his detriment, and Mars is in his fall.

Substances ruled by Cancer include caraway, honey, and moonstone.

♌ **Leo, the Lion:** "I will"

Ruled by the Sun, Leo is a sign of Fire, with all the energy and creative power the Sun traditionally symbolizes. In Leo, the Sun and Jupiter are in their triplicity, and Saturn is in his detriment; none of the planets have their exaltation or fall in this sign.

Substances ruled by Leo include angelica, onyx, and St. John's Wort.

♍ **Virgo, the Virgin:** "I analyze"

Methodical, critical Virgo, symbolized by a virgin bearing a sheaf of newly harvested grain, is attuned to the element of Earth and ruled by Mercury. In Virgo, Mercury is also exalted, Venus and the Moon are in their triplicity, Jupiter is in his detriment, and Venus is in her fall.

Substances ruled by Virgo include catnip, patchouli, and sardonyx.

♎ **Libra, the Scales:** "I balance"

Harmonious and aesthetic, Libra is an Air sign and is ruled by Venus. In Libra, Saturn is exalted, Saturn and Mercury are in their triplicity, Mars is in his detriment, and the Sun—which crosses into the cold half of the year in Libra—is in his fall.

Substances ruled by Libra include apple, jade, and rose.

♏ **Scorpio, the Scorpion:** "I transform"

The most complex of the signs, represented by the serpent and the eagle as well as the scorpion, passionate and secretive Scorpio is a Water sign ruled by Mars. In Scorpio, none of the planets are exalted; Mars is in his triplicity, Venus is in her detriment, and the Moon is in her fall.

Substances ruled by Scorpio include basil, jasper, and valerian.

♐ **Sagittarius, the Archer:** "I perceive"

An expansive and optimistic sign, Sagittarius—symbolized by the centaur—is attuned to Fire and ruled by Jupiter. In Sagittarius, the Sun and Jupiter are in their triplicity and Mercury is in his detriment; none of the planets are in exaltation or fall.

Substances ruled by Sagittarius include amethyst, hawthorn, and nutmeg.

♑ **Capricorn, the Fish-Tailed Goat: "I use"**

An Earth sign ruled by Saturn, Capricorn is patient, ambitious, and responsible; its enigmatic image spans the whole range of Earth's environments, from the mountain heights, where goats climb, to the depths of the sea. Mars is exalted in Capricorn; Venus and the Moon are in their triplicity, the Moon is in her detriment, and Jupiter is in his fall.

Substances ruled by Capricorn include comfrey, plantain, and yew.

♒ **Aquarius, the Water Bearer: "I know"**

Aquarius, innovative and idealistic, is an Air sign and is ruled by Saturn. In Aquarius, the Sun is in his detriment—this sign governs the bleakest part of winter—and Saturn and Mercury are in their triplicity, but none of the planets have their exaltation or fall in this sign.

Substances ruled by Aquarius include frankincense, iris, and obsidian.

♓ **Pisces, the Fishes: "I believe"**

Dreamy and imaginative Pisces is attuned to the element of Water and ruled by Jupiter. In Pisces, Venus is in her exaltation, Mars is in his triplicity, and Mercury has both his detriment and his fall.

Substances ruled by Pisces include horsetail, sapphire, and turquoise.

The Planetary Powers

In the ancient vision of the cosmos, the space between the distant sphere of the stars and the upper limit of Earth's atmosphere was ruled by seven great powers, who were the gods and goddesses of many of the old pagan religions. The existence of these deities did not have to be taken on faith. Anyone who went out on a clear night and looked up along the track of the zodiac could see them: five shining points of light against the backdrop of the constellations.

These, together with the Sun and Moon, shifted their positions in predictable ways relative to the background stars. In ancient Greece, when the first philosophers of the

West joined mages and theologians in thinking about these luminous beings, they came to call the Sun, the Moon, and these five lights *planetes,* "wanderers"—the origin of our word "planets."

People in the modern West have been taught for a long time now to think of the old veneration of the planets as so much blind superstition. In this light, it's worth taking a moment to realize just how much sound common sense was involved. As astrologers have always known, and as the new science of astrobiology is beginning to rediscover, the other bodies of the solar system have definite, measurable effects on Earth. Alongside the obvious examples—the seasons, driven by the Sun's heat, and the tides, set in motion by the Moon's gravity—modern researchers have begun to amass a long list of subtler biological and psychological effects on living beings, humans very much included. In doing so, they are following in the footsteps of other watchers of the heavens who tracked similar patterns in their own way a very long time ago.

From the point of view of natural magic, these subtle effects make the planets the major sources of energy for magical use. Most of the time, a natural magic working will be built up around a planetary correspondence, and in fact many of the old texts of natural magic ignore all other correspondences and simply discuss the planets and their powers. It's still possible to work with the tradition this way even today, though experience will show that the background patterns of the zodiac and the patterns of manifestation of the elements also add much to the work and its results.

One crucial insight shared by ancient astrologers and modern researchers alike is that each of the planets has its influences and effects most strongly focused on specific types of activity. In the old lore, this insight took the form of correspondences of the sort discussed earlier, in which each planet was held to correspond to different aspects of the spectrum of human life. A clear understanding of the different planets' realms of influence is thus highly important in working with natural magic.

As we've already seen, the planets have a series of possible relationships with the signs of the zodiac. Each planet also attunes with the four elements in two different ways. The first is an astrological correspondence, derived from the planetary relationship with the zodiacal signs; the second is a practical correspondence, and governs the way in which the planet best interacts with the elemental realm in magical workings.

There is also a pattern of interaction among the planets themselves, which can be used in work that involves more than one planet. Traditionally, the planets were divided into two groups: a solar group including the Sun, Venus, and Mars, and a lunar group including the Moon, Jupiter, and Saturn, with Mercury having a foot in both groups. You'll notice that these connections can be read in the traditional symbols of the planets as well: all of the solar planets have the circle of the Sun in their symbols, and all the lunar ones have the crescent of the Moon, while ambivalent Mercury has both circle and crescent.

♄ Saturn

Saturn governs all things concerning sorrow, death, old age, the past, limitation, stability, agriculture, and also abstract thought and philosophy. It was traditionally called the "Greater Misfortune," as it deals with many of the more difficult aspects of human existence. Its astrological element is Air; in practical magic, it resonates most closely with Earth.

Substances ruled by Saturn include comfrey, lead, onyx, and yew.

♃ Jupiter

Jupiter governs all things concerning good fortune, growth and expansion, formal ceremonies and rites of passage, charity, feasting, and advancement in one's profession or in bureaucratic contexts. It was traditionally called the "Greater Fortune" because of its association with success. Its astrological element is Fire; in practical magic, it resonates most closely with Water.

Substances ruled by Jupiter include almond, dandelion, jasper, and tin.

♂ Mars

The red planet Mars governs aggression, destruction, conflict, and violence in all their forms, as well as male sexuality and, oddly enough, all matters connected with livestock. It was traditionally called the "Lesser Misfortune," as its association with warfare made it understandably unpopular. Its astrological element is Water; in practical magic, it resonates most closely with Fire.

Substances ruled by Mars include basil, bloodstone, iron, and juniper.

☉ The Sun

The Sun governs power, leadership and all positions of authority, success of any kind, balance and reconciliation, and also sports and games involving physical exertion. Blending positive and negative, it was traditionally classed as neither fortune nor misfortune. Its astrological element is Fire; in practical magic, it resonates well with Air and Fire alike.

Substances ruled by the Sun include amber, cinnamon, gold, and saffron.

♀ Venus

Venus governs music, dance, all the arts, social occasions, enjoyments, all pleasures, love, the emotional life, and female sexuality. It was traditionally held to be the "Lesser Fortune." Its astrological element is Earth, and in practical magic it resonates with Earth and Water.

Substances ruled by Venus include catnip, copper, jade, and yarrow.

☿ Mercury

Quicksilver in every sense, Mercury governs learning and intellectual pursuits, messages and communication of all kinds, gambling, medicine and healing, commerce and economic matters, but also trickery, deception, and theft. Its ambivalence made it traditionally count as neither fortune nor misfortune. Its element, astrological as well as practical, is Air.

Substances ruled by Mercury include agate, fennel, jasmine, and parsley.

☽ The Moon

The Moon governs journeys, the sea, hunting and fishing, biological cycles, reproduction and childbirth, psychic phenomena, dreams, visions, the unconscious and the unknown. It was held to collect the influences of all the planets and pass them down to Earth, and so it was treated as neither fortune nor misfortune. Its astrological element is Earth; in practical magic, it resonates most strongly with Water.

Substances ruled by the Moon include camphor, lily, nutmeg, and silver.

The Magical Elements

The third of the main systems of correspondence in natural magic is based on the five elements of ancient magic and philosophy: Earth, Water, Air, Fire, and Spirit. The system of the magical elements has also had a good deal of scorn heaped on it in the last few centuries, and like the traditional theory of the planets, it also deserves a good second look.

The theory of the elements can be traced back to the Greek philosopher and mystic Empedocles of Acragas, who lived in the fifth century B.C.E., while it was Aristotle some two centuries later who defined the elements in ways that have been central to Western magic ever since. The basic intuitions underlying the elemental system, though, are probably much older, and ways of looking at the world that are very closely akin to magical elemental theory can be found in many different cultures around the world. Even the worldview of modern science, which discarded the elemental system hundreds of years ago, has had to let it in again through the back door: to describe the cosmos as matter-energy manifesting in the four forms of energy, gas, liquid, and solid, all moving against the curved and complex background fabric of space-time, is simply to restate the old intuition in new words.

It's a common mistake to think that the magical elements are identical to the material substances that bear the same names. Elemental Water, for instance, is not the fluid that comes out of your tap, but rather a much broader phenomenon that includes all fluids and many things besides. When the ancient lore states that Water (along with each of the other elements) is present in all things, it's not saying that the chemical compound dihydrogen oxide, H_2O, is contained in all other substances, but rather that all things in the universe of our experience have a "watery" side—an aspect or function that corresponds to the magical element of Water. It's best, in fact, to think of the elements primarily as patterns of experience that we encounter in one form or another at every moment.

As the scientists' four states of matter-energy may suggest, the four elements can best be understood on any level as four forms of one original substance, and this substance can pass from one form to another through patterns of transformation based on the qualities of the elements. Each element has two qualities, and each quality is shared by two elements. The qualities are warm, cold, dry, and moist, and relate to the elements in the following traditional diagram:

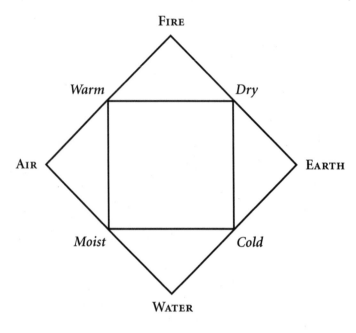

Diagram 1

Any element can change into another by giving up one of its qualities and replacing it with the opposite quality. For example, if Fire gives up its warmth and takes on cold, it transforms itself to Earth—a process that occurs symbolically every time a fire burns itself down to ash. An element can therefore transform itself directly into another if the two have a quality in common.

Between elements that have no quality in common, such as Water and Fire, transformations are indirect, and a third element plays the mediating role. For example, Water will not transform itself directly into Fire. If the Water first transforms itself into Air by changing cold for warmth, though, the Air can then become Fire by shedding moistness for dryness. (Even though the substances and the magical elements are not the same, this works just as well with the substances themselves; it's useless to try to light a glass of water with a match, but if the water is broken down into its airy components, the gases hydrogen and oxygen, the result will catch fire explosively.)

The fifth element, Spirit, represents the influence of higher levels of being on the interplay of the four other elements. If its influence is brought into the diagram shown above, another pattern emerges—one that is familiar to most modern practitioners of magic:

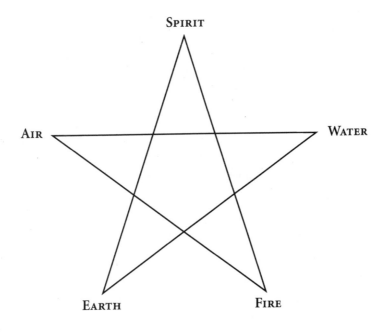

SPIRIT

AIR

WATER

EARTH

FIRE

Diagram 2

In practical use, since Spirit simply serves as a marker for whatever higher-level factors are in play in a given situation, it has few correspondences of its own, and none that are used in standard natural magic. Its presence should always be kept in mind, for it's often the effect of these higher-level factors that spells the difference between success and failure in magical workings. Still, in the material that follows, we'll mostly be discussing four elements, not five.

Like the planets, the four elements have their own realms of influence in human life and the world. They represent the basic realities of the universe as we experience it most of the time, and it's wise to keep them and their correspondences well in mind when planning any magical work that deals primarily with matter, or with the hard and fast details of everyday life.

Within our own consciousness, for example, the energizing force of will is like Fire, the agile and restless intellect is like Air, the fluid and responsive emotions are like Water, and the stable and usually predictable realm of the senses is like Earth. All four, in turn, are brought together into a world of meaning by the creative power of imagination, which serves as the equivalent of Spirit. Similarly, among living creatures, mammals with their warm blood are like Fire, birds with their wings and hollow bones are like Air, fish with their cold blood are like Water, and reptiles, insects, worms, and so forth are like Earth. (Note that in this scheme, the "warm" elements Fire and Air are assigned to warm-blooded creatures, while the "cold" elements Water and Earth are assigned to cold-blooded ones.) Here humanity, with its powers of awareness and communication, corresponds to the fifth element of Spirit.

In turn, among the seasons of the year—according to the traditional lore of natural magic, which differs from some more recent systems—the fickle weather of spring corresponds to Air, the steady heat of summer to Fire, the cooling days and drying leaves of autumn to Earth, and the cold and damp of winter to Water. Here the place of the element of Spirit is filled by the Sun, which remains central to the whole process and provides the energy that drives the changes of the seasons.

We can classify the four elements according to the aspects of life that they govern, and according to the set of qualities that define them.

 Earth—cold and dry

> The element of Earth governs solid physical matter and all things connected with it; agriculture, mining, and all that relates to the ground and what lies under it; the solid parts of the physical body, such as bones and muscles; and the sense of touch. It also governs employment, money, and physical property.
>
> Substances ruled by Earth include barley, coltsfoot, horsetail, mandrake, and patchouli.

 Water—cold and moist

> Water governs liquid physical matter and all related things; oceans, lakes, rivers, and streams; fertility and reproduction; the liquid parts of the physical body, such as blood and lymph; the emotions, and the sense of taste. It also rules social and sexual interactions between people, and is associated with happiness generally.
>
> Substances ruled by Water include iron, green jasper, lily, seashells, and turquoise.

Air—warm and moist

The element of Air governs gaseous physical matter and all associated things; the atmosphere, the winds and weather; the gaseous parts of the physical body, such as air in the lungs; and the nervous system; the intellect; and the sense of smell. In the social realm, it governs communication but also conflict, violence, and pain, and it is associated with suffering generally.

Substances ruled by Air include borage, elecampane, lapis lazuli, onion, and valerian leaf.

 Fire—warm and dry

Fire governs physical energy and all things related to it; heat, light, electricity, and radioactivity; the energetic aspects of the body, such as movement and body heat; the will, and the sense of sight. It also governs activity of all kinds, leadership, and personal and organizational power.

Substances ruled by Fire include bay laurel, cedar, frankincense, red jasper, and sage.

Step Three: Selecting the Materials

The third step in any natural magic working is selecting the specific material substances you intend to use, based on the purpose and symbolism you've already chosen, and settling on a form for the finished product. This process of selection can be a complicated one. Your goal is to choose a type of working that will be convenient and effective, and a substance or set of substances that will harmonize well with the purpose, the symbolism, and the kind of working you have in mind. The Encyclopedia section of this book is intended to make this as straightforward as possible, but even so you'll find that it may take you a good deal of time and plenty of hands-on experience to master the process.

Ethics and the Environment

Another aspect of magical ethics, however, applies at this stage of the process. The old traditions of natural magic made free use of every part of the animal, plant, and mineral kingdoms as magical resources. The age when these traditions evolved, it bears remembering, was long before the first stirrings of modern ecological consciousness in the West, and people—even intelligent, thoughtful, ethical people—commonly treated the natural world in ways many of us would find wasteful or even brutal today.

Be that as it may, this book is a practical handbook for modern magicians, not a museum of historical lore. The material given in this book has therefore been assembled with ecological values in mind. There are elements of the traditional lore that have been left out here for ecological reasons, and practices once common among natural magicians that have no place in modern magical work. The following notes may be of use in this context.

Minerals

It may seem strange to think of stones and other minerals as endangered but, here as in so many other cases, human overuse and exploitation have pushed the natural world close to its limits. Crystals and minerals that were once common are becoming hard to find as commercial interests haul them out by the truckload for industrial use or the rock shop trade.

The old traditions of natural magic and alchemy saw everything in the world as a living creature. In this way of looking at things, minerals are simply the slowest of all life forms, taking millions of years to sprout, blossom, and bear fruit. Every mineral used in natural magic should be treated with such considerations in mind. In gathering stones from the natural world, in particular, take only what you need, and if possible return what you take to its place when you are finished.

Plants

The situation with regard to plants is simpler in some ways, more complex in others. As far as I know, I have not included any information on the magical uses of endangered species in this book, simply because these need to be preserved, not exploited. I have given most space to those plants that can easily be grown by the home gardener, in the hope that magicians who want to make use of them will plant and harvest their own. This is not just a hobby for those with money and property; even a small window box or clay pot will provide room for many herbs, including some of the most magically powerful. The section on gardening in the workbook covers this side of natural magic in much more detail.

Those who prefer to "wildcraft"—that is, to gather their herbs directly from the natural world—need to be aware that even seemingly small actions can damage ecosystems beyond repair. Several North American herbs, the potent medicinal herb goldenseal among them, have already been wildcrafted so heavily that their survival is in danger. As we are finding out in so many ways just now, the natural world is not infinite, and if we treat it unthinkingly it begins to withhold its gifts. If a meadow has a hundred flowers growing in it, it's easy to think, "It won't matter if I just take one"—and just as easy to forget what will happen if ninety-nine other people walk through the same meadow and think the same thing.

Animals

For similar reasons, animal products play a very small part in this book. Vegetarians and animal-rights proponents would suggest that they should play no part at all, but with all due respect, this is something about which each person needs to make up his or her own mind. Those people who eat meat or use animal products such as leather have every right to know and use the magical effects of these things.

Furthermore, despite claims that have occasionally been made by vegetarians, it's simply not true that eating meat or other animal products is incompatible with an active spiritual or magical life. (Anyone who believes such claims should sit down with a copy of *Black Elk Speaks,* or some other accurate book on the spiritual life of the native peoples of the Great Plains, whose traditional diet was well over half meat, and who nonetheless had a spiritual life of dazzling intensity.) Some spiritual traditions consider vegetarianism to be necessary, and some do not. Since most magical teachings consider plants to be just as alive and conscious as animals, too, the absolutist ethical claims sometimes made for a vegetarian diet are at least open to question as well.

At present, however, most species of wild animals are under severe pressure as a result of human overpopulation and the destruction of wild habitat. It thus seems sensible, at least, to discourage the magical use of wild creatures under these conditions, and (with one exception, explained below) I have not discussed the magical use of wild animals in this book.

Domesticated animals like cows, pigs, and chickens are another matter. These animals are part of the human environment; the survival of their species is not at risk; ecologically sound ways of raising them are becoming increasingly common; and many people (including many magicians) use them already as sources of food and raw materials. It seems reasonable to include their magical uses here as well.

As mentioned above, one wild creature has been included in the Encyclopedia section of this book. Deer evolved together with large predators such as wolves and cougars, which play a crucial role in holding deer populations within the natural balance. Without predators to keep them in check, deer (like most species, including ours) overpopulate until they wreck the ecosystem that supports them, then die off from mass starvation, leaving a damaged environment behind.

Nowadays, wolves and cougars are rare, and the only large predator that can keep deer populations in check throughout most of North America is *Homo sapiens*. Until this changes, deer hunting by humans is probably going to have to play a part in many ecosystems. In the spirit of respect for the animal—a spirit long exemplified by the native peoples of this land—what is taken must be used completely, and natural magic is one respectful way in which that may be done.

Step Four: Working the Magic

Only after you finish all three of these steps—after you know why you are doing the working and exactly what it is intended to bring about, after you have selected the symbolism and correspondences you will be using, and after you have brought both the purpose and the symbolism "down to earth" in the form of some particular set of substances you will be using in a specific way—is it time to go on to the fourth step, the actual magical working itself.

The exact nature of the fourth step will vary widely depending on what form of finished product you've selected. If it's an amulet, you'll merely have to put the substances into an appropriate bag and place the bag where it's meant to go; if it's a potion or some other liquid form, you'll have to brew up the product and then put it to use; if it's something more complicated, such as pebble incense or a wax-dressed candle, there will be various different kinds of work involved. A wide selection of the possibilities is covered in the third part of this book, The Natural Magic Workbook.

Magical Timing

One thing that plays a central role all through this phase of traditional natural magic is timing. The different currents of magical power move through cycles of intensity over time, and it's a standard teaching of the lore—not to mention a routine experience of practicing magicians—that a working begun when its corresponding energy is at high intensity will produce better results than one started when the current of energy is weak.

There are three main ways to work out the proper timing for natural magic. The first, the solar-lunar method, tracks very broad shifts in energy cycles based on the phases of the Moon and the seasons of the year. The second, the method of electional astrology, involves paying attention to the movements of the planets and choosing a time accordingly. The third, the method of planetary hours and tattwas, involves working out the rise and fall of the different energies by way of certain traditional calculations. I personally prefer a combination of the first two methods, but all these methods are used successfully by modern natural magicians, and all three will be given here.

Method 1: Sun and Moon Cycles

The simplest approach of all has to do with the phases of the Moon and the seasons of the year. The rules are simple. Since the Moon is the most potent influence on the etheric realm of life energy, etheric energies are strongest at the Full Moon and weakest at the New Moon. When the Moon is waxing from new to full, the energies foster increase and upward motion, while the Waning Moon from full to new marks a time of decrease and downward motion. In magical practice, correspondingly, workings intended to bring growth and increase on any level are done while the Moon is waxing, while workings designed to cleanse, purify, and decrease are done while the Moon is waning. The last few days before the Full or New Moon are the strongest for either purpose.

The broader cycle of the solar year has its own tides, which relate to the cycle of the seasons and of the agricultural year; the same etheric patterns that influence magic also shape the life of the natural world, a point many traditions of folk magic have learned to use with a high degree of exactness. The fine details vary according to latitude and other local factors, but in general the time between the spring equinox and the summer solstice (March 21 to June 21, approximately, in the Northern Hemisphere) is a time of beginnings and of growth; that between the summer solstice and the fall equinox (June 21 to September 23), a time of completion and fruitfulness; that between the fall equinox and the winter solstice (September 23 to December 23), a time of preservation and taking stock; and that between the winter solstice and the spring equinox (December 23 to March 21), a time of destruction and purification. These four seasons have been called, respectively, the Tide of Sowing, the Tide of Reaping, the Tide of Planning, and the Tide of Destruction, and these names sum up their nature fairly well.

Example. Let's suppose that you meant to make an amulet to improve your physical and emotional health—a classic use for natural magic—and wanted to use this first system of timing. Since this purpose is associated with growth and increase, you would want to make the amulet while the Moon is waxing, preferably during the three days right before it's full. For best results, a Waxing Moon during the Tide of Sowing might be selected.

Method 2: Electional Astrology

To make use of this second method, you'll need an ephemeris or an astrological calendar so that you can track the movements of the Sun, the Moon, and the planets relative to the signs of the zodiac. A computer program that will allow you to generate astrological charts is useful but not necessary. You don't actually need to be able to cast a chart to use the magical side of electional astrology; all you need to know is how to look up a planet in the tables, find out what sign it's in, and see what aspects it makes with other planets.

The central principle of this method of timing is that the Moon and the planetary correspondence central to your working (if this is different from the Moon) should both be strong, as the old books phrase it, during the time when you do the working. In general, a planet is strong when it is in a sign that is one of its rulerships or its exaltation, or when its next aspect is one of the three favorable aspects (conjunction, sextile, or trine) with the Moon, Venus, or Jupiter. A planet is weak when it is in a sign that is one of its detriments or its fall; when its next aspect is one of the two negative aspects (square or opposition) with Mars or Saturn, or a conjunction with the Sun; or when it's retrograde. The Moon is also strong in the waxing half of its cycle, weak in the waning half, and very weak when it's "void of course"—that is, when it has passed the last aspect it will make with any planet before it passes into another sign.

The phases of the Moon and the position of planets relative to the signs can easily be looked up in your ephemeris, and you can also see whether the planet is retrograde—that is, apparently moving backward from Earth's perspective—and thus too weak to use. The aspects can also be looked up, but this is a little more complex. An aspect is a specific angle made between two planets, as seen from the perspective of the Earth. The aspect is "perfected"—that is, it actually takes place—at a particular moment in time, but its magical effects start before the actual moment of perfection.

To locate the time when the aspect begins to apply, start from the time of perfection and look back through the ephemeris or calendar until you find one of three things:

the perfection of another aspect involving the same planet, the time when the planet "stands direct" (that is, stops being retrograde and begins moving forward, as seen from Earth's perspective), or the time when the planet passes from one sign to another. Whichever of these you find closest to the aspect itself is the beginning of the time when the aspect applies.

Timing elemental workings by this method is a little easier. All that's necessary is that the Moon be strong and in a sign attributed to that element during the time of your working.

Example. Let's suppose that you wanted to make the same amulet as before, but this time using electional astrology for the timing. After careful consideration, you decided to base the amulet's symbolism on the Sun, and so the Sun and Moon both have to be strong at the time when you make the amulet. (For the sake of this example, two real months—November and December 1998—will be used; all times of astrological events are Pacific Standard Time.)

Looking at the ephemeris, you find that the Moon trines the Sun on November 29, a little after midnight, and there are no other lunar or solar aspects for over ten hours beforehand. This looks good, but the Moon is in its detriment in Aries at that point, and thus weak. Looking a little further reveals that the Moon and the Sun are sextile on November 24 at 4:33 A.M., with the Moon entering into Aquarius not quite four hours earlier. The Moon has no particular relation to Aquarius, but the Sun in Sagittarius is in its triplicity, and thus mildly strong; the Moon is strengthened because it is in the waxing half of its cycle, two days short of First Quarter, and the sextile aspect between Moon and Sun strengthens the Sun. Provided that you don't mind staying up past midnight to make the amulet, this would be a suitable time. If not, the afternoon and early evening of December 1 offers another possibility; the Moon is two days short of the full and enters into a sextile aspect with Jupiter at 7:43 P.M., making it very strong. The Sun remains mildly strong through its placement in Sagittarius, and finishes with a potentially complicated aspect with Uranus at 4:44 P.M.

Method 3: Planetary Hours and Elements in Course
The third method uses a set of calculations that, according to traditional lore, tracks the ebb and flow of planetary and elemental energies around the world. The most complicated of the three methods, this requires a certain amount of mathematical skill

to use, and it's rendered even more complex by the fact that completely different calculations are needed for planetary and elemental workings.

We'll begin with planetary hours. There are twelve planetary hours in a day and twelve in a night, just as with the ordinary kind. Unfortunately planetary hours change length with the seasons; a planetary hour in the day is precisely one-twelfth the time from sunrise to sunset, while in the night it is precisely one-twelfth the time from sunset to sunrise.

To calculate the planetary hours for any given day of the year, use the following process:

> **Step one:** Find the times of sunrise and sunset in an almanac or ephemeris.
>
> **Step two:** Figure out the total time from sunrise to sunset in hours and minutes.
>
> **Step three:** Multiply the number of hours by sixty; add this to the minutes to work out the total number of minutes between sunrise and sunset.
>
> **Step four:** Divide that total by twelve to get the number of minutes in a daytime planetary hour.

To calculate the planetary hours for any given night of the year, you have two possible approaches. If you've already worked out the hours of the day, subtract the total from step three from 1440, which is the total number of minutes in twenty-four hours. If you haven't worked out the hours of the day, simply go through the same process as above but start with the time from sunset to sunrise.

To figure out which planet rules any given hour, start with the day of the week:

> **Monday**—Moon
>
> **Tuesday**—Mars
>
> **Wednesday**—Mercury
>
> **Thursday**—Jupiter
>
> **Friday**—Venus
>
> **Saturday**—Saturn
>
> **Sunday**—Sun

The day of each planet runs from sunrise to sunrise, so that what we would call very early Monday morning is, in magical terms, the last hours of the day of the Sun. The first hour of each day, starting with sunrise, is ruled by the same planet that rules the day as a whole. The following hours are assigned to planets according to a repeating cycle, as shown in Diagram 3.

Thus on a Friday, since the first hour is governed by Venus, the second will be governed by Mercury, the third by the Moon, the fourth by Saturn, and so on around until the eighth hour of the day, when Venus comes up again. The hours of the night begin with the planet next in sequence after the twelfth hour of the day. In the case of Friday, again, the twelfth hour will always be ruled by Jupiter, and so the first hour of the night will be ruled by Mars. Following the cycle around, the last hour of the night on any Friday will be ruled by the Moon, and so the first hour of Saturday will be ruled by Saturn, the ruler of the day. (The whole process can be followed on the table of planetary hours, given on page 41.)

For best effects, a planetary working should be done on the day and hour of the planet in question, if the working uses only one planet. If more than one planet is involved, the day of one and the hour of another makes for a good balance of energies.

For the elements, a different set of calculations determines the element in course at any given time. Each of the five elements governs a period of twenty-four minutes, and the whole cycle thus takes place every two hours. The cycle starts at the dawn of each day with Spirit, with Air, Fire, Water, and Earth following in that order, each ruling for twenty-four minutes and then giving way to the next. The time of sunset has no effect on the process; to work out the element in course, simply find the time of sunrise and add two-hour increments to it until you have reached the part of the day in which you want to work, then count ahead by twenty-four-minute increments to assign the elements to their stations in the next two-hour cycle.

Example. Let's suppose once again that you wanted to make the same solar amulet, this time using the planetary hours to determine the timing. Right away you know that the working will need to be done on a Sunday, and we'll assume that the next convenient Sunday happens to be November 22. On that day, at the latitude of Seattle, the sun rises at 7:12 A.M. and sets at 4:18 P.M. This makes the day from sunrise to sunset a total of 9 hours 6 minutes long, or—multiplying 9 x 60, and then adding 6

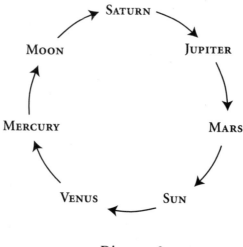

Diagram 3

to the total, to give the number of minutes—546 minutes. 546 divided by 12 is 45.5 minutes, which is therefore the length of a daytime planetary hour on that day.

The first planetary hour that day will be the hour of the Sun, and will run from sunrise at 7:12 A.M. for 45.5 minutes, ending at 7:57 and 30 seconds. The eighth planetary hour of the day will begin seven planetary hours, or 5 hours 18 minutes 30 seconds of clock time, after sunrise, at 30 seconds past 12:30 P.M., and go until 1:16 P.M. If neither of these will work, you'll have to calculate the third and tenth planetary hours of the night, which are also governed by the Sun. The hours of the night are much longer than the daytime hours at this season—there are 894 minutes between sunset and sunrise, and so each nocturnal planetary hour is a full 74.5 minutes long; the third hour of the night thus begins at 6:47 P.M. and runs until 8:01 and 30 seconds, while the tenth hour begins 30 seconds after 3:28 A.M. and runs until 4:43 A.M.

If you wanted to make the amulet with the element of Fire in course, and didn't care about the planetary hour, you would have twelve chances that day: from 8:00 to 8:24 A.M., from 10:00 to 10:24 A.M., from 12:00 noon to 12:24 P.M., and so on around the clock. If you wanted to have both the element and the planet in course, on the other hand, your only chance would be from 4:00 to 4:24 A.M. on Monday morning.

Planetary Hours

Hours of the Day

Hour	Sunday	Monday	Tuesday	Wednesday	Thursday	Friday	Saturday
1	Sun	Moon	Mars	Mercury	Jupiter	Venus	Saturn
2	Venus	Saturn	Sun	Moon	Mars	Mercury	Jupiter
3	Mercury	Jupiter	Venus	Saturn	Sun	Moon	Mars
4	Moon	Mars	Mercury	Jupiter	Venus	Saturn	Sun
5	Saturn	Sun	Moon	Mars	Mercury	Jupiter	Venus
6	Jupiter	Venus	Saturn	Sun	Moon	Mars	Mercury
7	Mars	Mercury	Jupiter	Venus	Saturn	Sun	Moon
8	Sun	Moon	Mars	Mercury	Jupiter	Venus	Saturn
9	Venus	Saturn	Sun	Moon	Mars	Mercury	Jupiter
10	Mercury	Jupiter	Venus	Saturn	Sun	Moon	Mars
11	Moon	Mars	Mercury	Jupiter	Venus	Saturn	Sun
12	Saturn	Sun	Moon	Mars	Mercury	Jupiter	Venus

Hours of the Night

Hour	Sunday	Monday	Tuesday	Wednesday	Thursday	Friday	Saturday
1	Jupiter	Venus	Saturn	Sun	Moon	Mars	Mercury
2	Mars	Mercury	Jupiter	Venus	Saturn	Sun	Moon
3	Sun	Moon	Mars	Mercury	Jupiter	Venus	Saturn
4	Venus	Saturn	Sun	Moon	Mars	Mercury	Jupiter
5	Mercury	Jupiter	Venus	Saturn	Sun	Moon	Mars
6	Moon	Mars	Mercury	Jupiter	Venus	Saturn	Sun
7	Saturn	Sun	Moon	Mars	Mercury	Jupiter	Venus
8	Jupiter	Venus	Saturn	Sun	Moon	Mars	Mercury
9	Mars	Mercury	Jupiter	Venus	Saturn	Sun	Moon
10	Sun	Moon	Mars	Mercury	Jupiter	Venus	Saturn
11	Venus	Saturn	Sun	Moon	Mars	Mercury	Jupiter
12	Mercury	Jupiter	Venus	Saturn	Sun	Moon	Mars

Table 1

Practicing Natural Magic

In the course of learning natural magic, you probably won't follow the four steps of the sequence we've just outlined all the time. It's a good idea, as part of the learning process, to spend time working intensively with one herb or stone, or with a single planetary or elemental correspondence, to broaden your knowledge and develop a clear sense of the potentials of one aspect of the universe of natural magic. When you set out to accomplish something through natural magic, though, the four steps given above will bring you the most reliable results.

Another issue you will need to explore is the role of ritual in your work. You may wish to combine your experiments in natural magic with ritual workings, or you may not. There are many different kinds and traditions of magical ritual, of course, ranging all the way from the very simple "kitchen magic" used by many pagan systems up to the complex occult disciplines of magical lodge traditions such as the Golden Dawn, the Aurum Solis, and others. All of these approaches, different as they are, can be effectively combined with the toolkit of natural magic. For this reason, I haven't included ritual methods to go along with the natural magic techniques in this book; my own training in ritual magic is in one particular tradition, the tradition of the Golden Dawn, and the methods it uses aren't really suited for everyone. It should be remembered, though, that natural magic can also be used on its own, without a ritual framework. While this may not be the best option in many cases—the union of ritual and natural magic can achieve results neither approach accomplishes by itself—it is a possibility, and one you may wish to explore.

One thing that should accompany all of your explorations of natural magic is a written record. It's a good idea to keep a magical journal in which all your recipes, workings, and experiences in natural magic can be written down and reviewed at intervals. It's also a good idea to put together a looseleaf notebook of magical recipes for easy reference. Both of these will help you learn from your successes and your mistakes alike.

PART 2

THE
NATURAL
MAGIC
ENCYCLOPEDIA

Using the Natural Magic Encyclopedia

In the pages that follow, 176 substances used in natural magic—herbs, trees, stones, oils, resins, and more—are described in detail. This is only a small portion of the whole range of raw material that can be used by the natural magician. I have focused on substances that can be used relatively easily and safely by the beginning student of this art, and for the most part on those with a solid history of use in traditional Western natural magic.

Information on each of the materials is listed here under the following headings:

Description: This is a basic, nontechnical description of the substance, giving its source, its appearance, and (where appropriate) a little bit of its history as well. This will not give you enough information to identify plants accurately in the wild, or for that matter in your backyard; for that, a good botanical handbook and a solid grasp of botany is a necessity.

Temperature: In the traditional lore of Western natural magic and medicine, each substance had a "temperature" corresponding to one of the four elements, and to two of the four qualities that make up the elements. Thus substances were seen as fiery (which is warm and dry), airy (warm and moist), watery (cold and moist), or earthy (cold and dry). Each of the qualities, in turn, could be present in one of four degrees, ranging from the first degree (very mild) to the fourth (very intense). Temperature deals with the elemental *effect* of the substance—that is, which direction it tends to pull the elemental balance of the human body. Temperature thus determines the element that will be strongest *in the magician* as a result of a working.

Astrology: This heading gives the planet and sign of the zodiac traditionally held to rule the substance. There are normally a range of different correspondences given in the old books; the process of working out these correspondences is an art, not an exact science. I have chosen the attributions that have proved most accurate and useful in my own experience, and provided alternatives when a substance seems to relate to more than one astrological factor. Note that the sign of the zodiac also gives another elemental correspondence, as each sign corresponds to one of the elements. This correspondence gives the elemental *nature* of the substance— that is, the element that will be strongest in the substance itself during the working.

Lore: This heading is simply a collection of some of the folklore and magical tradition surrounding the substance, and can be used as a guide to the subtleties of its magical use.

Safety Issues: The fact that a substance is "natural" doesn't necessarily make it safe! Poison hemlock, arsenic, and strychnine are all naturally occurring substances, and an herbal poison can kill you just as efficiently as one made from artificial chemicals. Most of the materials covered here are relatively safe, but the recommendations given under this heading need to be studied carefully *and followed* in order to prevent potentially serious problems from arising.

Parts Used: When a substance has different parts (herbs, for instance, have roots, seeds, leaves, flowers, and the like), some parts may be useful for natural magic, while other parts are not. The specific parts to be used are listed here.

How Used: There are various different ways to make use of any given substance in natural magic. The various kinds of preparations and their use in practical magic, are covered in detail in Part Three of this book, but this heading gives basic types of preparations as a guide to how the different substances are best put to work.

Magical Uses: Each substance, in turn, has certain specific effects—"occult virtues," to use the traditional term—when put to use in a magical working. It's often not enough to know the astrological and elemental symbolism of a given herb or stone, since any one planet, element, or sign can rule over many different aspects of life. This heading gives details of the magical effects of each substance and, when appropriate, some hints concerning the best way to put those effects to work.

The Encyclopedia

Acorn

Acorn

Description: The acorn is the nut of the oak tree. See *Oak*.

Temperature: Earthy—cold in the second degree, dry in the third.

Astrology: Jupiter in Sagittarius.

Lore: Acorns have been important symbols of fertility in Western magical traditions since ancient times; in fact, "glans," the medical term for the head of the penis, literally means "acorn" in Latin.

Safety Issues: Acorns contain large amounts of tannic acid, which will upset your stomach if eaten.

Parts Used: Whole acorn.

How Used: Amulets.

Magical Uses: Acorns may be put to use in any working intended to bring about fertility, whether in the most obvious sense or in the subtler realms of creativity and artistic innovation.

Agate

Description: This attractive translucent stone is a fine-grained variety of chalcedony, and may occur in several different colors. One type, called moss agate, has mosslike dark patterns.

Temperature: Airy—warm and moist in the second degree.

Astrology: Mercury in Gemini.

Lore: The agate is one of the classic protective stones in traditional Western natural magic, having power to banish hostile spirits and turn aside magical attack. It also had applications in weather magic, where it was used to halt storms.

Different colors of agate have different powers in traditional lore. The green variety was used to help both physical and nonphysical vision and to promote fertility, the red to banish venomous creatures and to calm storms. The tawny agate was credited with protective powers against every kind of evil, and gave its wearer both a bold heart and, paradoxically, the virtue of prudence. Moss agates are important in garden magic, and the wearer of one will always have a green thumb.

Safety Issues: None.

How Used: Amulets; water and oil infusions can be used in potions, baths, washes, oils, and scents.

Magical Uses: Agate is worth considering in any working meant to bring insight or to help someone deal with a dangerous situation. It may also be used for any of the traditional purposes listed above.

Agrimony

Agrimony (*Agrimonia eupatoria*)

Description: Agrimony is a common perennial weed found all over the world. Its leaves are divided into coarsely toothed leaflets that alternate long and short, and its flowers, which appear in a tall spike from May to September, are small, yellow, and five-petaled. It is also known as stickle-wort or cocklebur.

Temperature: Fiery—warm and dry in the first degree.

Astrology: Jupiter in Cancer.

Lore: Agrimony was traditionally used as a sleep charm to banish insomnia, especially the kind caused by worries and depression. An old tradition held that if it was laid under a sleeper's head, they would not awake until it was removed. It also has a long history as a charm against hostile magic. For strongest effect, it should be harvested at midsummer.

Safety Issues: None.

Parts Used: Entire herb.

How Used: Amulets, sachets, potions, baths and washes, oils and scents.

Magical Uses: Agrimony may be used for either of the traditional purposes just mentioned. It is particularly useful for dispelling hostile magic or turning it back against the sender.

Almond (*Amygdalus communis*)

Description: The almond tree is native to the Mediterranean countries but is cultivated in warm and relatively dry climates over much of the world. It grows ten to twenty feet high, with slender pointed leaves, pink or whitish flowers, and sharp thorns. The kernel produces a light, clear oil (sold as "sweet almond oil") when pressed. This should not be confused with the essential oil extracted from the bitter variety of almond, usually called "bitter almond oil," which is somewhat poisonous and must be rectified (purified of toxic compounds) to make it safe for use.

Temperature: Fiery—warm and dry in the first degree.

Astrology: Jupiter in Leo.

Alternative Correspondence: Sun.

Lore: A length of almond branch was one of the traditional materials for a magician's wand.

Safety Issues: The unrectified essential oil is toxic and should not be used.

Parts Used: Nuts, wood, oil, rectified essential oil.

How Used: Use the nuts in amulets and food, the wood in working tools, and the essential oil in incense, baths, washes, oils, and scents. Sweet almond oil is one of the standard carrier oils and may be used in making infused oils of any kind.

Magical Uses: Important as a correspondence of Jupiter, almond can be used whenever the energies of this planet need to be invoked into a working. It also helps foster clairvoyance and divination.

Almond

Amber

Description: True amber is the fossilized resin of ancient pine forests, mostly in lands now under the North Sea. Relatively soft for a stone, it will scratch easily unless handled with a certain degree of care. The resin of the storax tree is often sold as "amber" but has different magical powers; see *Storax*.

Temperature: Fiery—warm in the third degree and dry in the first.

Astrology: Sun in Leo.

Lore: Amber traditionally calms the nerves and brings mental clarity. It was worn by Roman women as protection against hostile magic, and has been used by many cultures for magical healing.

Safety Issues: None.

How Used: Amulets; water and oil infusions may be used in potions, baths, washes, oils, and scents.

Magical Uses: Amber is a magical amplifier, and a piece placed in an amulet or used in other forms of natural magic will make success more likely. Its solar connections also make it a good choice for any working drawing on the energy of the Sun.

Amethyst

Description: Amethyst is a variety of quartz crystal naturally tinted with violet or purple.

Temperature: Fiery—warm and dry in the first degree.

Astrology: Jupiter in Sagittarius.

Lore: The term "amethyst" comes from a Greek word meaning "not drunk," as it was believed that wearing an amethyst would prevent drunkenness. This stone was held to provide similar protection against any other form of intoxication, whether this be from drugs, from sexual desires, or from emotions, and would also banish nightmares and bring sound sleep. To give an amethyst to a lover or spouse was believed to make love lasting.

Safety Issues: None.

How Used: Amulets; water and oil infusions may be used in potions, baths, washes, oils, and scents.

Magical Uses: Use amethyst to invoke Jupiter, to bring mental clarity and peace of mind, to deal with any situation where confusion and intoxication would be a problem, and to improve the mind generally. Put an amethyst under the pillow to improve sleep and bring pleasant dreams.

Angelica (*Angelica archangelica, A. atropurpurea*)

Description: Angelica is a tall biennial or perennial herb that grows wild in damp places, and is also cultivated as a medicinal plant. It stands from three to seven feet high when mature, with large compound leaves and umbels of white or greenish-white flowers. The two species named here—the first European, the second native to North America—have the same medical and magical uses. An essential oil is extracted from the root; a gum for incense can also be gathered by making small cuts on the stem and root crown in spring and harvesting the hardened sap.

Temperature: Fiery—warm and dry in the third degree.

Astrology: Sun in Leo.

Lore: Angelica is traditionally attributed to the archangel Michael, ruler of Fire and of the Sun, and old herbals claim that it always bloomed on May 8, the feast of the Apparition of St. Michael. The root was worn about the neck to dispel hostile magic, evil spirits, and epidemic disease. It was also kept in the house for similar purposes.

Like many other solar herbs, it was also used to banish ill luck and bring a change in fortune for the better.

Safety Issues: Angelica should not be used internally by diabetics. The essential oil can cause photosensitivity, and should be avoided during pregnancy.

Angelica

Parts Used: Root, essential oil.

How Used: Amulets, sachets, incense, food, potions, baths, washes, oils, and scents.

Magical Uses: Angelica is one of the most powerful protective herbs known to Western natural magic, and it also serves to bring energies of blessing and healing to bear on a person or place. The root is the part most often used; pieces of root can be included in any kind of amulet, or a root can simply be used intact as an amulet in its own right. Angelica root may also be eaten, either straight or candied. Powdered, it can be used as an incense, while a potion made from the root may be used as a ritual drink or added to bath water to cleanse your aura. The essential oil may be used in baths and washes as well as amulets, oils, and scents.

Anise (*Pimpinella anisum*)

Description: Anise is a widely cultivated annual that can also be found wild in many places. It stands up to one-and-a-half feet high, has delicate leaves of several different shapes, and produces umbels of small white flowers in July and August. The seeds are commonly used as a baking spice, and an essential oil is extracted from them.

Temperature: Fiery—warm and dry in the second degree.

Astrology: Mars in Scorpio.

Lore: Anise is used to drive off obsessing spirits, especially those that focus on disrupting the emotional levels of the self. It stabilizes the emotions, clears away feelings of depression, and helps bring the conscious self in tune with the higher levels of the self. In many countries, it also has an important place in wedding lore, and is used to season wedding cakes.

Safety Issues: The essential oil is very potent and can be toxic in large doses.

Parts Used: Seeds, essential oil.

How Used: Amulets, sachets, food, potions, baths, washes, oils, and scents.

Magical Uses: Put anise in a dream pillow to chase off disturbing dreams and offer protection when using the dreaming state as a portal to the astral realm, and put it into any cake you bake for a wedding or handfasting. It may also be used in banishing and exorcism.

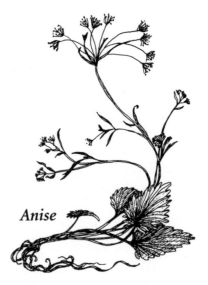

Anise

Apple

Apple (*Pyrus malus*)

Description: Like most of the common fruit-bearing plants of the Western world, the apple tree is a member of the rose family. It is common enough to need no description here.

Temperature: Sour apples such as Granny Smith are earthy—cold and dry in the second degree; sweet apples such as Delicious and Rome are airy— warm and moist in the second degree.

Astrology: Venus in Libra.

Lore: The apple has a wide range of traditional lore and magical customs connected with it in different countries. It is sometimes a faery tree, and the last apple of the year's crop should always be left in the tree to ensure good harvests.

Safety Issues: None.

Parts Used: Fruit, flowers, and wood.

How Used: Amulets, food, and potions.

Magical Uses: Apples are primarily useful in love magic.

Asafoetida (*Ferula foetida*)

Description: Asafoetida is the dried juice of a Central Asian perennial that has a stem from six to ten feet high and umbels of greenish flowers on top. I've never encountered the plant, but if it smells a tenth as bad as its dried sap, it's one to avoid. The gum has a pervasive rank scent, and when burnt it produces clouds of smoke that smell like an overpowering combination of very rotten onions and burning dung. Another name for the plant is "Devil's dung," which sums things up quite well. The sap is extracted by making incisions on the root and stem, allowing the sap to harden, and then gathering it.

Temperature: Fiery—warm and dry in the third degree.

Astrology: Saturn in Gemini.

Lore: Asafoetida has long been used in Europe and elsewhere to banish hostile spirits.

Safety Issues: None.

Parts Used: Dried sap, essential oil.

How Used: Incense, oils.

Magical Uses: Asafoetida is the supreme tool for banishing in natural magic. Burned as incense, it will drive off spirits, no matter how powerful; it will also clear objects and enclosed spaces of all magical energies. Magicians who take up the sometimes risky practice of summoning spirits often keep a bottle of powdered asafoetida on the altar in case things go completely awry. The one disadvantage to this useful habit is that if the asafoetida is ever used as an incense, every magical object present in the room when it is burned will be stripped of energies and will have to be reconsecrated.

The essential oil of asafoetida is somewhat less disruptive to magical energies than the burnt resin, and smells less vile as well, but it can be hard to obtain. It may also be used to banish and purify.

Ash

Ash (*Fraxinus spp.*)

Description: Ash is a deciduous tree, tall and straight, with smooth bark and leaves divided into narrow, pointed, sawtoothed leaflets.

Temperature: Fiery—warm and dry in the second degree.

Astrology: Sun in Sagittarius.

Lore: The ash is an elf tree, and was associated (like most things faery) with the lore of medieval witchcraft as well. The winged seeds (called "keys") of the ash, on the other hand, are protective against hostile magic. Wands made of ash branches were carried by Druids in ancient times, and more recently were used for healing and prosperity workings.

Safety Issues: None.

Parts Used: Wood, seeds.

How Used: Amulets, working tools.

Magical Uses: The traditional uses are a practical guide here.

Asphodel (*Asphodelus spp.*)

Description: There are various species of asphodels grown for their showy flowers, which are star shaped and may be white, yellow, or of mixed colors. All grow from bulbous roots and have long, narrow leaves. The flowers blossom in May and June.

Temperature: Fiery—warm and dry in the third degree.

Astrology: Saturn in Leo.

Lore: The asphodel is closely linked to death and the after-death state in traditional lore.

Safety Issues: None.

Parts Used: Whole plant or flower.

How Used: Living plants, amulets, baths, washes, and oils.

Magical Uses: Asphodel should be used in workings directed toward the dead—for example, in laying a ghost to rest or helping a newly dead person to finish the transition out of the physical world. It is also considered wise to plant asphodel around graves to assist the dead in their transition.

Barley (*Hordeum vulgare*)

Description: Like most of our grain crops, barley is simply a kind of grass; look at an unmowed vacant lot around August and you'll see the sort of seed heads our distant ancestors gathered and, in time, learned to plant. Barley was one of the earliest of these useful grasses to be cultivated, and from Sumerian times to the present it has been grown for bread and beer.

Temperature: Earthy—cold and dry in the first degree.

Astrology: Saturn in Virgo.

Lore: As an ancient grain, barley has traditional links to some of the oldest known agricultural rites of the Western world. Initiates of the Eleusinian mysteries of ancient Greece drank a ceremonial drink made of barley, pennyroyal, and water. In Egypt, figures of the god Osiris were made of soil and barley seeds and then watered, so that the sprouting of the barley would symbolize the resurrection of the god.

Safety Issues: None.

Parts Used: Grains, flour.

How Used: Amulets, food, potions.

Magical Uses: All grains are fertility charms, which is why newly married couples are pelted with rice on their way out the door, and barley shares this symbolism and use as well. Cakes of barley are a traditional offering to the faeries.

Basil (*Ocimum basilicum*)

Description: Basil is an annual of the mint family, originally native to India, which is grown in gardens over most of the world. One to two feet high when mature, it has paired leaves, clusters of white or red flowers, and a strong aromatic scent.

Temperature: Airy—warm and moist in the first degree.

Astrology: Mars in Scorpio.

Lore: The martial and energetic quality of basil gives it the power to dispel fears and bring courage. It is also known to banish hostile spirits, and has

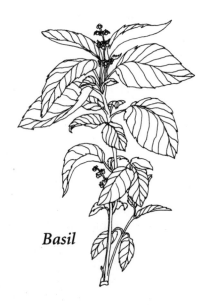

Basil

been used in many cultures to purify sacred spaces. Old books claim that too much use of basil will cause scorpions to breed in one's brain; the insight behind this symbolism is that, handled unwisely, the energies of the herb can lead to an overload of the passionate and belligerent qualities associated with Scorpio.

Basil should always be harvested in autumn for the best magical effect.

Safety Issues: The essential oil should be avoided during pregnancy.

Parts Used: Whole plant, leaves, and essential oil.

How Used: Living plants, amulets, sachets, incense, seasoning for food, potions, baths, washes, oils, and scents.

Magical Uses: Basil may be used in any working for protection, purification, or courage, or burned as an incense in invocations to Mars. Used occasionally and/or in combination with other less intense herbs, it can be valuable as a tool to banish fear, weakness, and confusion. Oil of basil may be blended with holy water to purify a working space before summoning spirits or engaging in other relatively dangerous forms of ritual magic.

Bay Laurel (*Laurus nobilis*)

Description: An evergreen shrub or small tree native to the Mediterranean basin, bay laurel has leathery dull-green leaves and small white flowers that bloom in clusters in spring, giving way to black berries in late summer.

Bay laurel should not be confused with West Indian bay (*Pimenta racemosa*), a tropical evergreen tree found in the Caribbean, or with bayberry (*Myrcia cerifera*), a North American tree with waxy berries. These are used in aromatherapy and perfumery, but their magical properties still await thorough exploration.

Temperature: Fiery—hot and dry in the third degree.

Astrology: Sun in Leo.

Lore: "Neither witch nor devil, thunder or lightning will hurt a man in the place where a bay tree is," runs an old saying. It was already in use as a protective incense in ancient Mesopotamia, and in Greece it was sacred to the solar god Apollo. The Greek magician-philosopher Proclus Diadochos, writing in the fourth century A.D., commented that branches of bay were a necessity in ritual work, as they allowed the magus to command and banish spirits.

The sudden withering of a bay laurel in a garden, on the other hand, was considered an omen of disaster for the garden's owner.

Safety Issues: The leaves and berries are mildly toxic and should not be taken internally, although a few leaves added to spaghetti sauce or other foods and set aside, uneaten, will provide seasoning without the least risk.

Parts Used: Leaves, essential oil.

How Used: Living trees, amulets, sachets, incense, seasoning for food, baths, washes, oils, and scents.

Magical Uses: Bay leaves, readily available at many grocery stores, are a powerful protective tool for the natural magician. They may be used in amulets and many other preparations, and they are often used as a flavoring for food, although it's unwise to eat them or drink a potion of the leaves as they are poisonous in concentrated doses. They also have divinatory powers. If you are thinking about a project, throw bay leaves onto the fire; if they crackle loudly, the project will be a success, while if they smolder and make no noise the omens are less favorable.

Bean, all varieties (*Phaseolus vulgaris*)

Description: For all their diversity, most of the varieties of bean currently grown in Western countries—navy beans, pinto beans, green beans, string beans, wax beans, and snap beans—are all descendants of the humble kidney bean, and share the same magical symbolism and uses. An annual, the bean plant has leaves divided into three-pointed leaflets, flowers of a range of colors, and green or yellow seed pods containing the beans themselves, of various colors depending on the variety.

Temperature: Airy—warm and moist in the first degree.

Astrology: Venus in Virgo.

Bean

Alternative Correspondence: Sun.

Lore: Beans, for all their homely reputation, are magical plants with a wide range of powers in traditional lore. The souls of the dead were said to hover around bean flowers in bloom, and it was believed that to sleep overnight in a bean field would bring madness, or at the very least terrifying dreams. On the other hand, beans were also used to chase away harmful spirits; a handful of beans thrown at a ghost, or a single bean spat out of the mouth, was thought to be sure protection against supernatural harm.

Safety Issues: None.

Parts Used: Whole plant, flowers, and seed.

How Used: Amulets, sachets, and food.

Magical Uses: Beans may be used, as in the traditional lore, to dispel spirits. Bean flowers may also be used, with care, for visionary workings.

Belladonna (*Atropa belladonna*)

Description: A perennial found in abandoned fields and wastes in Europe and eastern North America, belladonna has a fleshy, white rootstock, a stem that usually divides into three branches, and leaves in pairs with one twice the size of the other. It has brown or purple bell-shaped flowers and shiny, black, cherry-sized fruits.

Temperature: Earthy—cold and dry in the fourth degree.

Astrology: Saturn in Libra.

Lore: Belladonna was an important herb in the lore of medieval witchcraft, and an ingredient in some flying ointments. It was also used in love charms in some cultures. It should be picked at dawn for best magical effect.

Safety Issues: TOXIC. Belladonna is poisonous and should never be taken internally or used in a charm that will be in contact with your body.

Parts Used: Berries, root.

How Used: Amulets.

Magical Uses: Use belladonna, with care, in workings intended to bring love.

Belladonna

Benzoin (*Styrax benzoin*)

Description: The benzoin tree is a large tropical evergreen native to Southeast Asia, growing up to sixty feet tall. Its leaves, which resemble those of orange or lemon trees, are pale green above and whitish beneath. The resin used in natural magic is collected by making slits on the trunk and allowing the sap that flows out to harden on exposure to air and sun. The resin dissolves well in alcohol but hardens in water—a fact that needs to be kept in mind when considering its potential uses!

Temperature: Airy—warm and moist in the second degree.

Astrology: Sun in Capricorn.

Lore: One of the ancient incense resins, benzoin has been used for thousands of years to banish evil spirits. It also is known to improve one's mood and dispel depression.

Safety Issues: None.

Parts Used: Resin, essential oil.

How Used: Amulets, sachets, incense, oils, and scents.

Magical Uses: Benzoin makes a good resin for purifications, exorcisms, and protections, and may be used in oils and scents for the same purposes. Blend it in incenses for meditation and ritual workings, especially those focusing on balance and inner growth.

Beryl

Description: There are many colors of beryl, including the pale blue aquamarine and the golden heliodor, but the standard blue or blue-green type is the most suitable for magical uses. Chemically speaking, beryl is an aluminum beryllium silicate.

Temperature: Watery—cold and moist in the third degree.

Astrology: Mars in Scorpio.

Lore: The beryl is an elf stone, and was held to bring victory in war or legal conflict. More impressively, it is also credited with the power to cure stupidity. It was used to bring happiness, sharpen the mind, and stave off the effects of age; seafarers wore it to keep themselves safe from storms. In Christian magical lore, the beryl is assigned to St. Thomas and to the sixth order of angels, the Powers.

Safety Issues: None.

How Used: Amulets; water and oil infusions may also be used in potions, baths, washes, oils, and scents.

Magical Uses: Beryl is worth considering in any working meant to bring a successful end to conflict, and can also be used to attract faery contact. It also has general powers of protection, especially against hostile magic. Whether or not it is capable of overcoming stupidity, it does appear to sharpen the mind when worn as an amulet.

Betony (*Betonica officinalis*)

Description: A small perennial found in meadows, slopes, and forest edges in Europe, betony is also grown as a medicinal herb. Its leaves are opposite and hairy, and its flowers grow in whorls at the upper end of the plant during the summer months. It stands from six inches to two feet high.

Temperature: Fiery—warm and dry in the second degree.

Astrology: Jupiter in Aries.

Lore: A powerful protective herb, betony was often used to banish hostile magic, nightmares, and the evil creatures held to stalk the night. It was planted in churchyards to lay ghosts to rest, and worn in amulets of protection, especially by those who had to travel after dark. Like many magical herbs, though, it was held to lose all its virtue if touched with iron.

Safety Issues: None.

Parts Used: Whole plant.

How Used: Live plants, amulets, sachets, potions, baths, washes, and oils.

Magical Uses: Put the entire plant into amulets or sachets to banish hostile magic and malevolent spirits, or use an infusion for similar purposes. An herb pillow filled with betony will prevent nightmares. This herb may also be grown in the yard to protect a house and all who live in it from destructive magical forces.

Birch (*Betula spp.*)

Description: There are two different species of birch found wild in North America, white birch (*B. alba*) and black birch (*B. lenta*). Both are slender, deciduous trees with heart-shaped, finely toothed leaves and separate male and female catkins. Both have the same magical energies and effects.

Temperature: Fiery—warm and dry in the first degree.

Astrology: Venus in Sagittarius.

Lore: Birch was another source of protective magic in tradition, and birch twigs were kept in the house to turn aside the evil eye. A bundle of birch twigs beaten along the boundaries of a piece of property will drive away evil forces and bad luck. A birch tree decorated with red and white rags was often propped up near the stable door to keep the horses from being ridden by elves, who would not only drive the animals to the point of exhaustion but leave their manes knotted as well. On the other hand, the birch-spirit was held to be among the more dangerous tree-spirits, with the power to inflict madness or death with a touch of its long, white hand.

Safety Issues: The essential oil of sweet birch, which comes from the European species *B. lenta,* is somewhat toxic and should not be used in contact with the skin; the oil of white birch, by contrast, is entirely safe.

Parts Used: Twigs, whole tree, wood, and essential oil.

How Used: Living trees, amulets, working tools, incense, baths, washes, oils, and scents.

Magical Uses: Those who have easy access to birch should certainly keep it in mind for protective magic. Magicians who work with the faery

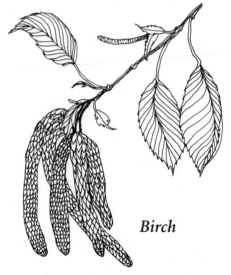

Birch

realm may find it useful to make a staff or wand of birch to protect themselves against the more dangerous of its inhabitants. The essential oil of white birch has the same effects, and may be used in any of the standard ways.

Blessed Thistle (*Cnicus benedictus*)

Description: An annual that grows wild in Europe and western Asia and is cultivated elsewhere, blessed thistle has the spiny leaves and flower heads common to all thistles. Its flowers are yellow and bloom from May to August.

Temperature: Fiery—warm and dry in the second degree.

Astrology: Mars in Aries.

Lore: Associated with St. Benedict in the lore of medieval Christian magic, blessed thistle was commonly used against hostile magic as well as against the less focused but still harmful force of simple hatred and ill will.

Safety Issues: Do not use while pregnant.

Parts Used: Flower, whole herb.

How Used: Amulets, incense, potions, baths, and washes.

Magical Uses: Blessed thistle may be used in all works of protection and blessing, especially when one is the target of envy, anger, or hatred.

Bloodstone

Description: Bloodstone is a deep green variety of chalcedony with flecks of red.

Temperature: Fiery—warm and dry in the second degree.

Astrology: Mars in Aries.

Lore: Bloodstone is a traditional talisman for warriors, granting courage, wisdom, and firmness of will, and was held to have the ability to stop bleeding. Traditional lore claims that it can be used in weather magic to call storms and thunder, and also to enable the wearer to read omens from the sounds of thunder and rain.

Safety Issues: None.

How Used: Amulets; water and oil infusions may also be used in potions, baths, washes, oils, and scents.

Magical Uses: Use bloodstone to invoke the energies of Mars, to summon rain, and to heighten awareness of the subtle messages of nature. Placed beneath the pillow, it will bring prophetic dreams.

Borage (*Borago officinalis*)

Description: Borage is an annual native to the Mediterranean region, hairy all over and growing up to two feet high. Its leaves form a basal rosette and grow alternately up the stem and branches. Its flowers are star-shaped, blue or purple, and bloom from June through August.

Temperature: Airy—warm and moist in the first degree.

Astrology: Jupiter in Leo.

Lore: "I, Borage, grant courage," runs an old proverb, and this points straight to the most important magical (and medical) function of the herb. Whenever one needs help overcoming fear or depression, borage is an excellent choice.

Borage

Safety Issues: Do not use long-term, during pregnancy, or while nursing.

Parts Used: Flowers.

How Used: Amulets, food, potions, incense, baths, and washes.

Magical Uses: Borage should be used in workings whenever courage is needed, and may simply be eaten for the same purpose; the flowers are traditional for this use, not to mention tasty!

Bracken Fern (*Pteridium aquilinum*)

Description: Bracken fern is one of the most common of all ferns, found in temperate climates around the world. An annual, it sends up fiddleheads each spring that unfold into spreading, multiply divided fronds that branch out from a single vertical stem. It is best when harvested in late spring or early summer. The brownish spores are hidden under the rolled edges of the fronds.

Temperature: Airy—warm in the first degree, dry in the third.

Astrology: Mercury in Taurus.

Lore: Like all of the ferns, bracken is associated with the art of magical invisibility, and those who wished to walk unseen were advised to gather fern seed and carry it with them. There is at least one level of irony at work here, as ferns have no seeds! (They are among the most ancient of all surviving plant types, and reproduce by means of spores.) It was probably the powdery spores, which grow on the bottom of the leaflets, that were gathered and pocketed by magicians from early times to the present. Traditionally, this had to be done at midnight; the spores were shaken out onto a sheet of virgin parchment or paper.

Safety Issues: Although a traditional wild food in many cultures, bracken fern can cause vitamin B deficiencies if eaten in large quantities.

Parts Used: Spores.

How Used: Amulets.

Magical Uses: Fern spores may be used whenever natural magic is used for invisibility workings, or simply in any situation where one would rather not be noticed.

Bryony (*Bryonia alba, B. dioica*)

Description: Bryony is a climbing plant with broad leaves and prickly stems. Native to central Europe, it is cultivated there and in North America as a medicinal and magical herb. Both species produce little greenish or yellowish flowers during the summer months; white bryony (*B. alba*) produces black berries, red bryony (*B. dioica*) red ones.

Temperature: Fiery—warm and dry in the third degree.

Astrology: Mars in Gemini.

Lore: Bryony is one of the chief magical herbs in European tradition. Its root was a common substitute for mandrake, with many of the same traditional powers. Little humanlike figures were often carved in bryony root and then buried in wet sand until the cut surfaces grew back over again; the resulting poppet was then used to house a familiar spirit, which was fed with daily offerings of wine. Other traditions claimed that bryony was protective against lightning, and one who wears a wreath of bryony leaves and flowers was thought to be safe during thunderstorms.

Safety Issues: TOXIC. Both types of bryony are poisonous and should not be taken internally or used in a charm that will come into contact with your body.

Part Used: Root.

How Used: Living plant, amulets.

Magical Uses: Like mandrake, bryony is a magical amplifier, and a small amount of the root placed in an amulet will increase its power. By itself, the root has protective powers and can be used for this purpose, but it seems to work best when combined with solar herbs or stones.

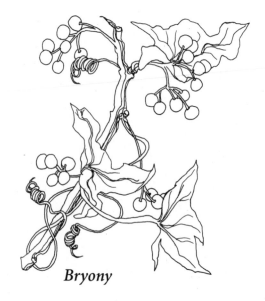

Bryony

Burdock

Burdock (*Arctium lappa*)

Description: Burdock is a common weed throughout the northern temperate regions of the world, with broad furry leaves and an edible taproot that may reach as far as six feet down into the soil. A biennial, it puts up a rosette of leaves at ground level the first year, and in the second year grows a stem several feet high on which purple flowers bloom, then turn to sticky burrs that fasten themselves tenaciously to hair, animal fur, and clothing. (The man who invented Velcro, it's claimed, first got the idea from burdock burrs.)

Temperature: Fiery—warm and dry in the first degree.

Astrology: Venus in Leo.

Lore: The root has been used as a protective amulet.

Safety Issues: None.

Parts Used: Root.

How Used: Amulets, food, potions, baths, and washes.

Magical Uses: Burdock root is worth considering as an ingredient in protective workings, as it seems to have definite positive effects in this direction, and it may also be eaten to draw on its magical and healing properties alike.

Camphor (*Cinnamomum camphora*)

Description: The camphor tree, a close relative of the cinnamon tree, is native to southern Asia and has been grown there for many centuries. An evergreen, it has clusters of small white flowers that mature into red berries. The wood of trees more than fifty years old contains a crystalline substance that is called raw or crude camphor; an essential oil can also be extracted from the wood.

Temperature: Watery—cold and moist in the third degree.

Astrology: Moon in Cancer.

Lore: Camphor was little used in traditional Western natural magic, but was believed to lessen sexual desire.

Safety Issues: Raw camphor is toxic in large doses and should not be taken internally. The essential oil is available in three different types, which represent different fractions of the very complex essence of the tree; white camphor, the lightest, is safe, but the other two (brown camphor and yellow camphor) are quite toxic and should not be used outside of a laboratory. Fortunately, nearly all the camphor oil sold by essential oil companies is white camphor.

Parts Used: Raw camphor, white camphor oil.

How Used: Amulets, sachets, incense, baths, washes, oils, and scents.

Magical Uses: Use camphor to invoke the Moon. Due to its mildly anaphrodisiac effects, it makes an excellent incense or scent for rituals involving the Greek goddess Diana, the Maiden phase of modern paganism's Triple Goddess, or any other virgin goddess associated with the Moon.

Caraway (*Carum carvi*)

Description: Caraway grows wild in the northern regions of North America, Europe, and Asia, and is cultivated throughout the northern temperate zone as a seasoning and a medicinal herb. Biennial or perennial, it puts up an angular, branched stem in the second year. Its small white or yellow flowers appear in umbels in May and June. An essential oil is extracted from the ripe seed or fruit.

Caraway

Temperature: Fiery—warm and dry in the third degree.

Astrology: Mercury in Cancer.

Lore: Caraway is commonly used as a magical herb for weddings in the same way, and for many of the same reasons, as anise. There is another side to this habit, though, for caraway was held to have the power to prevent all kinds of theft—including that of one's spouse! Traditional lore claims that objects containing caraway seed could not be stolen, and that the growing plant would prevent thieves from making their escape.

Safety Issues: None.

Parts Used: Whole plant, seed, and essential oil.

How Used: Living plants, amulets, sachets, seasoning for food, baths, washes, oils, and scents.

Magical Uses: Amulets of caraway seed can be worn or placed over doorways and windows to discourage thieves; a caraway wash may be used on the doorsill, or the plant itself can be grown in the yard, for the same purpose. Use an oil of caraway in blessing personal possessions that you wish to keep safe from theft.

Carnelian

Description: Another variety of chalcedony, carnelian is red and hard, qualities that pass over into its magical powers.

Temperature: Fiery—warm and dry in the third degree.

Astrology: Sun in Virgo.

Lore: Like most red stones, carnelian was seen in the traditional lore as a source of energy; it was recommended as a magical cure for shyness and a weak voice, and was also said to keep the wearer from harm as a result of collapsing houses or falling walls. Additionally, it protected the wearer against forgetfulness and anger. The opaque variety of carnelian, which is called sard, offers protection against sorcery, and also counteracts the negative qualities of onyx (see *Onyx*); in Christian magical lore, sard is associated with the first order of angels, the Seraphim.

Safety Issues: None.

How Used: Amulets; water or oil infusions may also be used in potions, baths, washes, oils, and scents.

Magical Uses: Carnelian may be used to help overcome shyness and to increase confidence in a wide array of circumstances, and it also makes a good basis for an amulet of mental clarity. Sard should always be around when onyx is used for natural magic, to protect against the latter's disruptive and depressive effects.

Cassia (see Cinnamon)

Catnip (*Nepeta cataria*)

Description: Catnip is a member of the mint family, with the telltale square stem and strong, aromatic flavor. A perennial, it has oblong, scallop-edged leaves with white fur on the underside. Its flowers, white with purple spots, grow in spikes from June to September.

Catnip

Temperature: Fiery—warm and dry in the third degree.

Astrology: Venus in Cancer.

Lore: Catnip was used traditionally in fertility charms, and its connection with cats was also made use of by those who practiced shapeshifting and other forms of animal magic.

Safety Issues: Do not take internally during pregnancy.

Parts Used: Whole plant, leaves.

How Used: Amulets, sachets, potions, baths, and washes.

Magical Uses: Any magical working involving cats or cat-related deities should involve catnip in one form or another. It may also be used to good effect as a relaxant to use before clairvoyant or visionary work, and a sachet or herbal pillow of catnip will protect sleepers if placed in or near the bed. It also makes an effective charm for a woman who wishes to become pregnant, but should not be taken internally in this case because of potential effects on the developing child.

Cattle (*Bos spp.*)

Description: Modern domesticated cattle are descended from the aurochs, the wild cattle of the Eurasian plains.

Temperature: Beef is airy—warm in the first degree, moist in the second.

Astrology: Moon in Taurus.

Lore: Cattle are lunar creatures par excellence, revered as such by many ancient cultures; their strength and the sharp horns of the older breeds are a reminder that the Moon was not always seen as a passive force!

Safety Issues: Live cattle should be treated with the respect that any other creature weighing half a ton would merit. If you eat beef, organically raised and grass-fed beef are less chemically and biologically contaminated than the ordinary feedlot-raised variety, as well as far more humane.

Parts Used: Meat, milk, cheese, horns, leather, hooves.

How Used: Food, working tools.

Magical Uses: Beef, milk, and cheese may be eaten as communion foods of the Moon; horns, leather, and hooves make good raw materials for lunar working tools.

Cedar (*Cedrus* and *Thuja spp.*)

Description: There are several different families of tree that bear the name "cedar," all of them evergreens with scaly needles and the familiar, strong cedar scent. All share the same broad magical symbolism and energies. An essential oil extracted from the Atlantic cedar (*C. atlantica*) is sold under the name "Atlas cedarwood" and works well for magical purposes.

Temperature: Fiery—warm and dry in the fourth degree.

Astrology: Jupiter in Sagittarius.

Lore: In Europe, cedar is often called *arbor vitae* ("tree of life"), but its traditional symbolism has much more to do with death. Cedars, like yews (which share a similar symbolism—see *Yew*), were routinely planted

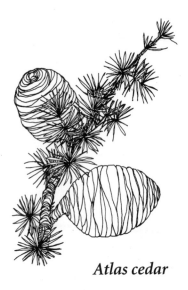

Atlas cedar

around cemeteries to symbolize eternal life but also more practically to keep the ghosts of the dead in their proper place.

It's worth noting that the Western red cedar (*Thuja occidentalis*) plays the same role in the Native American cultures of the Pacific Northwest; cedar bark and needles were used to purify those who had contact with the dead. The ancient Egyptians also made much use of cedar oil in their rituals of mummification.

Safety Issues: The essential oil is mildly toxic and should be avoided during pregnancy.

Parts Used: Needles, essential oil.

How Used: Amulets, sachets, incense, baths, washes, oils, and scents.

Magical Uses: Cedar's intensely fiery energy is a powerful tool for purification in any of its applications. It will banish hostile spirits and is invaluable in exorcism. It is also a powerful tool for workings aimed at success and the attainment of magical power.

Celandine

Description: Celandine is a common plant in damp places and roadsides all through northeastern North America and Europe. It has spreading, irregular leaves and bright yellow, four-petaled flowers that grow in umbels from April to September. All parts of the plant contain a bitter, yellow juice that turns red when it comes into contact with air.

Temperature: Fiery—warm and dry in the third degree.

Astrology: Sun in Leo.

Lore: Celandine should be gathered for magical purposes at dawn on a day when the Sun is in Leo and the Moon is in Aries.

Safety Issues: None.

Parts Used: Whole plant.

How Used: Amulets, sachets, potions, baths, and washes.

Magical Uses: Celandine is an important visionary herb. It can be used to fill dream pillows, or taken as a tea a short time before bed to bring prophetic dreams.

Centaury (*Centaurium umbellatum*)

Description: Centaury is found all over Europe in meadows and open woodlands. Six to eighteen inches tall, it has a rosette of basal leaves, and its stem leaves are opposite and sessile. Its flowers are red and cone-shaped, and bloom in the fall.

Temperature: Fiery—warm and dry in the third degree.

Astrology: Sun in Sagittarius.

Lore: Associated with Chiron the Centaur, the legendary healer and tutor to a whole generation of heroes in ancient Greek myth.

Safety Issues: None.

Parts Used: Flowers, whole plant.

How Used: Amulets, baths, and washes.

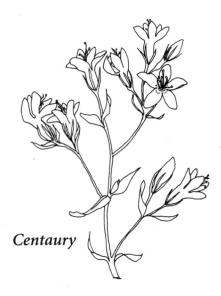

Centaury

Magical Uses: Centaury is a good plant for general magical purposes, used to banish hostile magic and to open up magical states of consciousness. Add some to workings based on other materials in order to give them additional force.

Chalcedony

Description: Many semiprecious stones are varieties of chalcedony, which is itself a translucent variety of quartz crystal. The variety generally sold under the name "chalcedony" is usually pale blue or gray, with a smooth, waxy shine.

Temperature: Airy—warm and moist in the second degree.

Astrology: Mercury in Cancer.

Lore: Traditionally a powerful healing stone, chalcedony is especially powerful against mental disturbances. It was also credited with the power to banish ghosts and harmful magic, which in some cases is another way of saying the same thing. It was also often used as an amulet to keep children from drowning.

Safety Issues: None.

How Used: Amulets; water and oil infusions may be used in potions, baths, washes, oils, and scents.

Magical Uses: Chalcedony can be used for any working of Mercury, as it concentrates the powers of this planet to high intensity. It is also well worth using to counteract a tendency to mental imbalance.

Chamomile (*Anthemis nobilis, Matricaria chamomilla*)

Description: There are two different plants called chamomile, belonging to different botanical genera but sharing the same magical symbolism and most of the same medical effects. The first (*A. nobilis*) is a creeping perennial with ferny leaves and daisylike flowers rising up on solitary stalks; the second (*M. chamomilla*) is an annual that can grow up to eighteen inches tall, with more substantial leaves and very similar flowers. Both are used as a source for essential oils.

Temperature: Fiery—warm and dry in the first degree.

Astrology: Sun in Leo.

Lore: Like most solar plants, chamomile has protective powers, and it was often grown in the garden to keep evil and ill luck away.

Safety Issues: Do not use while pregnant.

Parts Used: Whole plant, flower, and essential oil.

How Used: Living plants, amulets, sachets, potions, baths, washes, oils, and scents.

Magical Uses: Chamomile may be used in any working or preparation meant to protect and bless; it has potent healing powers, magical as well as medicinal, and it is also an important ingredient in fluid condensers. Use it whenever melancholy or stress are making some other problem worse. It also has visionary effects, and may be included in sachets or herbal pillows for magical dreamwork.

Chamomile

Chicken

Chicken (*Gallus domesticus*)

Description: The common domestic chicken is descended from the jungle fowl, a wild bird native to India, which was domesticated thousands of years ago and has since spread over much of the world.

Temperature: Fiery—warm and dry in the second degree.

Astrology: Sun in Aries.

Lore: Chickens were used in ancient times for divination; the diviner would trace a circle in the dirt with all the letters of the alphabet around it, put a grain of wheat on each letter, and then set a chicken in the middle. The order in which the chicken ate the grains spelled out the answer to the divination. They were also the classic sacrifice to solar gods and goddesses throughout the Mediterranean world.

Safety Issues: Both chicken meat and eggs should be cooked thoroughly to cut down on the risk of salmonella infection, which causes severe diarrhea. Handwashing with soap before and after handling chicken is a good idea, too. As with any other domestic animal, organically raised, free-range chicken is a good idea for a variety of reasons.

Parts Used: Meat, eggs, and feathers.

How Used: The meat and eggs may be used for food; the feathers may be used in amulets or as quills for drawing solar talismans.

Magical Uses: Chicken makes a useful correspondence to the Sun and may be used appropriately in any solar working.

Chicory (*Chicorium intybus*)

Description: Chicory, a relative of dandelion, can be found wild in Europe and North America and is also cultivated as a coffee substitute and a medicinal herb. It has long, narrow leaves, toothed around the base and smooth-edged higher up the plant, and its flowers are blue or violet, with toothed ends to the rays. It blooms from July well into the fall months.

Temperature: Earthy—cold and dry in the second degree.

Astrology: Jupiter in Virgo.

Lore: Chicory was said to grant the power of invisibility, and was one of the herbs that was believed to magically open locks. In order to have these powers, however, it supposedly had to be harvested on July 23 with a golden knife, in perfect silence.

Safety Issues: None.

Parts Used: Whole plant, flower.

How Used: Amulets, sachets, potions, baths, washes, and oils.

Magical Uses: A herb of silence and secrecy, chicory can be used in any working where these concepts are central.

Chicory

Chrysolite

Description: A semiprecious variety of olivine, a magnesium iron silicate, chrysolite is a translucent golden color—in fact, its name comes from the Greek words for "golden stone."

Temperature: Fiery—warm and dry in the third degree.

Astrology: Sun in Leo.

Lore: Chrysolite's traditional uses come primarily from its ancient place as the most important stone of the Sun. Worn as an amulet, it grants the solar qualities of dignity and charisma. In Christian magical lore, chrysolite is assigned to the fourth order of angels, the Dominations.

Safety Issues: None.

How Used: Amulets; water and oil infusions can be used in potions, baths, washes, oils, and scents.

Magical Uses: Chrysolite may be used to invoke the Sun and to give confidence and dignity, especially when dealing with large groups of people. Use it whenever you need help with leadership skills or wish to overcome shyness.

Cinnamon (*Cinnamomum zeylanicum*)

Description: Cinnamon is the powdered inner bark of a tree native to southern Asia, a tropical evergreen that grows up to fifty feet tall. It has thick bark, leathery leaves that let out a spicy smell when bruised, and small white flowers that mature into bluish-white berries. Essential oils are extracted from the leaves and the bark. Much of what is sold as "cinnamon" nowadays is actually from a related tree, cassia (*C. cassia*); this has most of the same characteristics, although its magical symbolism is a little different.

Temperature: Fiery—warm and dry in the second degree.

Astrology: True cinnamon is Sun in Aries, while cassia is Sun in Capricorn.

Cinnamon

Lore: Another solar plant with purifying and protective qualities, cinnamon was also often used in medieval love potions and amulets.

Safety Issues: The essential oil from the bark is a strong irritant, and should never be used in anything that will come into contact with bare skin. The essential oil from the leaf is much safer and is generally better for magical use, but—like any essential oil—should always be diluted before being applied to bare skin.

Parts Used: Powdered bark, essential oil of leaf.

How Used: Amulets, sachets, seasoning for food, incense, washes, oils, and scents.

Magical Uses: Use cinnamon to bring solar force to bear on any magical working, or to invoke the element of Fire. It has a strong expansive quality, and should be on the short list whenever magic is to be done to expand one's horizons or clear away limits, inner or outer. It may also be used for its protective virtues.

Cinquefoil (*Potentilla anserina*)

Description: Cinquefoil is a creeping perennial found in open ground throughout North America and Europe. Its leaves, divided into an odd number of toothed leaflets dark green above and silver below, grow in a basal rosette; its yellow flowers bloom on a long slender stalk from May through September. Two other species of cinquefoil, *P. canadensis* (found in eastern North America) and *P. reptans* (found in Europe), differ in that they always have five leaflets; they have the same magical uses as *P. anserina*.

Temperature: Earthy—cold and dry in the second degree.

Astrology: Mercury in Taurus.

Lore: For magical uses, cinquefoil should always be gathered at midnight beneath a waxing moon. It seems to strengthen nearly any form of magic, and for this reason was added to a dizzying range of natural magic workings. The root was also used by itself, carried in a pocket or hung around the neck to improve one's powers of communication and persuasion and to protect against hostile magic.

Safety Issues: None.

Parts Used: Root.

How Used: Amulets, baths, and washes.

Magical Uses: Another general magical herb, cinquefoil may be put into nearly any magical working or preparation to increase its strength. Its traditional uses are also worth putting to work.

Cinquefoil

Clary Sage (*Salvia sclaria*)

Description: A close relative of common sage, clary sage is a biennial that grows up to three feet high. Its leaves are fuzzy and slightly purplish, and it has small blue flowers.

Temperature: Fiery—warm in the first degree, dry in the second.

Astrology: Jupiter in Taurus.

Lore: Clary sage is traditionally associated with the eyes both magically and medicinally.

Safety Issues: None.

Parts Used: Leaves, essential oil.

How Used: Amulets, sachets, potions, baths, washes, oils, and scents.

Magical Uses: Clary sage may be used in any magical working where clarity of sight is needed, whether of the physical eyes or of subtler forms of vision. It also has calming and relaxing properties, and this may well play an important role in its visionary powers. An infusion of the leaves may be used to bathe the eyes or the forehead; the essential oil is also effective. The essential oil may also be used in place of ordinary sage oil, which is somewhat toxic.

Colors

Description: Color plays an important role in natural magic, and the skilled natural magician will always consider it as a resource. The fine gradations of color scales used in some traditions of ritual magic are rarely used in natural magic, however. Three colors—red, white, and black—form the essential palette of the natural magician.

Red corresponds to the life force, blood, Fire, and the Sun. In traditional natural magic, it is the standard color to use in works of protection, love, blessing, fertility, and healing.

White corresponds to the intuition and the psychic realm, to clarity, Water, and the Moon. It is the standard color to use in works of purification, consecration, and divination, as well as for spiritual development.

Black corresponds to death, night, sorrow, Earth, and the Underworld. It is the standard color to use in works of binding, exorcism, and invisibility. It was also traditionally used in works of malediction, destruction, and death by those selfish and foolish enough to engage in them.

For workings specially consecrated to one of the elements or planets, a somewhat more complex color system can be used.

Elements
Spirit: White

Air: Yellow

Fire: Red

Water: Blue

Earth: Green

Planets
Saturn: Black

Jupiter: Purple

Mars: Red

Sun: Orange

Venus: Green

Mercury: Yellow

Moon: Blue

How Used: Cloth bags for amulets and sachets, candles for oil dressings and rituals generally, garments and equipment for ritual wear.

Coltsfoot (*Tussilago farfara*)

Description: Coltsfoot is a perennial found in Europe, Asia, and North America, growing mostly in damp places. Each year the rootstock puts up a fuzzy white stem topped by a large yellow flower, and then large leaves whose shape—like a horse's hoof—give the plant its name.

Temperature: Earthy—cold in the first degree, dry in the second.

Astrology: Mercury in Taurus.

Lore: I have been able to find little in the way of traditional magical lore concerning coltsfoot, although it was often used as a healing herb.

Safety Issues: Use with caution. Avoid excessive or long-term use, and don't use while pregnant or nursing.

Parts Used: Leaves.

How Used: Amulets, sachets, incense, potions, baths, and washes.

Magical Uses: Coltsfoot is a visionary plant, and may be used to heighten visionary experience or to assist magical dreamwork. It also has a calming influence.

Comfrey (*Symphytum officinale*)

Description: Comfrey is a perennial that grows in damp places in North America and Europe, and is widely cultivated as well for its healing virtues. Its leaves are large, deeply veined and bristly, and its flowers—purple to white, and shaped like the finger of a glove—bloom from May to the end of summer.

Temperature: Earthy—cold and dry in the first degree.

Astrology: Saturn in Capricorn. It is associated with the fixed star Algorab.

Lore: Comfrey seems to have been used almost entirely as a medicinal plant in earlier times.

Safety Issues: Comfrey contains compounds that can harm the liver; it should not be taken internally on a regular basis, although occasional use seems to be relatively safe. It's best used externally; even so, it should not be used excessively, and should be avoided during pregnancy.

Parts Used: Root.

How Used: Amulets, potions, baths, and washes.

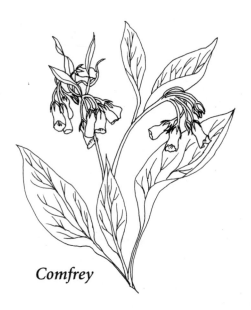

Comfrey

Magical Uses: Comfrey is one of the best options for workings connected with Saturn. Unlike many Saturnine plants, its energies highlight the more beneficial qualities of this often difficult planet. Use it for workings of stability and endurance, and in any magic connected to real estate.

Copper

Description: Once among the most common metals on the planet, copper has become rare after thousands of years of intensive mining and use by human beings. Red, easily shaped, and good at conducting energy, its surface will turn greenish with corrosion unless protected against contact with air.

Temperature: Earthy—cold in the third degree and dry in the first.

Astrology: Venus.

Lore: An important metal in alchemy, copper has been used for a wide range of magical purposes in many cultures.

Safety Issues: Like most metals, copper is somewhat toxic, and items of copper should not be used to hold food or drink for human consumption.

How Used: Amulets, working tools.

Magical Uses: Strongly associated with the element of Earth, copper can be used to invoke Earth energies, and it makes a good metal for a pentacle or other magical working tool of Earth.

Coriander (*Coriandrum sativum*)

Description: Coriander is an annual cultivated for its seeds since ancient times, and currently grown in Europe, the Mediterranean basin, and North and South America. One to two feet high, it has finely divided leaves and white or red flowers that bloom in umbels during the summer months. An essential oil is extracted from the seeds.

Temperature: Fiery—warm and dry in the first degree.

Astrology: Mars in Aries.

Lore: Coriander is a powerfully protective herb, and a generous bunch of it tied with red ribbon was often hung inside the house to banish dangers and bring peace. If grown in the garden, it was also held to protect both the house and its inhabitants. It should not be used as incense, as this can amplify anger and other destructive passions.

Safety Issues: None.

Parts Used: Whole plant, seeds, essential oil.

How Used: Living plants, amulets, sachets, seasoning for food, baths, washes, oils, and scents.

Magical Uses: Primarily a protective herb, coriander may be used in any working for this purpose. It is especially useful for workings in which the magician (or the person he or she is helping) needs to preserve independence against outside pressure to conform or obey.

Cumin (*Cuminum cyminum*)

Description: A low-growing plant native to the Middle East, closely related to coriander, cumin has been grown for its spicy seeds for thousands of years. It has feathery leaves and small pink or white flowers. An essential oil is extracted from the seeds.

Temperature: Fiery—warm and dry in the third degree.

Astrology: Mars in Aries.

Lore: Cumin's fiery energy was often used in charms to bring good fortune.

Safety Issues: The essential oil should be avoided during pregnancy, and can also cause phototoxicity; skin that comes in contact with it should be kept out of sunlight.

Parts Used: Powdered seed, essential oil.

How Used: Amulets, sachets, seasoning for food, baths, washes, oils, and scents.

Magical Uses: Cumin's magical uses are identical to those for coriander (see *Coriander*).

Daffodil (*Narcissus spp.*)

Description: All the many varieties of daffodil grow from bulbs, with long, slender leaves and showy flowers of various shades of yellow, orange, and white.

Temperature: Fiery—warm and dry in the second degree.

Astrology: Sun in Leo.

Lore: A powerful solar herb, daffodil was used to banish evil spirits from a house and to exorcise cases of obsession. If a daffodil bulb is carried in the pocket, the bearer will be safe from fear and harm by night. It should always be gathered on the night of the Full Moon.

Safety Issues: The daffodil bulb, and to a lesser extent the plant as a whole, is mildly toxic and should not be taken internally in any form.

Parts Used: Flower, bulb.

Daffodil

How Used: Live plants, amulets, sachets, baths, washes, oils, and scents.

Magical Uses: Daffodil can be put to good use in amulets of protection. The bulb holds the most concentrated form of its energy. It is also a good plant to have in the garden to banish hostile energies and bring protection.

Daisy (*Bellis spp., Chrysanthemum spp.*)

Description: There are a number of different species of plants that carry the name of daisy; the two most important are the English daisy (*Bellis perennis*) and the oxeye daisy (*Chrysanthemum leucanthemum*). All are relatively small flowers borne singly on the end of stalks, with white (or sometimes pink) rays and yellow centers.

Temperature: Watery—cold and moist in the second degree.

Astrology: The English daisy is Sun in Cancer, the oxeye Venus in Cancer.

Lore: Daisies are commonly used in various kinds of love divination. In Christian magic, the daisy was associated with St. John.

Safety Issues: Most daisies are mildly toxic, and should not be taken internally in any form.

Parts Used: Flower.

English Daisy

How Used: Living plants, amulets, sachets, baths, and washes.

Magical Uses: A faery plant, the daisy can be grown to attract positive attention from nature spirits of all kinds, and also has a place in love workings. The English daisy is also a solar plant and has the usual protective qualities of that planet.

Dandelion (*Taraxacum officinale*)

Description: Perhaps the world's most widespread plant, dandelion grows over most of Earth's temperate areas and needs no introduction to anyone who has ever had to weed a yard! Several other closely related plants are often mistaken for it, however. True dandelion has hollow, round, smooth flower stems that bear only one flower each.

Temperature: Earthy—cold and dry in the second degree.

Astrology: Jupiter in Libra.

Lore: Like many bright yellow flowers, dandelion was gathered on St. John's Eve (June 23) as a charm against hostile magic.

Safety Issues: None.

Parts Used: Flower, root.

How Used: Amulets, sachets, food, potions, baths, and washes.

Magical Uses: Common as it is, dandelion is a good protective herb and can be used in any preparation meant to overcome negative energies. Dandelion wine makes an excellent addition to a magical meal, and can also be used as a communion wine in rituals of Jupiter; the leaves may also be used for a Jovian salad. Dandelion also has visionary powers, and the root can be used in workings to facilitate visionary experience and to amplify the effect of telepathy.

Deer (*Cervus spp., Odocoileus spp.*)

Description: These beautiful and gentle animals, through no fault of their own, must be controlled by human hunting through much of North America to keep them from overpopulating and exhausting their habitat. There are various species, of which whitetail (*O. virginianus*) and mule deer (*O. hemionus*) are the most common in North America. Stags (male deer) grow and then shed antlers each year, and these can sometimes be gathered by the attentive wilderness traveler.

Deer

Temperature: Venison is fiery—warm and dry in the second degree.

Astrology: Sun in Sagittarius.

Lore: Among the most magical of living creatures, deer have been hunted for food and other purposes since human beings first reached the temperate regions. Antler is the standard material for the hilts of magical knives and daggers in many traditions.

Safety Issues: The safety issues affecting deer are simply those involved with hunting, on the one hand, and meat preparation, on the other.

Parts Used: Meat, skin, and antlers.

How Used: Amulets, food, and working tools.

Magical Uses: Use venison, deerskin, and antler for solar forces in the same way that beef, leather, and cowhorn are used for lunar ones.

Dew

Description: Dew is water that condenses out of the air onto leaves, grass, and other surfaces. It should always be gathered before the direct rays of the Sun touch it.

Temperature: Watery—cold in the first degree, moist in the second.

Astrology: Moon in whatever sign the Moon is in when dew is collected.

Lore: In traditional magical and alchemical theory, dew carries the subtle energies of life, forming one of the main pathways by which these energies complete their cycles between Earth and sky. When the Sun is in the zodiacal signs Aries and Taurus (roughly March 21–May 20), the intensity of these energies is at their highest in the Northern Hemisphere as the sleeping Earth wakes from winter. (The equivalent period in the Southern Hemisphere is when the Sun is in Libra and Scorpio, roughly September 21–November 20.) At this time, alchemists gather dew at dawn from the leaves of lady's mantle (see *Lady's Mantle*), from mirrors or sheets of glass left out overnight, or simply by dragging clean cotton sheets over the grass until the sheets are dripping with moisture. Similar methods can be used to provide the natural magician with water that is already charged with energy. Dew cannot be kept for more than a few days at most, though, before the energies depart.

Safety Issues: Use dew collected only in places where the air is relatively pure. If the collection method involves contact with the ground, make sure the area has not been sprayed with chemicals and is upwind of major roads and pollution sources.

How Used: Potions, baths, and washes.

Magical Uses: Dew may be used as the base for any working that would normally call for water.

Diamond

Description: The rarest and most precious form of the polymorphous element carbon, diamond is a cubic crystal formed at enormous temperature and pressure deep within the Earth. It is the hardest of stones, and will cut or scratch most other gems.

Temperature: Earthy—cold in the fourth degree and dry in the second.

Astrology: Mars in Taurus.

Lore: The lore of the diamond is surprisingly mixed; it has many virtues, but is something of an unlucky stone, bringing unhappiness to its wearer; as the magician Jerome Cardan suggested in his book *On Gems and Colors*, its brilliance irritates the soul the way too much sunlight irritates the eyes. At the same time, it gives the wearer unconquerable courage and victory in all manner of conflicts, banishes ghosts, prevents nightmares, and can be used to heal many mental illnesses. In order to have magical powers, it must be received as a gift rather than purchased. Water infusions of diamond were said to heal most diseases.

Safety Issues: None.

How Used: Amulets; water and oil infusions may be used in potions, baths, washes, oils, and scents.

Magical Uses: If you should be fortunate enough to have a diamond given to you, it may be used as a banishing tool and as a source of energy for help in facing conflicts.

Dill

Dill (*Anethum graveolens*)

Description: Dill is cultivated as a spice, and also grows wild in many parts of the Americas and Europe. An annual reaching two to three feet in height, it has blue-green, narrow, spreading leaflets and puts out umbels of yellow flowers in late summer and early fall. An essential oil is extracted from the seeds.

Temperature: Fiery—warm and dry in the third degree.

Astrology: Mercury in Cancer.

Lore: A strong protective herb, dill was used to break hostile enchantments and obsessions, and was also often used in blessings of places, especially homes and kitchens. Bundles of dill placed over windows and doors will keep hostile entities out.

Safety Issues: None.

Parts Used: Seed, essential oil.

How Used: Amulets, sachets, seasoning for food, baths, washes, oils, and scents.

Magical Uses: Dill may be used for protection, banishing, and blessing. It is especially useful when mental clarity and the ability to think rationally are what is most needed.

Dittany of Crete (*Origanum dictamnus*)

Description: A close relative of oregano, dittany of Crete has the mint family's square stem and strong scent.

Temperature: Fiery—warm and dry in the third degree.

Astrology: Sun in Capricorn.

Lore: The scent of dittany is said to drive off venomous beasts. More useful to the magician, though, is its power to enable spiritual beings to take on embodiment in the world of our ordinary experience.

Safety Issues: None.

Parts Used: Leaves.

How Used: Amulets, sachets, incense, potions, baths and washes.

Magical Uses: Dittany has a powerful materializing effect, and is used as an incense in rituals of evocation when the spirit is summoned into full visible appearance, rather than into a crystal or mirror. It can also be used in any workings directed toward results on the physical level.

Dittany of Crete

East Wind

Description: In the windlore of Western natural magic, there are three east winds found everywhere on Earth: Subsolanus blowing from due east, Eurus from the southeast, and Caecias from the northeast.

Temperature: Fiery—warm and dry.

Astrology: Subsolanus is Mars in Aries, Eurus is Sun in Leo, and Caecias is Jupiter in Sagittarius.

Lore: These fiery winds were associated with clear weather and heat. In traditional imagery, they were portrayed with dark skin and hair, sky-blue robes, and crowns bearing the sun.

Safety Issues: None.

How Used: Wind can serve as a source or vehicle for magical energies. See *Wind*.

Magical Uses: See *Wind*.

Elder (*Sambucus spp.*)

Description: There are several different species of elder in North America, of which black elder (*S. nigra*), a variety imported from Europe, is the most magical. A shrub or small tree fond of damp areas, elder has pointed, saw-toothed leaflets, clusters of white flowers, and berries that range from black (in the European species) to purple and red (in the American ones).

Temperature: Fiery—warm in the second degree, dry in the third.

Astrology: Mercury in Sagittarius.

Lore: A powerful and magical tree, elder has both helpful and harmful powers. It was held to be unlucky to bring elder into the house, and to burn an elder log in the fireplace was a traditional way to summon evil spirits; if elder was used to build a crib or cradle, the tree spirit would attack the child placed there and pinch it black and blue. In some areas it was claimed that elder only grew where blood had been shed. To fall asleep under an elder tree was to risk madness.

Elder

On the other hand, it was a powerful source of magical protection; an elder tree planted near the house would keep hostile magic at bay, elder branches were placed near graves to keep the corpse from being inhabited by an evil spirit, and if a door was pinned shut with a green elder twig neither elves nor workers of harmful magic could open it. The leaves of elder were also gathered on May Eve and fastened to doors and windows to banish hostile magic. In some areas, elder boughs were hung above houses and stables to keep flying dragons out.

Safety Issues: All North American species of elder are at least mildly poisonous and should not be taken internally or used in a charm that will come into contact with your body. The one exception is that the berries of most species are edible when properly cooked. Buying commercially processed elderberry preserves or syrup is probably the safest approach here.

Parts Used: Whole plant, twigs, and berries.

How Used: Live trees, amulets, and food (cooked berries only).

Magical Uses: Elder may be used for protective purposes, and a living tree planted by one's house makes a particularly effective way to do this. Otherwise, it should be used only for magical workings out of doors, as the traditional prohibition against bringing it indoors seems to have some validity.

Elecampane

Elecampane (*Inula helenium*)

Description: Elecampane is a perennial native to Europe but it can also be found wild in eastern North America. Its leaves, olive-colored with white veins and toothed edges, grow from a thick furry stalk that can reach six feet in height. Its flowers, which are large and yellow, bloom in summer and early fall. An essential oil is extracted from the root and stem.

Temperature: Airy—warm in the second degree, moist in the first.

Astrology: Mercury in Virgo.

Lore: Elecampane is deeply associated with the faery folk, as its other names elfdock and elfwort suggest.

Safety Issues: Do not use during pregnancy or while nursing.

Parts Used: Leaves, essential oil.

How Used: Amulets, sachets, incense, food, potions, baths, washes, oils, and scents.

Magical Uses: Elecampane should be considered by any natural magician who seeks contact with nature spirits.

Elm (*Ulmus spp.*)

Description: Two species of elm are found in North America, the English elm (*U. campestris*) and the American or slippery elm (*U. fulva*). Both are stately deciduous trees, once very common in the eastern half of the conti-nent but rarer now because of the ravages of Dutch elm disease. Rough, thick bark, roughly oval leaves with sawtoothed edges, and clusters of small flowers that bloom in early spring mark both types.

Temperature: Fiery—warm in the second degree, dry in the third.

Astrology: Saturn in Capricorn.

Lore: This tree was originally called "Elven" because of its association with the faery. It also has a traditional link with dreaming: dreams are said to dwell under every leaf of an elm tree.

Safety Issues: None.

Parts Used: Whole tree, leaves.

How Used: Live trees, amulets, sachets, baths, and washes.

Magical Uses: Planting an elm is one of the best ways to attract faery contact. The leaves can also be used to heighten dreamwork.

Elm

Emerald

Description: Emerald is a rare and precious variety of beryl, notable for transparency and a deep green color.

Temperature: Earthy—cold in the first degree and dry in the third.

Astrology: Venus in Cancer.

Lore: Emerald has a very long history as a magical stone. It was held to strengthen the eyes and the memory. It brings success in love, yet—surprisingly, perhaps, for a stone of Venus—calms passion and helps preserve chastity. The emerald is above all a stone of truth, and was credited with the power to banish illusions and protect the wearer against trickery. Some emeralds are said to change color when a lie is told in their presence. Placed under the tongue, it gives power to foretell the future.

In the lore of Christian magic, the emerald was associated with the ninth and lowest angelic order, the Angels.

Safety Issues: None.

How Used: Amulets; water and oil infusions may be used in potions, baths, washes, oils, and scents.

Magical Uses: Use emerald to heighten awareness of Earth energies, to focus love magic into channels that will be beneficial for all concerned, to banish illusions, and to heighten the clarity of divinations. It can also be placed in a working tool of Earth, such as a pentacle, to strengthen the link with the magical energies of that element.

Epsom Salt

Description: Named after the once-famous springs at Epsom in England, whose waters are rich in this compound, Epsom salt is a common mineral salt used for various medicinal purposes. Its proper name in chemical jargon is magnesium sulfate.

Temperature: Watery—cold in the second degree, moist in the first.

Astrology: Saturn in Pisces.

Lore: As far as I have been able to find, Epsom salts were not used in magic before the development of purified essential oils in modern times.

How Used: Medium for essential oils.

Safety Issues: Epsom salts can cause diarrhea when taken internally.

Magical Uses: Epsom salt and common table salt (see *Salt*) are used in modern natural magic as a medium for magical baths and washes that involve essential oils; see Baths and Washes in Part Three of this book.

Eyebright (*Euphrasia officinalis*)

Description: Eyebright is a small annual found in grassy places throughout Europe and western Asia. It has a square stem, stiff oval leaves, and little red and white flowers that bloom from June to September.

Temperature: Fiery—warm and dry in the first degree.

Astrology: Sun in Leo.

Lore: As the name suggests, eyebright was traditionally used to heal eyes, as well as to provide magically enhanced vision. It also was held to stimulate the memory and the mind.

Safety Issues: None.

Parts Used: Whole plant.

How Used: Amulets, potions, baths, and washes.

Magical Uses: An important ingredient in fluid condensers, eyebright is also valuable when used in charms directed toward clarity and insight. Use an infusion of eyebright as a ritual drink when beginning a period of intense study, or when suffering from depression.

Fennel (*Foeniculum vulgare*)

Description: Native to the Mediterranean region, fennel has been cultivated for its root and seeds for thousands of years. Its sturdy stems, which have bluish stripes, grow as much as six to eight feet tall. Its leaves are delicate and ferny, and its yellow flowers bloom in large umbels in late summer and early fall. The whole plant has a strong licoricelike scent. An essential oil is extracted from the seeds or the whole plant.

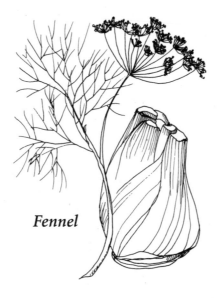

Fennel

Temperature: Fiery—warm and dry in the second degree.

Astrology: Mercury in Virgo. It is traditionally associated with the Pleiades.

Lore: Fennel was used in charms for fertility and virility, and it also was credited with protective powers; harvested on Midsummer's Eve and hung above the door, it kept hostile beings and ill luck out of the house. At the same time, it was traditionally held to be bad luck to grow the plant itself; "to sow fennel," an old proverb had it, "is to sow sorrow." It should not be used as an incense, as this will tend to amplify anger and other destructive passions.

Safety Issues: None.

Parts Used: Seeds, essential oil.

How Used: Amulets, sachets, seasoning for food, potions, baths, washes, oils, and scents.

Magical Uses: Fennel may be used for protection, blessing, and magical healing, and those who fast for magical reasons will certainly wish to drink fennel tea to settle their stomachs before ritual or meditative work. Its Mercurial symbolism also makes it a good choice for workings aimed at success, especially in business.

Fish

Description: There are many species of edible fish, but with few exceptions the lore of Western natural magic treats all fish as essentially the same. Since most species are under severe pressure from overfishing in the wild, the ethical natural magician should strongly consider using farm-raised fish only.

Temperature: Fresh fish is watery—cold and moist in the third degree; salted fish is fiery—warm and dry in the second degree.

Astrology: Varies, depending on the fish, but most white fish used for human food can be treated as Moon in Pisces, and most red fish are Sun in Pisces.

Lore: Fish have a complex place in the old lore. Cold as death, and surviving without breathing, they are often death symbols, and yet the phallic shape of many fish has earned them a symbolism that points in the opposite direction. They partake of the paradox and complexity of the magical lore of the sea, in which they have an important place.

Safety Issues: Many wild-caught fish, especially those from inland waters, contain large amounts of heavy metals and other toxic pollutants—another argument in favor of the farm-raised variety.

Parts Used: Meat, bones.

How Used: Amulets, food.

Magical Uses: Eat saltwater fish as a communion food of the sea; use fish bones in amulets and other preparations of sea magic.

Fish

Foxglove

Foxglove (*Digitalis purpurea*)

Description: Foxglove grows wild in Europe and along the Pacific coast of North America, and is grown as an ornamental throughout North America. A biennial, it stands two to six feet tall, with wavy-edged leaves and distinctive bell-shaped flowers, pink or purple on the outside and white with red spots inside.

Temperature: Fiery—warm and dry in the second degree.

Astrology: Venus in Libra.

Lore: The name "foxglove" is actually a contraction of "little folks' glove," and this points to its primary use in natural magic as a means of contact with nature spirits. Those who sought dealings with the faery realm commonly grew it in their gardens.

Safety Issues: TOXIC. Foxglove contains toxic amounts of powerful heart stimulants, and may also cause dermatitis. It should never be taken internally or used in any charm that will come into contact with your body.

Parts Used: Whole plant.

How Used: Live plants.

Magical Uses: The highly poisonous nature of this plant makes it difficult to use safely; furthermore, the nature spirits may react unpredictably to those who cut or harvest a plant which, at least in their opinion, is their property. The safest and most effective way to use it is simply to plant it in one's garden as an invitation to faery contact.

Frankincense (*Boswellia thurifera*)

Description: Frankincense is the resin of a small tree native to northeast Africa and the Arabian peninsula, with leaves divided into narrow leaflets and white or pink flowers. The resin is collected by making cuts on the bark and allowing the milky sap to dry and harden in the sun. An essential oil is also extracted from the resin.

Temperature: Fiery—warm and dry in the third degree.

Astrology: Sun in Aquarius; associated with the Pleiades.

Lore: Frankincense has powers of protection, blessing, and elevation of consciousness that have made it prized since the days of ancient Egypt. It is the most famous of the ancient incense resins.

Safety Issues: None.

Parts Used: Resin, essential oil.

How Used: Amulets, sachets, incense, baths, washes, oils, and scents.

Magical Uses: It can be used in almost any working of ritual magic, and is especially relevant for those directed toward spiritual development. Because of its solar correspondences, it is used in charms directed toward success in any field. Its best and strongest use, though, is in spiritual matters, and it will tend to bring spiritual energies to bear even in the most material aspects of life.

Fumitory (*Fumaria officinalis*)

Description: An annual weed found in nearly all parts of the world, fumitory is a low plant with gray-green leaves and small flowers that can be any color from purple to white, but which always have a red-black spot at the tip. It blossoms from May to September and should be gathered while flowering.

Temperature: Fiery—warm and dry in the first degree.

Astrology: Saturn in Capricorn.

Lore: A plant associated with the Underworld and with the deep energies of the Earth, fumitory was traditionally said to grow not from a seed but from vapors rising from underground; its name, in fact, is a garbling of the Latin *fuma terrae*, "earth smoke."

Safety Issues: None.

Parts Used: Whole plant.

How Used: Amulets, sachets, incense, baths, and washes.

Magical Uses: Fumitory is a useful herb for exorcism and purification, and is used to banish hostile spirits or to purify a ritual space. It has a special connection to the subtle energies of the Earth and may be used in any working where these play a central role.

Garlic (*Allium sativum*)

Description: Garlic began its career as a variety of wild onion in Siberia, but is now grown as a seasoning in most of the world. One of the most common of all kitchen herbs, garlic has the tubular stem and long thin leaves of the onion family, and produces a cluster of small white flowers at maturity. The bulbs should be harvested in the fall.

Temperature: Fiery—warm and dry in the fourth degree.

Astrology: Mars in Aries.

Garlic

Lore: Like all members of the onion family, garlic has been used for protection against hostile magic and malevolent spirits since ancient times. Its role as vampire repellent in horror fiction and movies is one of the few remnants of authentic natural magic that survives in modern popular culture. Oddly, it has also been used as an aphrodisiac since the days of ancient Egypt.

Safety Issues: Concentrated forms such as capsules or extracts should not be taken internally while pregnant or nursing.

Parts Used: Bulb.

How Used: Amulets, seasoning for food.

Magical Uses: Garlic bulbs are protective amulets in their own right, and a braid of garlic hung up in the kitchen will keep hostile forces at bay and bring health and happiness. Garlic's strong connections to Mars also make it a good choice whenever the energies of the warrior planet are to be invoked, whether to face a conflict or to stimulate male sexual energies.

Garnet

Description: This glassy silicate derives its name from a garbling of the word "pomegranate," which shares its red color and transparent sheen. It is common enough to be used as an abrasive in sandpaper and grinding wheels.

Temperature: Fiery—warm and dry in the second degree.

Astrology: Mars in Aquarius.

Lore: Garnets have the power to strengthen the will, and an oath sworn over a garnet is said to be all but impossible to break. Stones of constancy and fidelity, garnets also offer protection against nightmares, depression, and wounds, and are said to turn dull at the approach of danger.

Safety Issues: None.

How Used: Amulets; water and oil infusions may be used in potions, baths, washes, oils, and scents.

Magical Uses: Use garnets to bring strength to the will and to reinforce magical oaths. They may also be put to use as protective gems.

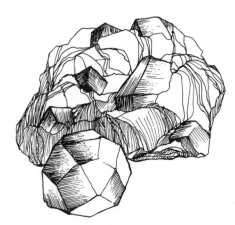

Garnet

Ginger (*Zingiber officinale*)

Description: Native to the jungles of South Asia, ginger is grown nowadays in most tropical and semitropical regions and will often flourish as a house plant in a sunny location. Each root puts up one or more stems that can be up to four feet tall, festooned with long narrow leaves and spikes of showy white and purple flowers. An essential oil is extracted from the root.

Temperature: Fiery—warm and dry in the second degree.

Astrology: Mars in Aries.

Lore: A ginger root planted in the garden was held to foretell, by its flourishing or failing, the health of the gardener. Although it does not seem to have been much used in traditional Western natural magic, Arab wizards have used it for centuries as an aphrodisiac and a source of magical protectio.

Safety Issues: Do not take in capsule form while pregnant, and people with gallstones should consult a health-care practitioner before using.

Parts Used: Root (whole or powdered), essential oil.

How Used: Amulets, sachets, incense, seasoning for food, potions, baths, washes, oils, and scents.

Magical Uses: Ginger has protective and healing properties, besides its ability to stimulate sexual energies, and a whole dried root may be used as an amulet for any of these purposes. Powdered or grated ginger root may also be eaten, to make use of its potent medicinal properties as well as the magical ones.

Gold

Description: The most precious of the metals known to the ancient world, gold is heavy, soft, and yellow or red in color.

Temperature: Temperate—a perfect blending of all of the elemental qualities.

Astrology: Sun.

Lore: The most perfect metal, according to alchemical lore, gold fills the same place among the minerals as the lion among animals, the eagle among birds, the salmon among fish, and the Sun among the bodies of the solar system. It is held to bring health to the physical body.

Safety Issues: None. Gold is one of the most nonreactive of metals, and unless you are practicing alchemy and working with strong acids and gold salts, your chances of harming yourself with it are small.

How Used: Amulets, working tools; water and oil infusions may be used in potions, baths, washes, oils, and scents. Water infusions of heated gold are the central ingredient in fluid condensers (see Fluid Condensers in Part Three).

Magical Uses: Use gold to invoke the Sun and for healing and blessing. Small quantities of gold can also be included in any magical preparation to balance the energies and amplify the effect.

Grape (*Vitis vinifera*)

Description: The grape vine, originally native to the eastern Mediterranean area, is now grown in warm climates all over the world. When grape juice was first fermented to produce wine is anyone's guess; the ancient Egyptians and Sumerians were doing so by the time of their first records. Grape seeds are pressed to extract an oil that makes a good base for oil infusions.

Temperature: Airy—warm in the first degree, moist in the second.

Astrology: Sun in Pisces.

Lore: The grape vine, and wine made from grapes, have been treated as magical substances since the beginning of recorded history. Grapes were traditionally sacred to Bacchus and Dionysus, and grape wine was called "the blood of the Earth" by the ancient Greeks. Grape vines have long been used as a material in love magic.

Safety Issues: None, except for those involved with drinking any alcoholic beverage.

Parts Used: Whole fruit, raw or fermented juice, leaves, vines, seed oil.

How Used: Grapes themselves are used in food and potions, and the seed oil is a good infusion base for magical oils. Wine may be used as the basis for

Grape

any potion, while grape leaves and vines may be used in amulets, sachets, baths, and washes. The leaves also make a good wrapping for appetizers, as anyone fond of Greek cooking knows well.

Magical Uses: Grape has little in the way of specific energy of its own, but carries other energies very well; almost any magical working can be done in a way that involves grape in some form. In particular, wine is the standard base for many herbal potions, as well as the most traditional communion beverage.

Hawthorn (*Crataegus oxyacanthus*)

Description: A shrub or small tree native to Europe but widely grown in temperate parts of North America, hawthorn has smooth gray bark, small leaves with three lobes, and clusters of white or pink flowers that bloom in late spring. The scarlet, berrylike fruits (which are called "haws," whence the name of the tree) mature in the autumn; they are edible, although the seeds are not and will cause gastric trouble if swallowed.

Temperature: Fiery—warm in the second degree, dry in the third.

Hawthorn

Astrology: Mars in Sagittarius.

Lore: One of the most sacred of trees in Western natural magic, the hawthorn is said to be so holy that no malicious spirit can so much as approach it. It was also associated with the faery.

Safety Issues: Hawthorn thorns are not to be trifled with, as they are tipped with irritant compounds. The seeds are mildly toxic and should be removed from the fruit before cooking or eating.

Parts Used: Whole tree, wood, flowers, and fruit.

How Used: Live trees, amulets, sachets, working tools, food, potions, baths, and washes.

Magical Uses: Hawthorn is a potent source of magical protection and an equally potent connection with the realm of nature spirits. Its faery connections make it unwise to cut down a living tree; one that is damaged beyond recovery may be used as a source for wood, but a new tree should certainly be planted in its place. The fruit and flowers are less problematic to gather, but a gift of food should be left at the foot of the tree.

Hazel (*Corylus spp.*)

Description: A shrub or small tree found in temperate areas throughout the Northern Hemisphere, hazel is a tall shrub, often growing in clusters. It has rounded, lobed, finely toothed leaves, long slender catkins, and nuts covered with a sheath that often has short hairs on it. Witch hazel (*Hamamelis virginiana*), a related shrub of much the same appearance and magical uses, is found all over the eastern third of North America; it may be used for the same purposes, and is also the preferred source of hazel twigs for dowsing.

Temperature: Earthy—cold and dry in the third degree.

Astrology: Mercury in Virgo.

Lore: The traditional tree of wisdom in Celtic countries, hazel has long been used by magicians of every kind throughout the Western world. Wands and divining sticks are often made of hazel, which (for best effect) should be cut with a single stroke of a consecrated knife at sunrise on a Wednesday.

Safety Issues: None.

Parts Used: Live shrub, wood, nuts.

How Used: Living plants, amulets, working tools, incense, food, baths, washes, and oils.

Magical Uses: Hazel may be used to invoke Mercurial energies. The nuts (often sold as "filberts") make an excellent communion food of that planet. Any part of the plant may be used for a working to invoke wisdom, and the traditional use of hazel wood for magical wands is well worth continuing, as the wood conducts energies cleanly and effectively.

Hazel

Hellebore niger

Hellebore (*Helleborus spp.*)

Description: There are several species of hellebore in Europe, of which one—black hellebore or Christmas rose (*H. niger*)—has been introduced to North America as a garden plant. Black hellebore grows about a foot high, with spreading leaflets and showy white flowers that bloom during the winter.

Temperature: Fiery—warm and dry in the third degree.

Astrology: Saturn in Libra; associated with the fixed star Algol, the "demon star."

Lore: Hellebore was used to drive off evil influences and break hostile spells, especially curses placed on livestock and pets. The root was held to have protective qualities and was used to purify buildings of unwanted influences, although it was said that anyone digging up the root should beware of eagles, who would try to kill the digger if they saw him or her at work. In addition, the leaves were used in workings for invisibility.

Safety Issues: TOXIC. Hellebore contains poisonous amounts of powerful heart stimulants, and should never be taken internally or used in a charm that will come into contact with your body.

Parts Used: Whole plant, leaves, and root.

How Used: Amulets.

Magical Uses: Use hellebore for rituals of magical invisibility—that is, for gaining the ability not to be noticed—and for blessings and protections placed on animals. It should be gathered fresh for each use, preferably somewhere out of sight of eagles.

Hemlock, Poison (*Conium maculatum*)

Description: A relative of carrot and parsley, poison hemlock can grow up to eight feet tall, with large, finely divided leaves and umbels of small white flowers that bloom in the summer months. Purplish blotches mark the stem, and the whole plant when bruised has an unpleasant odor reminiscent of dead mice.

It should not be mistaken for the evergreen tree called Western hemlock (*Tsuga heterophylla*), which grows on the Pacific coast of North America. These two plants are completely unrelated magically as well as botanically.

Temperature: Earthy—cold and dry in the fourth degree.

Astrology: Saturn in Scorpio.

Lore: Traditionally, hemlock was used to consecrate magical working tools. It was sacred to Hecate, the Greek goddess of sorcery.

Safety Issues: TOXIC. As the name suggests, poison hemlock is extremely dangerous—the poison that killed the Greek philosopher Socrates was extracted from it. It can quite easily cause severe illness or death if used carelessly, and even touching it with bare skin can cause dermatitis. It should never be taken internally in any form, or used in a charm that will come into contact with your body.

Parts Used: Whole plant.

How Used: Amulets, oils.

Magical Uses: Use hemlock, with care, as an herb of Saturn. A few drops of a cold oil infusion can be mixed with other oils and used to consecrate magical tools; it will lend stability to the consecration, and give the tool power over spirits.

Hemp (*Cannabis sativa, C. indica*)

Description: Hemp is a tall, sprawling annual native to south and east Asia. It has been domesticated for at least 5,000 years, and is now grown on every continent except Antarctica (and possibly even there, under artificial light). It can grow as high as ten feet, with leaves made up of the familiar spreading, sawtoothed leaflets and little green flowers that bloom in the autumn months in most climates. A resin, better known as hashish, is extracted from the female flowers.

Temperature: Fiery—warm in the second degree and dry in the third.

Astrology: Saturn in Aries.

Lore: Hemp has been used as a magical herb for thousands of years by cultures all over the world. Due at least in part to its psychoactive properties, it was often used as an aid to divination, and hemp seed also plays a part in many traditional love spells.

Safety Issues: While hemp is apparently as safe as any herb in existence—there has never been a confirmed case of fatal hemp poisoning—it cannot be legally grown or possessed in many parts of the world.

Parts Used: Leaves, female flowers, seed, and resin.

How Used: Amulets, incense, food, potions, oils, and scents.

Magical Uses: If you live in an area where the possession and use of hemp is legal, it may be burnt as an incense for visionary work, included in amulets, and put to use in other applications. Otherwise, due to the legal difficulties involved, it should be replaced by an herb you can use without risking time behind bars.

Henbane (*Hyoscyamus niger*)

Description: Perhaps the strangest-looking of all herbs, henbane has an appearance to match its deservedly sinister reputation. It has sticky, hairy, fleshy, grayish-green leaves, dull yellow flowers with purple veins, and a foul, rotting smell. Its fondness for once-disturbed soils, just to finish off the picture, makes it a common plant in graveyards and old ruins.

Henbane

Temperature: Earthy—cold and dry in the fourth degree.

Astrology: Saturn in Aquarius; associated with the fixed star Algorab.

Lore: If the root is carried by a man it is said to promote sexual vigor and make him attractive to women. Henbane also is associated with the Underworld and was used in rituals of necromancy and evocation, as well as in the lore of medieval witchcraft.

Safety Issues: TOXIC. Henbane is highly poisonous and can cause severe illness or death if used carelessly. It should never be taken internally in any form, or used in a charm that will come into contact with your body.

Part Used: Root.

How Used: Amulets.

Magical Uses: Use henbane, with care, to invoke Saturn and deal with Earth energies and the powers of the Underworld.

High John the Conqueror (*Ipomea jalapa, I. purga*)

Description: A member of the bindweed family and a close relative of the sweet potato, High John the Conqueror is a native of Mexico and South America; it also grows wild in the warmer parts of eastern North America, and is grown as an ornamental in much of southern Europe. Its twining stems, bearing heart-shaped leaves and red or purple funnel-shaped flowers, rise from a wrinkled, brown, tuberous root that may range from the size of a walnut to that of an orange.

Temperature: Fiery—warm in the fourth degree, dry in the third.

Astrology: Sun in Leo.

Lore: High John the Conqueror root is far and away the most important herbal charm in North American folk magic, and took its colorful name from an African-American folk hero, an African prince sold into slavery who time and again managed to get the upper hand over his captors. Hoodoo doctors and other magical practitioners use the root to dispel bad luck, banish hostile spells, bring success in gambling, and attract members of the opposite sex. Kept in a red cloth bag or simply carried in the pocket, the root might be "fed" by rubbing it with an infused oil of the root at regular intervals. The same infused oil, and various other preparations used as baths and washes, also have important roles in hoodoo and related traditions.

Safety Issues: TOXIC. The root contains an extremely strong laxative and should not be taken internally.

Part Used: Root.

How Used: Amulets, sachets, baths, washes, and oils.

Magical Uses: Like nearly all solar herbs, High John the Conqueror has powerful protective effects and can be used to banish hostile magic and spirits. It also works well in charms for love, for luck, and for success of any kind.

Holly

Holly (*Ilex spp.*)

Description: There are several different species of holly found in North America; the most familiar is English holly (*I. aquifolium*), which is native to Europe but is grown widely as an ornamental plant and for holiday decorations. The shiny, spiny dark green leaves and bright red berries are familiar to most people; less familiar are the magical traditions connected with this plant.

Temperature: Fiery—warm and dry in the second degree.

Astrology: Saturn in Leo.

Lore: Holly is protective, and is said to banish both lightning and hostile magic.

Safety Issues: Holly berries are somewhat toxic and should not be eaten.

Parts Used: Whole plant, wood, leaves, and berries.

How Used: Living plant, amulets, working tools, washes, and oils.

Magical Uses: A strong source of protection, holly may be used to banish hostile spirits and spells; a wand of holly will command evoked entities.

Honey

Description: The common honeybee (*Apis mellifera*) gathers flower nectar and, by an alchemy human beings have never been able to duplicate, turns it into sweet, sticky, golden honey as stored food for the cold months when no flowers bloom. Honey gathered from different kinds of flowers has different properties, based largely on the flower source.

Temperature: Fiery—warm and dry in the second degree.

Astrology: Sun in Cancer.

Lore: Mead, which is fermented from honey, is an ancient ritual beverage with a long history in pagan religious traditions. Honey, and baked goods made with it, is also among the standard traditional offerings to the faery folk.

Safety Issues: None.

How Used: Amulets, food, potions, and scents.

Magical Uses: A deeply solar substance, honey may be used as a communion food of the Sun or as an offering to nature spirits (who are generally quite fond of it).

Hops (*Humulus lupulus*)

Description: A climbing vine found in temperate climates all over the world, hops have been cultivated intensively in North America and Europe as a flavoring agent for beer and ale. Hop vines grow up to twenty feet long, with three- to five-lobed sawtoothed leaves and clusters of yellow-green flowers that mature into the papery, conelike "hops" used in brewing, herbal medicine, and magic. An essential oil is extracted from the hops.

Temperature: Fiery—warm and dry in the second degree.

Astrology: Mars in Aries.

Lore: Hops have been used for centuries in making beer and ale, which in ancient times were important ritual beverages used in many religions. (It may be worth mentioning that hops are only one of the herbs that have

Hops

been used in this way; some others included in beer in early times—notably henbane and mandrake—produced beverages that combined intense psychoactive effects with a moderately high casualty rate.)

Safety Issues: The essential oil and flowers should be avoided by those suffering from depression.

Parts Used: Hops, essential oil.

How Used: Amulets, sachets, potions, baths, washes, oils, and scents.

Magical Uses: Hops are an important asset in visionary work, and may be included in an herbal pillow to promote magical dreams or in an oil or bath used before astral projection or scrying. Magical beer is also an option, particularly for those who are willing to take up home brewing; other herbs besides hops may be included, although this should be done with care.

Horehound (*Marrubium vulgare*)

Description: A perennial belonging to the mint family, fond of roadsides and disturbed ground, horehound can be found wild in the coastal regions of North America and Europe, and is grown for medicinal purposes over much of the world. Its fuzzy, square stems bear equally fuzzy leaves in pairs and small white flowers that bloom in the summer months.

Temperature: Fiery—warm in the second degree, dry in the third.

Astrology: Mercury in Scorpio; associated with the fixed star Capella.

Lore: A bitter herb eaten at Passover in Jewish tradition, horehound was once sacred to the Egyptian god Horus. It seems to have had little use in Western natural magic, though.

Safety Issues: Do not use while pregnant.

Parts Used: Leaves.

How Used: Amulets, potions, baths, washes, and oils.

Magical Uses: Horehound is strongly mercurial, and will bring the energies of Mercury to bear in most kinds of natural magic. It will bring clarity to the mind and heighten intuition.
It can be drunk as an infusion, although it is very bitter.

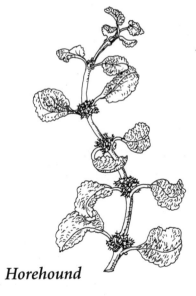

Horehound

Horsetail (*Equisetum spp.*)

Description: This ancient plant, sole survivor of an age so far in the past that it makes dinosaurs look like the new kids on the block, is found in several different species all through the Earth's temperate zones. Its creeping rootstock sends up two different kinds of shoots—fertile ones, which are flesh-colored and have conelike heads containing spores, and sterile ones, which are green and look like miniature pine trees with whorls of small branches.

Temperature: Earthy—cold and dry in the second degree.

Astrology: Saturn in Pisces.

Lore: The phallic shape of the fertile shoots has brought them into use as a charm for fertility.

Safety Issues: None.

Parts Used: Fertile or sterile shoots.

How Used: Amulets, potions, baths, and washes.

Magical Uses: Horsetail may be used for fertility magic or for invocations of Saturn.

Houndstongue (*Cynoglossum officinale*)

Description: This biennial herb grows as a weed in Europe and northeastern North America. Its leaves are shaped like a dog's tongue, as the name of the plant might suggest, and are covered with fine hairs on both sides. Its flowers, which are reddish-purple and funnel shaped, bloom in clusters in late spring and summer.

Temperature: Earthy—cold and dry in the second degree.

Astrology: Mercury in Virgo.

Lore: A leaf of houndstongue put inside each shoe, under the sole of the foot, was said to keep dogs from barking at the wearer.

Safety Issues: Mildly toxic, houndstongue should not be taken internally. It can also cause dermatitis in some people.

Parts Used: Leaves.

Houndstongue

How Used: Amulets, washes, and oils.

Magical Uses: Use houndstongue in workings of silence and secrecy. It may also be used effectively to control the energies of Mercury in ritual.

Houseleek (*Sempervivum tectorum*)

Description: This odd-looking perennial is native to Europe, where it can often be found growing on the walls and roofs of old houses as well as on stone walls and dry, rocky soil. Its leaves, which are fleshy and come to sharp spiny points, grow in a rosette directly from the rootstock, and the plant also produces a stem covered with little green scales, topped by a cluster of rose-colored blossoms each summer.

Temperature: Earthy—cold in the third degree, dry in the first.

Astrology: Jupiter in Sagittarius.

Lore: Houseleek has also been called "thunder plant" and "Jove's beard," and tradition had it that lightning would never strike a house that had houseleek growing on its roof.

Safety Issues: None.

Parts Used: Whole plant.

Houseleek

How Used: Live plants, amulets.

Magical Uses: Its chief use remains as a protection against lightning and storms, and more generally as an aid to weather magic.

Hyacinth

Description: The flower with this name is important in legend but has little magical power. The stone of the same name, by contrast, is a valuable addition to the natural magician's toolkit. A variety of zircon, hyacinth is a hard, purple or violet semiprecious stone much prized in ancient times.

Temperature: Earthy—cold in the first degree and dry in the second.

Astrology: Jupiter in Sagittarius.

Lore: A powerful stone useful in a range of magical applications, hyacinth (also called jacinth) was often used as a talisman by travelers in earlier times, as it provided protection against disease and injuries and made the wearer safe from lightning. It was also credited with the ability to banish insomnia and bring restful sleep. It was used to banish grief and melancholy, and was held to grant the wearer second sight if placed under the tongue.

Safety Issues: None.

How Used: Amulets; water and oil infusions may also be used in lotions, baths, washes, oils, and scents.

Magical Uses: Hyacinth is an excellent protective stone and visionary stone, and may be used by itself or in combination with other ingredients. As the traditional lore suggests, it makes a particularly effective amulet for safety in traveling.

Hyssop (*Hyssopus officinalis*)

Description: Hyssop is an evergreen shrub native to southern Europe and grown as an ornamental in North America. It has square woody stems, narrow leaves, and flowers that can be any color from rose pink to bluish purple; these latter grow in whorls at the branch tops and bloom all through the summer and early fall. An essential oil is extracted from the leaves and flowering tops.

Temperature: Fiery—warm and dry in the third degree.

Astrology: Jupiter in Cancer.

Lore: Hyssop has been an herb of purification since ancient times; "Cleanse me with hyssop, Lord," says Psalm 51, "and I shall be clean." It was generally used in the ancient Near East to sprinkle consecrated water.

Safety Issues: The essential oil is mildly toxic and should be avoided during pregnancy and by epileptics.

Parts Used: Leaves, essential oil.

How Used: Amulets, sachets, potions, baths, washes, oils, and scents.

Magical Uses: Hyssop is an important herb of protection, and may be hung above windows and doors to keep all unwelcome beings and energies outside. Other preparations can be used to good effect for the same purposes.

Hyssop

Iris

Iris (*Iris spp.*)

Description: Iris is a perennial found in wetlands throughout the temperate zone. There are various species; the most common in North America is blue flag (*I. versicolor*). All have sword-shaped leaves, and bear two or three large, showy flowers on each stalk. The root, the most magically important part, is often called orris root, and is the source of an essential oil.

Temperature: The root is fiery—warm and dry in the second degree. The flowers are watery—cold and moist in the third degree.

Astrology: Moon in Aquarius.

Lore: Iris is associated with the Greek goddess of dawn. The root has a long history of use in love magic.

Safety Issues: Fresh iris will cause dermatitis in some people. The powdered root can cause nausea and vomiting in large doses. *Iris versicolor* is poisonous.

Parts Used: Root, essential oil.

How Used: Amulets, sachets, incense, baths and washes (root only), oils, and scents.

Magical Uses: Iris has protective powers, and the flower, dried and ground root, or essential oil may be used for this purpose, or in rituals to bring a love relationship into one's life.

Iron

Description: The most common metallic element in the Earth's crust, iron was among the last metals known to the ancients to be discovered and used, as it occurs in pure form only in meteorites and has to be smelted out of its ores at high temperature. Gray or bluish in color, and much tougher than any of the other common metals, it has generally been used for tools and weapons rather than for decoration.

Temperature: Watery—cold in the third degree and moist in the first.

Astrology: Mars.

Lore: An ill-omened metal in many traditions, at least in part because of its role as the supreme material for weapons in ancient times, iron also traditionally banishes spirits of all kinds.

How Used: Amulets, working tools.

Magical Uses: Iron makes one of the most effective banishing tools known to Western natural magic. Its specific powers have to do with its effects on etheric substance (see The Theory of Natural Magic in Part One of this book). Iron, especially when honed to a sharp edge or point, will "short out" etheric patterns on contact. Most spirits with etheric bodies know this and will avoid cold iron; faeries in particular hate and fear it, and will flee from it.

Fruiting Ivy

Ivy (*Hedera helix*)

Description: A climbing evergreen vine native to the Old World but common all through the temperate regions of North America, ivy has spreading leaves with anything from three to seven lobes, small greenish flowers that bloom in the autumn, and black berries.

Temperature: Fiery—warm and dry in the second degree.

Astrology: Saturn in Scorpio; it is associated with the fixed star Alphecca.

Lore: Traditionally associated with the gods Bacchus and Dionysus, ivy was plaited into garlands and worn by worshippers of these deities of revelry. Paradoxically, it was also held to prevent drunkenness!

Safety Issues: Ivy is somewhat toxic and should not be taken internally.

Parts Used: Whole plant.

How Used: Amulets.

Magical Uses: Ivy is best used for its Saturnine qualities; a garland of ivy may be worn during any working involving Saturn's energies, and ivy can be put into any amulet made for a Saturnian purpose.

Jade

Description: There are actually two minerals sharing the common name "jade," a magnesium silicate more properly called nephrite and an aluminum silicate called jadeite. Both are hard, translucent stones that can have a variety of green or blue-green shades, and that are capable of being polished to a very fine degree of smoothness and shine.

Temperature: Earthy—cold and dry in the third degree.

Astrology: Venus in Libra.

Lore: The most important of magical stones in East Asian lore, jade is less central to Western natural magic but it is credited with significant powers nonetheless. It was said to have power to grant victory and repel hostile magic, and was used to send magical attacks back to their senders. Another traditional use was to bless gardens and growing things. Green jade was credited with the power to bring rain.

Safety Issues: None.

How Used: Amulets; water and oil infusions may be used in potions, baths, washes, oils, and scents.

Magical Uses: Use jade in amulets meant to turn hostile workings back on their senders. Green jade may also be used in weather magic.

Jasmine (*Jasminum officinale*)

Description: A delicate vine native to southern Asia but naturalized in the American South as well, jasmine has dark green leaves that grow in pairs and white five-petaled flowers with a sweet scent. An essential oil is extracted from the flowers, but this can be prohibitively expensive in a pure form.

Temperature: Airy—warm and moist in the second degree.

Astrology: Mercury in Cancer.

Lore: Jasmine is often used in traditional American folk magic, especially as an oil for dressing candles.

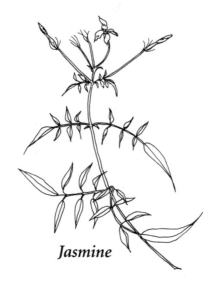

Jasmine

Safety Issues: None.

Parts Used: Flowers, essential oil.

How Used: Amulets, sachets, incense, baths, washes, oils, and scents.

Magical Uses: Jasmine has aphrodisiac qualities, and may be used effectively in any kind of sexual or love magic. It also has useful protective and healing powers, and banishes melancholy.

Jasper

Description: Like so many semiprecious stones, jasper is a form of chalcedony. It has several different colors, of which red and green are the most magically important.

Temperature: Red jasper is fiery—warm and dry in the second degree; the green variety is watery—cold in the first degree and moist in the third.

Astrology: Jupiter in Scorpio.

Lore: One of the classic amulet stones, jasper was often worn to protect the wearer against supernatural evil. It also has an old reputation, dating back to ancient Greek times, as a rain-bringer for use in weather magic. In

Christian magical lore, jasper is associated with the third order of angels, the Thrones.

Traditionally, any given piece of jasper had as many magical virtues as it had veins or distinct colors.

Safety Issues: None.

How Used: Amulets; water and oil infusions may also be used in potions, baths, washes, oils, and scents.

Magical Uses: Jasper is among the most useful stones for the practicing magician, as it dispels destructive magic and drives off hostile spirits. Worn in rituals of evocation, it will help the magician retain control of summoned spirits. It may be put to good use any time one must deal with the shadowy and dangerous side of the magical realm. The red variety is the most useful for this purpose; the green variety has similar properties to a somewhat lesser degree, but can also be used, like green jade, to bring rain.

Jet

Description: Jet is a hard, dense, and polishable variety of coal, velvet-black in color.

Temperature: Earthy—cold and dry in the fourth degree.

Astrology: Saturn in Aquarius.

Lore: Traditionally used to make rosaries, jet was also much used in earlier times for protective amulets. It was considered very potent against all kinds of supernatural evil. As a variety of coal, it can be burnt, and burning powdered jet as an incense was an effective way to break even very strong hostile magic.

Safety Issues: None.

How Used: Amulets; water and oil infusions may be used in potions, baths, washes, oils, and scents.

Magical Uses: Jet may be used for protection against harm from any source, and to banish destructive energies. It makes a good addition to a magical sword or any other working tool used to command or banish.

Juniper (*Juniperus communis*)

Description: An evergreen shrub found in dry, rocky areas throughout the Northern Hemisphere, juniper has chocolate-brown bark and needles with a pale stripe on the upper surface. Juniper cones, which look rather like berries, are green in the first year and ripen to purple or blue-black in the second year. An essential oil is extracted from the berries; an oil extracted from the needles and wood is also available, but this is often adulterated with turpentine and should be avoided.

Temperature: Fiery—hot in the third degree, dry in the first.

Astrology: Mars in Aries.

Lore: Juniper was used in spells to recover stolen property. It was also credited with important purifying and protecting virtues, especially when dealing with spirits.

Safety Issues: The essential oil and berries should be avoided during pregnancy, and by anyone with kidney disease. Also, the berries should not be used for longer than six weeks.

Parts Used: Leaves, wood, and essential oil.

How Used: Amulets, sachets, incense, baths, washes, oils, and scents.

Magical Uses: Juniper is a valuable resource for the practicing magician, as an incense of purification as well as in other preparations. Burn it at the close of evocation rituals to chase off lingering spirits. Its traditional use as a deterrent to theft may also be worth exploring.

Juniper

Lady's Mantle

Lady's Mantle (*Alchemilla vulgaris*)

Description: A perennial found in moist places in eastern North America, Europe, and northern Asia, lady's mantle has broad fanlike leaves up to six inches across, edged with a sawtooth fringe, and little green flowers that blossom from late spring well into the fall.

Temperature: Fiery—warm and dry in the second degree.

Astrology: Venus in Scorpio.

Lore: An important herb for women's health, lady's mantle has another importance in Western esoteric lore, one hinted at by its scientific name *Alchemilla*, "little alchemist." The edges of the leaves collect dew in large droplets, and alchemists—who made much use of dew in their secret art— would plant beds of lady's mantle in their gardens and collect the dewdrops each morning at sunrise during those months of the year when dew was held to contain subtle energies central to the alchemical Great Work.

Safety Issues: None.

Parts Used: Leaves, whole plant.

How Used: Living plants, amulets, incense, potions, baths, washes, scents, and oils.

Magical Uses: Lady's mantle may be used for invoking any feminine form of the divine. Added to any natural magic mixture, it will strengthen the working and improve its focus.

Lapis Lazuli

Description: This stone, a form of calcite with iron pyrite inclusions, has been prized since ancient times; the pharaohs of Egypt and the kings of Sumeria both hoarded it and used it for magical purposes. It is an intense blue in color, with flecks of gold.

Temperature: Airy—warm and moist in the second degree.

Astrology: Jupiter in Sagittarius.

Lore: Lapis lazuli is another stone much used for magical protection since ancient times. It was also held to banish melancholy.

Safety Issues: None.

How Used: Amulets; water or oil infusions may also be used in potions, baths, washes, oils, and scents.

Magical Uses: A valuable protective stone, lapis lazuli can be used in any working for this purpose.

Lavender (*Lavendula spp.*)

Description: An evergreen shrub native to the Mediterranean, lavender is cultivated all over Europe and North America for its fragrant flowers. It grows one to two feet high, with slender gray-green leaves and light purple flowers that bloom in the summer months. Its essential oil is one of the very few that can be safely used on the skin in pure form, without dilution.

Temperature: Fiery—warm and dry in the third degree.

Lavender

Astrology: Mercury in Leo.

Lore: Lavender has an old reputation as an anaphrodisiac—that is, a substance that inhibits sexual arousal—and in earlier times, those who needed help maintaining vows of chastity would wear lavender garlands.

Safety Issues: None.

Parts Used: Flowers, essential oil.

How Used: Living plants, amulets, sachets, incense, potions, baths, washes, oils, and scents.

Magical Uses: Lavender is a valuable stimulant to the psychic and visionary senses, and can be used for visionary work, for magical dreamwork, or as an incense for meditation. It is also good for the nerves, calming yet at the same time energizing, and a drop or two of the essential oil rubbed onto the temples or the base of the skull will help cure the nervous exhaustion that sometimes comes after intensive magical work.

Lead

Description: Gray, heavy, extremely soft, and relatively common in the Earth's crust, lead has rarely been used for anything more exalted than plumbing.

Temperature: Earthy—cold and dry in the fourth degree.

Astrology: Saturn.

Lore: Lead, the coldest and heaviest of the metals known to the ancients, was often used as a symbol of Earth and what lies beneath it. Greek and Roman magicians used tablets of lead, written with incantations and words of power, to communicate with the powers of the Underworld.

Safety Issues: TOXIC. Lead is a poison, and dissolves readily in even the mildest acids (such as wine or tomato juice). It should never be used in any preparation that will be taken internally or brought into direct skin contact, and vessels made of lead or alloys containing lead (such as pewter) should never be used to hold food or drink for human consumption.

How Used: Amulets, working tools.

Magical Uses: Use lead for Saturnine magical workings, for Earth magic and contact with the Underworld, and for anything you wish to endure.

Leek (*Allium porrum*)

Description: A member of the onion family widely cultivated in northwest Europe, the leek looks like an overgrown onion stem without the onion, and has the familiar onion scent found throughout the allium family. Its flower is a spherical cluster of white or pink blossoms, which blooms in June and July.

Temperature: Fiery—warm in the third degree, dry in the second.

Astrology: Jupiter in Gemini.

Lore: The leek, according to tradition, will protect a home from lightning and dispel electrical charges.

Safety Issues: None.

Parts Used: Whole plant.

How Used: Living plant, food.

Magical Uses: The leek's primary use is in weather magic, as a protection against lightning.

Lemon Balm (*Melissa officinalis*)

Description: Another useful member of the mint family, lemon balm is native to the Middle East and Mediterranean basin but can be found growing wild in many places as an escapee from gardens. It has the square stem and paired leaves of the other mints, with clusters of flowers that may be any color from pink through yellow to blue-white. The whole plant has a lemony scent when bruised, and is a favorite of bees.

Temperature: Fiery—warm and dry in the second degree.

Astrology: Jupiter in Cancer.

Lore: One of the oldest of medicinal herbs, lemon balm is important in medical alchemy (spagyrics), and the preparation of an alchemical tincture of lemon balm is one of the first tasks set for beginning alchemists in many present-day schools of the Hermetic art.

Lemon Balm

Safety Issues: None.

Parts Used: Whole plant, leaves, and essential oil.

How Used: Amulets, sachets, potions, baths, washes, oils, and scents.

Magical Uses: Primarily used in love magic, lemon balm can be included in amulets and other magical workings. Steep lemon balm leaves in your bath water to attract a love relationship into your life. It also banishes melancholy and revives the vital spirits.

Lettuce (*Lactuca sativa*)

Description: Most people, thinking of lettuce, call to mind the leaves of the immature plant sold in grocery stores. Left to itself, lettuce produces a stem up to three feet tall, topped with loose clusters of yellow flowers that bloom in summer.

Temperature: Watery—cold and moist in the second degree.

Astrology: Moon in Leo.

Lore: In ancient Egypt, lettuce was sacred to Min, the god of fertility, and the plant itself was considered an aphrodisiac. The ancient Greeks, by contrast, considered it an anaphrodisiac. The sap from the mature plant's stalk has been collected and dried in several different cultures as an incense and a mild intoxicant.

Safety Issues: None.

Parts Used: Leaves, root, and dried sap.

How Used: The root can be used in amulets, potions, baths, washes, and oils; the dried sap makes a useful incense, while the leaves themselves are mostly useful as food.

Magical Uses: Lettuce is among the most effective plants for magical work with the element of Water. The confusion over its sexual effects seems to arise from the fact that the sap contains mild sedatives, which can cause arousal or its opposite depending on circumstances and individual body chemistry.

Lignum Aloe (*Aquilaria agallocha*)

Description: A large tree native to much of Southeast Asia, and grown commercially in northwestern India and certain regions of China, lignum aloe is completely unrelated to the common aloe plant (*Aloe vera*) so commonly used nowadays as a cosmetic and as a treatment for cuts and burns. When infected with a particular fungus, the wood produces a yellowish oil, usually called agar oil, which is the source of scent and magical effects alike.

Temperature: Fiery—warm in the third degree, dry in the second.

Astrology: Jupiter in Sagittarius.

Lore: One of the ancient incense woods, lignum aloe was traded westward from India in Egyptian times and is referred to in the Old Testament. It was used as an incense offering to divinities, as well as an ingredient in perfumes and scents.

Safety Issues: The essential oil is mildly toxic and should not be used by pregnant women.

Parts Used: Powdered wood, essential oil.

How Used: Sachets, incense, baths, washes, oils, and scents.

Magical Uses: Primarily spiritual in its focus, lignum aloe may be used in incense or other preparations aimed at higher modes of consciousness. It is especially useful as an incense in ritual magic, and several traditional incense blends for ritual work make use of it.

Lily (*Lilium spp.*)

Description: There are a good many species of lilies, wild and domesticated, in North America, and a range of other flowers (such as lily of the valley, *Convallaria majalis*) that are more or less distantly related to lilies but share versions of the same name.

Temperature: The bulb is fiery—hot in the second degree and dry in the first; the flower is watery—cold and moist in the second degree.

Lily

Astrology: White lilies are Moon in Scorpio, yellow lilies Moon in Pisces.

Lore: The second most important symbolic flower in Western tradition, lily represents purity—which should not be taken in the simple-mindedly sexual sense. The purity of the lily is like the purity of clean water, or of a powerful medicine; in magical terms, it represents singleness of purpose, of will, and of desire. For magical purposes, lilies should always be gathered when the Sun is in Leo.

Safety Issues: Lilies are mildly to significantly toxic, and should never be taken internally in any form.

Parts Used: Flowers, bulb.

How Used: Amulets, sachets, washes, and oils.

Magical Uses: Use lilies to call up singleness of will and purpose, and to inspire creativity and fertility. Goddesses such as Diana, who are traditionally virginal, should be invoked with lilies.

Linden (*Tilia europaea*)

Description: Also known, confusingly, as lime (although unrelated to the tree that produces the fruit of that name), linden is a European deciduous tree that can reach 100 feet in height. Common in forests and mountain areas, it is also among the trees most often planted along European city streets, and has been used in many American cities in the same way. Its heart-shaped, somewhat asymmetrical leaves are bluish-green in color; its flowers, greenish or brownish, blossom during early summer. An essential oil is extracted from the dried flowers.

There is also an American species (*Tilia americana*), which is often called basswood, and which has yellow or white flowers.

Temperature: Fiery—warm in the first degree and dry in the second.

Astrology: Mercury in Taurus.

Lore: Linden was often used as a relaxant and a psychic stimulant in Central European magical traditions.

Safety Issues: None.

Parts Used: Flowers, essential oil.

How Used: Amulets, sachets, potions, baths, washes, oils, and scents.

Magical Uses: Linden makes a good relaxant for magical dreamwork and other visionary states. It may be taken in the form of tea, sewn into an herbal pillow, or used in any other preferred form.

Linden

Lovage

Lodestone (see Magnetite)

Lovage (*Levisticum officinale*)

Description: This parsley relative, notable for its strong, aromatic scent, is native to southern Europe and Asia Minor but grown in gardens all over the Old World. Its round, hollow stem grows up to six feet high and bears large carrotlike leaves and umbels of pale yellow flowers in the summer. An essential oil is extracted from the root or the whole plant.

Temperature: Fiery—warm and dry in the second degree.

Astrology: Sun in Taurus.

Lore: Traditionally, lovage was steeped in bath water to bring romance into one's life. The stalks are highly nutritious and were once a common vegetable.

Safety Issues: The essential oil should be avoided during pregnancy. Lovage is also not recommended for use by people taking blood-thinning agents or with impaired or inflamed kidneys.

Parts Used: Leaves, essential oil.

How Used: Amulets, food, potions, baths, washes, oils, and scents.

Magical Uses: Primarily used in love magic, lovage may also be used in fertility charms for gardens and fields.

Mace (*Myristica fragrans*)

Description: Mace is the dried and powdered husk around the seed of an evergreen tree native to Indonesia but now grown in many tropical countries. The tree grows up to seventy-five feet high, with smooth grayish bark, thick foliage, and small yellow flowers. The seed within the husk is the source of the spice nutmeg (see *Nutmeg*).

Temperature: Fiery—warm and dry in the second degree.

Astrology: Jupiter in Sagittarius.

Lore: Mace was little used in traditional Western natural magic.

Safety Issues: Mace is toxic in large quantities and can cause nausea, vomiting, dizziness, stomach pains, rapid pulse, anxiety, liver pain, double vision, and coma.

Mace

Parts Used: Powdered husk.

How Used: Amulets, sachets, incense, seasoning for food, baths, washes, oils, and scents.

Magical Uses: Mace may be used to invoke the energies of Jupiter. It may also have protective powers, but this still needs further research.

Magnetite

Description: This black, moderately hard, and naturally magnetic iron ore was the source of the first magnets known to human beings.

Temperature: Fiery—warm and dry in the third degree.

Astrology: Mars in Aries; associated with the fixed star Polaris.

Lore: Magnetite, often under its common name lodestone, has long been one of the standard tools of folk magic in North America, especially for love spells. In many of these traditions, magicians who have a lodestone feed it iron filings once a week and treat it as the dwelling of a familiar spirit.

The traditional lore of Western natural magic likewise gives magnetite a wide array of uses. It was often a protective amulet against hostile spirits, and was used to dispel melancholy. Worn around the neck, it strengthens the memory. Lore holds that it attracts lightning, though, and should never be worn outside during a storm.

Safety Issues: None.

How Used: Amulets; water and oil infusions may be used for potions, baths, washes, oils, and scents.

Magical Uses: The role of magnetic fields in magic was researched intensively in some European traditions, but little of this lore has been made public in the English-speaking world. While most of this material is outside the realm of natural magic, magnetite is in some ways the bridge connecting these realms. It can be used as a source of magical power in many applications; oil and water infusions of magnetite are naturally charged and may be used as a basis for other infusions and preparations. The traditional uses given above are also worth further exploration.

Maidenhair Fern (*Adiantum pedantum*)

Description: A delicate fern found in damp places in the temperate zones of North America and Asia, maidenhair fern has shiny, dark stems and tapering fronds, with leaflets that are smooth-edged on the side nearer to the root but ragged on the other.

Temperature: Earthy—cold in the first degree, dry in the second.

Astrology: Mercury in Gemini.

Lore: Like all ferns, the seed (or rather spores) of the maidenhair fern are held to contain the gift of invisibility. The leaves of maidenhair appear silver when immersed in water, and water will not cling to them; Roman mythologists connected this property of the plant to the birth of Venus, who was born of sea foam.

Safety Issues: Don't use while pregnant. Large doses may act as an emetic.

Parts Used: Spores.

How Used: Amulets.

Magical Uses: Maidenhair fern can be used in an amulet of invisibility or for any working done to deal with situations where you would rather not be noticed.

Malachite

Description: An ore of copper (technically, a basic copper carbonate), malachite has a deep green color.

Temperature: Fiery—warm and dry in the second degree.

Astrology: Sun in Sagittarius.

Lore: This stone was often used to protect children from the attacks of hostile spirits and magic, and it was also believed to preserve the wearer against injuries caused by falling.

Safety Issues: None.

Malachite

How Used: Amulets; water and oil infusions may also be used in potions, baths, washes, oils, and scents.

Magical Uses: As the traditional lore suggests, malachite is best used as a protective stone, with particular powers against accidents.

Mandrake (*Mandragora officinarum*)

Description: Mandrake is a relative of tomato and deadly nightshade native to the Mediterranean countries and the Middle East, but grown in gardens in medieval Europe. Its leaves, large and dark, rise directly out of the rootstock and often lay flat along the ground when the plant is mature; it produces bell-shaped flowers, yellow or purple, on stalks a few inches high, and these mature into fleshy yellow berries. The root, which may be up to three feet long, often forks into two or three parts resembling the legs of a man.

There is also an American mandrake (*Podophyllum peltatum*), also known as mayapple, which is somewhat less dangerous and has similar magical effects. It grows in the eastern third of the continent in deciduous forests.

Temperature: Earthy—cold in the fourth degree, dry in the second.

Astrology: Saturn in Taurus; associated with the fixed stars Deneb Algedi and Spica.

Lore: The traditional lore surrounding the mandrake begins with the process of harvesting the root. A complicated ritual was used to extract it from the ground, for it was believed that the plant itself would run away if not properly approached. It had to be dug up with an ivory staff, after a circle was first traced around it with a sword, and the harvester had to be careful not to allow the wind to blow in his or her face during the process. Furthermore, whoever actually pulled the root free was said to die at once, either from a terrible cry let out by the plant or from the sheer intensity of the mandrake's poison. The trick of getting a dog to do the deed, by tying it to the plant and then luring it with meat, was one common way around this problem.

The forked root of the plant often has some resemblance to a human being, and illustrations in medieval herbals usually pictured mandrake simply as a naked human figure with leaves and berries sprouting from its head. This reflects a common magical practice in which a mandrake root was treated like a living being, given food and clothing and bathed in wine once a week; the spirit of the plant would then reveal the future, bring harm to enemies, and make its owner wealthy.

More generally, mandrake root has been used for nearly any imaginable magical purpose. Western natural magic includes a dizzying array of uses for it, and many of these have been carried over into American folk magic, where the American mandrake is used for protection and love magic.

Safety Issues: TOXIC. European mandrake is highly poisonous and should never be taken internally or used in any preparation that may come into contact with your body. The American species is a little less toxic, and its fruit is edible; the rest of the plant causes violent nausea and diarrhea and can kill in sufficient dosages.

Parts Used: Root.

How Used: Amulets.

Magical Uses: Dangerous as it can be, mandrake does have definite uses in natural magic. It is probably the strongest magical amplifier in the natural magician's toolkit, and a few slivers of mandrake root added to an amulet will increase the effectiveness of the charm dramatically. The root itself can also be used as a protective amulet.

Marigold

Marigold (*Calendula officinalis*)

Description: The source of the "calendula" products so important in modern medicinal herbalism, marigold is an annual with narrow, hairy, roughly toothed leaves and showy orange or yellow flowers that bloom from summer into early fall. An essential oil is extracted from the flowers; this can be difficult and expensive to obtain, as a very large number of flowers produces a very small amount of oil.

Temperature: Airy—warm in the second degree, moist in the first.

Astrology: Sun in Leo. It is associated with the fixed star Procyon.

Lore: When used for magical purposes, marigold should always be gathered when the Sun is in Leo, at the height of its strength. It was often used for protections and blessings in folk magic.

Safety Issues: None.

Parts Used: Flowers, essential oil (if you can get it).

How Used: Amulets, sachets, incense, potions, baths, washes, oils, and scents.

Magical Uses: Marigold has important powers of protection and consecration, and may be used for these purposes whenever a solar influence is desired.

Marjoram (*Majorana hortensis*)

Description: Marjoram is yet another member of the mint family, with the square stem and paired leaves to prove it. Its stem and leaves are covered with gray wooly down, and its small white or pink flowers bloom in the summer. Some marjoram is annual, some perennial, depending on the variety and the climate.

Temperature: Fiery—warm and dry in the third degree.

Astrology: Mercury in Aries. It is associated with the fixed star Deneb Algedi.

Lore: Despite its astrological attribution, marjoram has a special relationship with the Greek goddess Aphrodite, whose touch was said to give it its sweet scent. It was made into chaplets for newlyweds, and also planted on graves to help the newly dead sleep in peace.

Safety Issues: An essential oil is extracted from the flowers; this should be avoided during pregnancy.

Parts Used: Whole plant, essential oil.

How Used: Amulets, sachets, incense, seasoning for food, potions, baths, washes, oils, and scents.

Magical Uses: Marjoram is particularly useful in love magic, whenever the goal is to create a permanent relationship (rather than to pursue more short-term pleasures).

Mistletoe (*Viscum album*)

Description: A parasitic plant found on various kinds of deciduous trees in Europe and northern Asia, European mistletoe is yellow-green and leathery, with narrow leaves, yellow or green flowers, and sticky white berries. There is also an American species (*Phoradendron flavescens*), which has rounder leaves but is otherwise similar.

Temperature: Fiery—warm and dry in the third degree.

Astrology: Sun in Leo.

Lore: The most important sacred plant of the Druids, mistletoe was known by the ancient Celts as "all-heal." Even today, in parts of Germany, the

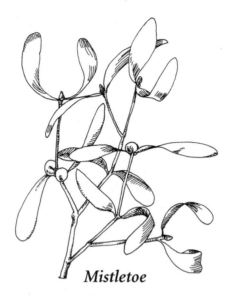

Mistletoe

mistletoe is called Drudenfuss—"Druid's foot"—which is also the common term for the pentagram. A mistletoe plant worn about the neck was held to dispel hostile magic. The most powerful mistletoe is found on oak trees, but this is also among the rarest.

Safety Issues: Both kinds of mistletoe are somewhat toxic and should not be taken internally in any form.

Parts Used: Whole plant, berries.

How Used: Amulets, sachets, washes, and oils.

Magical Uses: A powerful herb with many uses, mistletoe has particular connections with fertility and creativity on all levels. It can be used by those who desire children, but also by those who have some other form of creative act in mind. It is also a magical amplifier, and may be added to almost any magic for constructive and creative purposes for added effect. Finally, it has potent protective powers, and may be used to turn aside all forms of hostile magic and banish disruptive spirits.

Moonlight

Description: The light of the Moon is reflected sunlight, but its effects are wholly different from those of the Sun's direct rays. The most important influence on the Earth's etheric body, the Moon generates etheric tides that are precisely equivalent to the physical tides of the ocean, and this tidal force is especially strong when moonlight reaches the Earth's surface unhindered by clouds. Objects exposed to moonlight will pick up an etheric charge that mirrors the Moon's influence at the time.

Temperature: Watery—cold and moist in the second degree.

Astrology: Moon, in whichever sign the physical Moon is located at the time.

Lore: The lore of the moon and moonlight is ancient and complex, linking up with astrology, alchemy, and pagan spirituality as well as magic. Countless spells rely on the moon's beams, especially for divination, visionary experience, and sea magic.

Safety Issues: None.

How Used: Source of energies.

Magical Uses: Moonlight is a potent source of energy that may be used for any working related to the Moon, to water, or the sea, or to the intuitive and visionary senses. Any preparation exposed to moonlight will take on its energies, especially if it contains lunar herbs or stones, or includes an etheric condenser—a special form of magical preparation that will be covered in detail in the Workbook section.

Moonstone

Description: Moonstone is a translucent or transparent variety of feldspar, an aluminum silicate that is part of nearly all crystalline rocks. True moonstone is white and lustrous, and may have a pearly or opaline shimmer of other colors when exposed to light.

Temperature: Watery—cold and moist in the third degree.

Astrology: Moon in Cancer.

Lore: Moonstones are said to change color with the phases of the Moon. They are beneficial to plants, and orchard keepers in the Middle Ages would hang moonstones on trees to bring abundant crops. They were held to prevent insanity and grant good fortune, and are also credited with the power to arouse love.

Safety Issues: None.

How Used: Amulets; water and oil infusions can be used in potions, baths, washes, oils, and scents.

Magical Uses: As their name suggests, moonstones are most important magically as vessels of the Moon's power. They may be used in any lunar working, and should certainly be part of any working tool meant to call on the Moon's energies. Those who have gardens may also wish to use moonstone to foster the health and growth of plants.

Motherwort (*Leonurus cardiaca*)

Description: Motherwort is a perennial native to North America and Europe, found in abandoned places and along roads and paths. Its stems are square, hollow, and usually reddish; its leaves splay out into multiple sharp points, and its flowers—red, pink, or white—bloom in clusters around the stem during summer.

Temperature: Fiery—warm and dry in the third degree.

Astrology: Venus in Leo.

Lore: Motherwort was once held to drive away venomous beasts by its scent.

Safety Issues: Touching the plant can cause dermatitis in some people. Do not use while pregnant.

Parts Used: Whole plant.

How Used: Amulets, sachets, washes, and oils.

Magical Uses: Useful for protection, especially against hostile magic, motherwort also strengthens the wearer and helps banish depression.

Mouse-ear

Mouse-ear (*Hieracium pilosella*)

Description: A little perennial plant that grows wild in Europe and the eastern half of North America, mouse-ear has hairy leaves that form a rosette at ground level and yellow flowerheads that rise up to a foot above the ground on slender stalks.

Temperature: Fiery—hot and dry in the first degree.

Astrology: Moon in Aries.

Lore: A plant widely used in alchemy, mouse-ear—together with another herb, moonwort—was believed to accomplish the crucial step of fixing mercury. Edged tools taken red-hot from the anvil and quenched in mouse-ear juice were said to cut through iron as easily as through soft lead.

Safety Issues: None.

Parts Used: Whole plant, juice.

How Used: Amulets, sachets, baths, washes, and oils.

Magical Uses: Mouse-ear controls the energies of Mars, and can be used to banish hostility, quarreling, and the threat of violence and to dispel hostile magic. It should also be used in consecrating magical working tools of edged iron or steel.

Mugwort (*Artemisia vulgaris*)

Description: A common wayside weed in Europe and eastern North America, mugwort grows up to five feet tall; its deeply divided leaves are dark green above and downy-white underneath. Its flowers, like little yellow buttons gathered into long spikes, bloom between July and October. An essential oil is extracted from the leaves and flowers.

Temperature: Fiery—hot and dry in the second degree.

Astrology: Venus in Cancer.

Lore: In traditional natural magic, mugwort had an important role as a protective herb. Its leaves were traditionally harvested on St. John's Eve, June 23, and its root was gathered in the autumn. It was set over fires on St. John's Eve so that its smoke would protect the herds and banish misfortune. A branch of mugwort kept in the house, especially one that had been "smoked" in this way, was held to dispel hostile magic and drive away evil spirits. Mugwort was also put up over the door to preserve a house from being struck by lightning, and hidden under the doorstep to ensure that no annoying person would come to visit. It was also used as a visionary herb; placed in a pillow, it was said to bring strange dreams in which the dreamer might see events from his or her future life.

It may also be worth noting that all the various species of the *Artemisium* genus—including wormwood and southernwood, both covered in this Encyclopedia—share similar magical powers.

Safety Issues: The essential oil is somewhat toxic and should be avoided during pregnancy.

Mugwort

Parts Used: Leaves, flowers, and essential oil.

How Used: Amulets, sachets, incense, potions, baths, washes, oils, and scents.

Magical Uses: An important herb for the natural magician, mugwort is of great benefit in workings for protection as well as for enhanced awareness and psychic powers. The traditional habit of putting mugwort under the doorstep to keep annoying visitors away also seems to have a definite magical basis, and may be worth trying if your neighborhood is infested with door-to-door solicitors or the like.

Mullein (*Verbascum thapsus*)

Description: Mullein is a tall biennial found wild in Europe and the eastern half of North America, and grown widely as a medicinal herb. The leaves, which are so fuzzy they look like felt, grow in a rosette around the base and also on the tall stem, which can reach six feet in height. Spikes of yellow flowers bloom atop the stem in the summer months.

Temperature: Earthy—cold in the first degree and dry in the third.

Astrology: Saturn in Gemini.

Mullein

Lore: In earlier times, the flower stalks of mullein were dried, dipped in oil, and used as torches for ceremonial use. Mullein was also much used in protective magic, especially to banish hostile spirits.

Safety Issues: None.

Parts Used: Leaves, whole plant.

How Used: Living plants, amulets, sachets, incense, potions, baths, washes, and oils.

Magical Uses: Mullein leaves are valuable in amulets of protection, and the plant may also be grown in the garden to bring protection to the house.

Myrrh (*Balsamodendron spp.*)

Description: Like frankincense, and many other incenses used in ancient times, myrrh is a resin exuded by trees native to Arabia and eastern Africa. There are several species of trees that produce myrrh; all are small and shrubby, with gnarled branches, triple leaves, and small white flowers. The resin weeps naturally from the trunk, but small cuts are often made in the bark to increase the yield. An essential oil is extracted from the resin.

Temperature: Fiery—warm and dry in the third degree.

Astrology: Saturn in Aries.

Lore: One of the ancient incense resins, myrrh has a bitter edge that has long made it a symbol of sorrow and mourning.

Safety Issues: The essential oil should be avoided during pregnancy.

Parts Used: Resin, essential oil.

How Used: Amulets, sachets, incense, baths, washes, oils, and scents.

Magical Uses: Myrrh has a potent purifying influence, and may be used to purify, to protect, and to bless.

Nettle (*Urtica dioica*)

Description: There are several different species of nettle, all closely related and all armed with the stinging hairs that give the plant its character and much of its symbolism. The species listed here is the most common. A perennial comfortable in many different environments, it has a square, bristly stem and heart-shaped, saw-toothed leaves with pale down on the undersides. Its flowers are small and greenish, and appear in clusters hanging from beneath the leaves during the summer months.

Temperature: Fiery—warm and dry in the second degree.

Astrology: Mars in Aries.

Lore: There is surprisingly little magical lore about nettle, although it has been an important healing herb for centuries.

Safety Issues: The dried plant is perfectly safe, but touching the live plant will result in a painful skin reaction.

Parts Used: Leaves.

How Used: Amulets, potions, baths, and washes.

Magical Uses: Nettle is an excellent plant to use in workings involving the energy of Mars to strengthen the will and handle crisis situations more deftly, or to invoke Martial energies for other purposes.

Stinging Nettle

Nightshade

Nightshade (*Solanum dulcamara, S. nigrum*)

Description: These poisonous plants are found twining about fences and shrubs in many parts of North America. *S. dulcamara*, bittersweet nightshade, has purple flowers shaped like stars and brilliant, translucent red berries; *S. nigrum*, black nightshade, has clusters of white or pale violet flowers.

Temperature: Earthy—cold and dry in the fourth degree.

Astrology: Mercury in Libra.

Lore: Nightshade has important links to the lore of witchcraft, and was an ingredient in some flying ointments. Despite its poisonous effects and baleful reputation, it was held to remove hostile magic from humans and animals alike.

Safety Issues: TOXIC. Both kinds of nightshade are poisonous and should never be eaten or used in any preparation that will come into contact with your body.

Parts Used: Berries.

How Used: Amulets.

Magical Uses: Nightshade can be valuable in amulets to protect against magical attack.

North Wind

Description: There are three north winds in the traditional lore: Boreas blowing from due north, Corus from the northwest, and Aquilo from the northeast.

Temperature: Earthy—cold and dry.

Astrology: Boreas is Saturn in Capricorn, Corus Mercury in Virgo, and Aquilo Venus in Taurus.

Lore: These earthy winds brought cold winter weather down from the north. In traditional imagery, they were shown as strong, muscular figures with gray hair and wings, dressed in robes the color of storm clouds. Boreas had the additional peculiarity of legs and feet in the form of serpents' tails.

Safety Issues: None (beyond the risk of catching cold).

How Used: Winds can be used as sources or carriers of magical energies. See *Winds*.

Magical Uses: See *Winds*.

Numbers

Description: The lore of numbers overlaps in various ways with that of natural magic. In many traditional amulets and charms, numbers play an important role. Amulets often contain some specific number of seeds, leaves, or the like; many charms have to be made or consecrated a set number of times, and so on. While the meaning of some of these number-symbolisms is hard to ferret out, there are two major factors that can be traced.

First of all, there are what folklorists call "pattern numbers"—numbers that underlie the way people in different cultures think. In most Western societies, three is the most common pattern number. "Third time's the charm," as many people say; people count to three before opening their eyes or throwing a hand grenade; Christians worship a Holy Trinity, and most modern pagans revere a Triple Goddess.

In most of the native cultures of North America, by contrast, four is the principal pattern number; in China and much of the rest of eastern Asia, the same role is filled by the number five, while seven played much the same role in the cultures of the ancient Middle East.

The second factor, more complex, is the developed number symbolism of Western high magic, which has its roots in Greek philosophy and evolved into its modern form during the Renaissance. In this system, each number from one to ten has a specific meaning, corresponding to the ten Spheres of the Cabalistic Tree of Life and the ten celestial orbs of ancient cosmology.

Magical Uses: Each of these two factors involves a different approach to the use of numbers in natural magic. The first, the use of pattern numbers, fits well with the various modern revivals of pagan magic. A magician working in a specific tradition—Wiccan, Celtic, Norse, or what have you—simply needs to use the pattern numbers of that tradition in important amulets, just as those who once practiced the same approaches to magic would have done. A thorough study of the tradition's mythology and magic will reveal the numbers to use.

The number symbolism of high magic requires a more complex approach. Here the symbolism of the planets and elements, as outlined in The Theory of Natural Magic in Part One, is the controlling factor. The numbers of the planets are as follows:

Saturn—3

Jupiter—4

Mars—5

Sun—6

Venus—7

Mercury—8

Moon—9

Earth—10

The numbers four and ten are also the governing numbers of the elements—four corresponding to the elements on their own terms, ten to their role as components of the material world.

In any work of natural magic, then, the magician can simply use a number corresponding to the planet that governs the working, or one corresponding to the elements if the work is an elemental one. Three different plants may go into an amulet of Saturn, six drops of an essential oil may be added to a bath or wash meant to invoke the Sun, nine leaves of a lunar herb can be placed into a charm of the Moon, and so on. A little experimentation will teach the process quickly enough.

Nutmeg (*Myristica fragrans*)

Description: Nutmeg is the nut of the same tropical tree that also provides mace (see *Mace*). It has been exported from its native Southeast Asia for thousands of years as a cooking spice, and is now grown over much of the tropical world. An essential oil is extracted from the nut.

Temperature: Fiery—warm and dry in the second degree.

Astrology: Moon in Sagittarius.

Lore: Nutmeg, like mace, has been traditionally used in love magic of various kinds.

Safety Issues: Both nutmeg and its essential oil are somewhat toxic in large doses and will cause nausea, vomiting, dizziness, stomach pains, rapid pulse, anxiety, liver pain, double vision, and coma.

Parts Used: Whole or powdered seed, essential oil.

How Used: Amulets, sachets, incense, seasoning for food or drink, baths, washes, oils, and scents.

Magical Uses: Nutmeg is particularly suited to Moon magic and sea magic, and its unusual combination of lunar and fiery energies can be an important help in keeping workings of this sort within a healthy elemental balance. Like many lunar herbs and stones, it can also be used in magical dreamwork, as it intensifies dreams, especially when eaten or used as an incense.

English Oak

Oak (*Quercus spp.*)

Description: This mightiest of deciduous trees—growing as high as 150 feet—has gray bark and leaves with rounded or fingerlike lobes. Its seed, the acorn, has a special symbolism of its own (see *Acorn*).

Temperature: Earthy—cold and dry in the second degree.

Astrology: Jupiter in Sagittarius.

Lore: The most powerful of trees in Northern European tree magic, the oak is associated with the Indo-European god of thunder—Thor, Taranis, Perun, and Zeus, to give some of his names in different cultures. Mistletoe that grows on oak (see *Mistletoe*) was held to contain the essence of the oak's power, and was thus the most prized of herbs to ancient and modern Druids alike.

Safety Issues: Preparations made of white oak should not be applied to extensively damaged skin.

Parts Used: Whole tree, wood, leaves.

How Used: Living trees, amulets, working tools.

Magical Uses: Oak is the preeminent tree of power in ancient symbolism, and its wood may be used to direct and channel high levels of energy; a wand or staff of oak is a most useful tool for those who practice weather magic or Earth magic. A chaplet of oak leaves may be worn when invoking Jupiter or any of the pagan gods of thunder. Place an amulet or talisman beneath the roots when you plant an oak tree and the magical working will endure long after your death.

Obsidian

Description: Obsidian is a natural glass formed by cooling lava from volcanic eruptions. Black and shiny, it can be worked to an edge sharper than any metal can achieve.

Temperature: Watery—cold and moist in the first degree.

Astrology: Saturn in Aquarius.

Lore: A rare stone in the Old World, obsidian was little used in traditional Western natural magic, though it found some use as a way of invoking Saturnine energies.

Safety Issues: None.

How Used: Amulets; water and oil infusions may be used in potions, baths, washes, oils, and scents.

Magical Uses: Obsidian may be used magically to invoke Saturn, especially for that planet's intellectual gifts of depth, focus, logical precision, and contemplative insight.

Olive (*Olea europaea*)

Description: The olive tree, native to the Mediterranean countries but grown in warm regions around the world at present, is an evergreen growing up to twenty-five feet tall. Its leaves are long, leathery, and pointed, dark green above and silvery beneath; its flowers are white and fragrant, and its fruit is the familiar edible olive, which is green when young and black when ripe. The oil pressed from the berries is a staple for food and other uses throughout the Mediterranean countries and the Middle East.

Temperature: The ripe fruit and oil are airy—warm and moist in the first degree; the leaves, branches, and bark are earthy—cold and dry in the second degree.

Astrology: Jupiter in Cancer.

Lore: According to Greek mythology, the olive tree was the creation and special emblem of the goddess Athena.

Safety Issues: None.

Parts Used: Berry, oil.

How Used: Food, base for infused oils.

Magical Uses: Olive oil is the most common base for infused oils, as its own characteristics blend well with those of almost any other substance.

Onion (*Allium cepa*)

Description: This familiar garden vegetable also grows wild over much of the world. The bulb, the part normally eaten, is the underground part of the stem; above ground, the stem is hollow and green, surrounded by long thin leaves of similar color and structure. The flowers are pale green, and bloom in a round cluster during the summer months.

Temperature: Airy—warm in the fourth degree, moist in the third.

Astrology: Mars in Taurus.

Lore: One of the most common traditional protective herbs, onion shares many of the same magical effects as garlic. Half an onion placed on a saucer on the mantle, cut side up, is a traditional (and effective) response to hostile magic in many cultures.

Onion

Safety Issues: None.

Parts Used: Bulb.

How Used: Amulet, food.

Magical Uses: Like garlic, onion is best used for protection; it also has a place as a communion food of Mars.

Onyx

Description: Yet another semiprecious variety of chalcedony, onyx is translucent and has many layers of different colors.

Temperature: Fiery—warm in the second degree and dry in the third.

Astrology: Saturn in Leo.

Lore: Onyx was believed to bring melancholy and bad dreams, and was also used to counteract the effects of romantic love and sexual attraction. It was often held to be an unlucky stone, bringing discord and conflict to the wearer, although all its negative effects could be counteracted by wearing it together with sard, the opaque variety of carnelian (see *Carnelian*). The traditional lore warned pregnant women to avoid it, as it was believed to cause premature labor, but if it was placed on or near a woman actually in labor it brought about a quick and safe delivery.

In Christian magical lore, onyx was associated with the fifth order of angels, the Principalities.

Safety Issues: None.

How Used: Amulets; water and oil infusions may also be used in potions, baths, washes, oils, and scents.

Magical Uses: The various specific powers of onyx can all be summed up by the word "separation," and are best used in those situations when a connection of some sort needs to be brought to a quick and definite end. A variety of chalcedony should certainly be worn with onyx to counteract its tendency to cause depression.

Opal

Description: Opal is a form of silica, the same mineral that makes up quartz crystals, but is softer and less dense than quartz. Its subtle structure produces an iridescent play of colors in its depths.

Temperature: Airy—warm and moist in the second degree.

Astrology: Moon in Libra.

Lore: A traditionally unlucky stone, opals were claimed to bring misfortune of many kinds to their wearer. The one exception is the very rare black opal, which is held to be exceedingly lucky. Opals are also dreamstones and were used to call forth divinatory dreams.

Safety Issues: None.

How Used: Amulets. Water and oil infusions may also be used in potions, baths, washes, oils, and scents.

Magical Uses: The chief use of opal is in visionary work, in and out of the dream state. Use an opal to stimulate the visionary senses, to heighten scrying and Pathworking, or to learn the art of conscious or lucid dreaming. It should be kept in a silk bag when not in use, and one or more stones that tend to bring good fortune should be worn to counteract its effects.

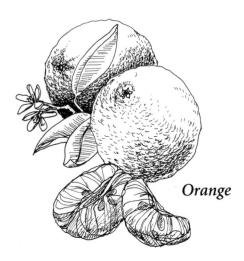

Orange

Orange (*Citrus aurantium, C. sinensis*)

Description: An evergreen native to Asia, the orange tree is cultivated in warm countries all over the world. It reaches thirty feet in height, with shiny green leaves, sweet-smelling white flowers, and the familiar orange-skinned fruits. A variety of essential oils are extracted from oranges—bitter and sweet orange oil from the peels of different varieties, petitgrain oil from the leaves, and neroli from the blossoms.

Temperature: Watery—cold and moist in the third degree.

Astrology: Sun in Cancer.

Lore: Oranges may have been the original of the "Golden Apples of the Hesperides" in Greek myth. Orange flowers and their oil, neroli, were used in rituals surrounding weddings.

Safety Issues: The essential oils from orange skins and leaves are phototoxic, and skin treated with them should be kept out of direct sunlight for several hours or until the oil has been washed off.

Parts Used: Fruit, peel, and essential oils.

How Used: Amulets, sachets, food, potions, baths, washes, oils, and scents.

Magical Uses: The energy of oranges has a strong solar quality, and may be used to invoke the Sun in any suitable context. The Sun's usual protective powers are also present, especially in the oil extracted from orange skins.

Oregano (*Origanum vulgare*)

Description: A close relative of marjoram and one of the many members of the mint family with a place in herbal lore, oregano is a perennial native to the Mediterranean area and much of Asia. Its square, purplish stem bears paired oval leaves dotted with small depressions. Its flowers are purple and appear in clusters at the ends of stems in late summer and early fall. An essential oil is extracted from the dried herb.

Temperature: Fiery—warm and dry in the third degree.

Astrology: Mercury in Gemini.

Lore: The lore of oregano and that of marjoram are thoroughly mixed together; in many sources, in fact, it's impossible to tell which of the two is being discussed. See *Marjoram*.

Safety Issues: The essential oil is toxic; it should never be applied to the skin, and should be avoided altogether during pregnancy.

Parts Used: Leaves, whole plant.

How Used: Living plant, amulets, sachets, incense, seasoning for food, potions, baths, washes, oils, and scents.

Magical Uses: Oregano's uses are essentially the same as marjoram's (see *Marjoram*).

Parsley (*Petroselinum sativum*)

Description: Parsley's crinkly leaves and distinctive scent are familiar all over the world. Biennial in most climates, it produces umbels of small white or greenish flowers in the summer months. Essential oils are extracted from the seeds and leaves.

Temperature: Airy—warm and moist in the third degree.

Astrology: Mercury in Libra.

Lore: Familiar as it is, parsley carries a remarkably sinister symbolism. In Greek and Roman times, parsley was a death symbol, used to decorate graves. Its connection to mortality was so strong that, according to the

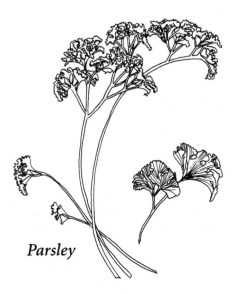

Parsley

Greek philosopher Plutarch, a group of soldiers who were on their way to a battle once encountered a donkey carrying a load of parsley, and ran away in a state of panic; such an omen, they were convinced, could mean nothing but imminent death.

Later, in the Middle Ages, parsley became one of the plants closely associated with Satan, and Christian folklore had it that the only way to plant parsley without diabolic interference was to sow the seed on Good Friday at moonrise. Old-timers still claim that the seed has to travel to Hell and back seven times in order to get the devil's permission to sprout, but this has more to do with parsley's very long germination time than with anything more straightforwardly magical.

Safety Issues: Essential oil of parsley is mildly toxic and should be avoided during pregnancy. The root, which has little magical value anyway, should not be taken internally during pregnancy or by people with inflammatory kidney disease.

Parts Used: Leaves.

How Used: Amulets, seasoning for foods, potions, baths, washes, oils, and scents.

Magical Uses: Parsley may be used when dealing magically with the souls of the dead or the afterlife.

Patchouli (*Pogostemon patchouli*)

Description: Patchouli is a low, bushy perennial herb native to Southeast Asia, grown for its fragrant leaves all over the tropical regions of the globe. An essential oil is extracted from the leaves.

Temperature: Earthy—cold in the first degree and dry in the second.

Astrology: Saturn in Virgo.

Lore: Patchouli has long been used as an aphrodisiac in tropical Asia, but it seems to have been unknown to the West until recent times.

Safety Issues: None.

Parts Used: Leaves, essential oil.

How Used: Amulets, sachets, incense, baths, washes, oils, and scents.

Magical Uses: Patchouli is a useful addition to any form of natural magic relating to sex or to the element of Earth. It helps to ground consciousness in the physical body and amplify the sense of touch.

Pennyroyal (*Mentha pulegium* or *Hedeoma pulegioides*)

Description: The candy-cane scent of pennyroyal, like its square stem and paired leaves, are signs linking it to the mint family. True pennyroyal, *M. pulegium*, is a very close relative of familiar mints such as spearmint and peppermint; American pennyroyal, *H. pulegioides*, belongs to a different genus but has the same scent and magical properties. An essential oil is extracted from true pennyroyal.

Temperature: Fiery—warm and dry in the third degree.

Astrology: Venus in Scorpio; associated with the fixed star Procyon.

Lore: Pennyroyal, in very small amounts, was one of the ingredients in the sacred drink given to initiates of the Eleusinian Mysteries.

Safety Issues: TOXIC. Pennyroyal is poisonous in strong doses, and should never be used in any form during pregnancy. The essential oil is highly toxic and should never be taken internally or used in any preparation that will come into direct contact with your body.

Parts Used: Whole plant, essential oil.

How Used: Amulets, sachets, baths, washes, scents, and oils.

Magical Uses: Pennyroyal has traditional links to the lore of immortality and reincarnation, and may be used in ceremonies intended to lessen the fear of death or to help the recently dead finish their transition to the afterlife.

Pig (*Sus scrofa*)

Description: Another common farm animal with a very uncommon history and symbolism, the pig descends from the fierce wild boars of ancient Europe, now all but extinct as a result of hunting. Modern notions of pigs as naturally dirty are a product of the unnatural conditions of most modern farms; left to themselves, pigs are clean animals who prefer a diet of fallen nuts and other foods of the forest floor.

Temperature: Pork is airy—warm and moist in the first degree.

Astrology: Saturn in Scorpio.

Lore: As the horse and stag in ancient symbolism represent the Sun, and cattle the Moon, pigs represent the Earth, and in particular the forces of the Underworld.

Safety Issues: Pork should always be cooked thoroughly to prevent food poisoning.

Parts Used: Meat, leather.

How Used: Food, working tools.

Magical Uses: Pork has been used as a communion food in Earth magic for thousands of years, and pig leather, pig bone, and boar tusks make excellent raw materials for working tools consecrated to Earth magic. The pig's connections with the symbolism of death also make it suitable for similar applications involving the Underworld and the dead.

Pig

Plantain

Plantain (*Plantago major, P. lanceolata*)

Description: There are two common varieties of plantain, with differently
shaped leaves—one, broadleaf plantain, broad and rounded and the other,
lance-leaf plantain, long and pointed. The first was held to have more virtue,
but both have the same uses in medicine and magic. Both kinds grow close
to the ground, with the leaves spreading out directly from the rootstock, and
both produce tall brown-tipped flower stalks from the middle of spring
until the first frosts. Leaves for drying should be collected in the early spring,
before the first flowers appear, but for immediate use leaves and root can be
gathered at any time. Its older name, waybread, was given it because it is
highly nutritious and was often gathered and eaten by travelers.

Temperature: Earthy—cold and dry in the third degree.

Astrology: Mars in Capricorn.

Lore: Plantain, according to a medieval legend, was once a maiden whose
faithless lover set out on a journey, promising to return. She waited for
him by the road for so long that eventually she turned into this most
common of roadside plants.

Safety Issues: None.

Parts Used: Whole plant.

How Used: Amulets, potions, baths, and washes.

Magical Uses: Plantain can be placed under the pillow to drive away night-mares and evil spirits. Those who want to maximize its powers should gather it during the last quarter of the Moon's cycle, during the planetary hour of Mercury, and tell the plant what it will be asked to accomplish before gathering it.

Quartz

Description: This is the generic "crystal" of modern New Age practice, as well as the material from which most crystal balls are made. Chemically speaking, it is pure or nearly pure silica (silicon dioxide), which naturally forms hexagonal crystals.

Temperature: Watery—cold in the first degree and moist in the third.

Astrology: Moon in Cancer.

Lore: A sacred substance in many shamanic traditions, quartz crystal is less important in Western natural magic but still has a significant place. It was considered to be congealed water by many of the old loremasters, and was used for scrying and other divinatory work requiring the receptivity of water. It was also held to have protective qualities, especially against spirits of the night.

Water infusions of quartz crystal were held to have healing properties, and the stone itself was sometimes used in weather magic meant to bring rain.

Safety Issues: None.

How Used: Amulets, working tools; water and oil infusions may also be used in potions, baths, washes, oils, and scents.

Magical Uses: The purity of quartz makes it a very good stone for holding magical energy; it will take and hold patterns well with little interference. For this reason a quartz crystal can be added to nearly any consecrated amulet to help it hold its charge. Once energized, though, a quartz crystal should never be exposed to direct sunlight unless you intend to erase its charge (see *Sunlight*). Quartz is also among the best of stones for use in scrying and other kinds of visionary workings.

Rain

Description: All forms of water that fall from the sky, including rain, snow, hail, and sleet, share a connection with the subtle forces of life. In magical and alchemical theory, these forces gather in the clouds as part of a subtle cycle of energies linked to the seasons, and during the zodiacal signs of Aries and Taurus (roughly March 21–May 20) these forces descend in the rain to bring renewed life to the soil. Rain caught in clean containers, especially during these months, has special magical properties and will give additional strength to any magical working that includes water. It cannot be stored for more than a few days, however.

Temperature: Watery—cold and moist in the second degree.

Astrology: Moon in Pisces.

Lore: Rainwater plays an important part in many traditional spells, especially as a basis for potions and as a reflecting surface for visionary work. In the days before air pollution, it was commonly used in any magical working where pure water was especially necessary. Like dew and other forms of water from the sky, it also has a long history as an ingredient in alchemical processes.

Safety Issues: Rain should only be used if it can be gathered in a place with relatively pure air.

How Used: Potions, baths, and washes.

Magical Uses: Rain may be used to add additional energy to any water-based working of natural magic, especially when gathered in the time period described in the traditional lore. It may also be put to use in fertility workings.

Rose (*Rosa spp.*)

Description: There are over a hundred different species of rose, ranging from little five-petaled wild roses to lush cabbage roses, and within these there are countless varieties, with flower colors from white through yellow and pink to deep reds on the edge of black. Some roses are shrubs, others creeping vines; most have thorns but a few types do not; all have some variation of the unmistakable scent of roses, and bear edible hips rich in vitamin C. Several different grades of essential oils are extracted from roses.

Rose

Temperature: Earthy—cold in the first degree, dry in the third.

Astrology: Venus in Libra.

Lore: The rose is the most important symbolic flower in the Western tradition, with the same kind of importance and range of symbolism the lotus has in Eastern cultures. Different colors have different symbolic meanings—the white rose represents innocence and silence, the pink rose simplicity and love, the yellow rose jealousy, the red rose passion and sacrifice.

Safety Issues: While the rose itself is entirely safe, many rose gardeners use extremely toxic pesticides. Unless you can be sure the roses you use were grown organically, it's usually wisest not to use them in any preparation that will be taken internally.

Parts Used: Flowers, leaves, hips, and essential oil.

How Used: Amulets, sachets, incense, food, potions, baths, washes, oils, and scents.

Magical Uses: The principal use of the rose is in love magic of various kinds. Rose petals are a common and effective ingredient in amulets for bringing a love relationship into one's life; oil of rose can be used in the same way. Equally, rose can be used to help awaken deeper aspects of love, such as compassion and devotion to the Higher.

Rosemary (*Rosmarinus officinalis*)

Description: This evergreen shrub is native to the lands around the Mediterranean Sea, but is grown in gardens over much of the world. Its narrow, needlelike leaves are dark green above and white beneath, with a clearly visible vein down the center and edges that roll down. Its flowers, white or pale blue, bloom in the spring in most climates. Rosemary is mildly poisonous in large doses, and should be taken internally only in small amounts. An essential oil is extracted from the flowers.

Temperature: Fiery—warm and dry in the second degree.

Astrology: Sun in Aries. It is associated with the fixed star Alphecca.

Alternative Correspondence: Moon.

Lore: Rosemary's name comes from the Latin *ros marinus*, "dew of the sea," and in its native habitat it flourishes on seaside cliffs. The most important traditional use for rosemary was to strengthen the memory; students in ancient Greece would wear rosemary garlands while preparing for examinations, and in the Renaissance rosemary gardens were a favored location for practicing the magical Art of Memory. It was also held to clear the mind, prevent giddiness, and banish depressed moods.

Safety Issues: Rosemary is somewhat poisonous in large doses. The essential oil should be avoided during pregnancy and by epileptics.

Parts Used: Leaves, root, and essential oil.

How Used: Living plant, amulets, sachets, seasoning for food, incense, baths, washes, oils, and scents.

Magical Uses: For all its fiery and solar symbolism, rosemary has an important magical link to the Moon, and through it to the ocean and to oceanic energies; use it whenever you need a solar force compatible with Moon magic or sea magic. At the same time, like most solar herbs, it has substantial protective powers and can be used to banish nightmares and hostile spirits. The root makes a fine incense, with a similar scent to frankincense and many of the same magical effects.

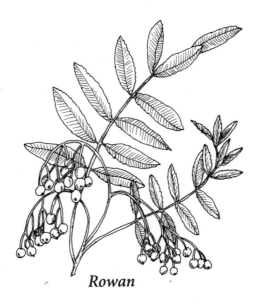

Rowan

Rowan (*Sorbus aucuparia, S. americana*)

Description: Two species of rowan (also called mountain ash) are found in
North America, the European (*S. aucuparia*), which is grown as an ornamental, and the American (*S. americana*), which is found wild in the eastern half of the continent. Both are small trees or shrubs, with leaves
divided into odd-numbered, toothed leaflets, clusters of white flowers
blooming during late spring, and red berries the size of peas that ripen in
the fall.

Temperature: Fiery—warm and dry in the second degree.

Astrology: Sun in Sagittarius.

Lore: One of the most powerful of protective trees in the Western tradition,
rowan was used to break hostile magic and chase off destructive spirits all
over Europe. A rowan branch in bed preserved the sleeper from nightmares, and a twig in the pocket kept the bearer safe against enchantment,
while a branch hung over the door and tied with red thread would keep
hostile magicians from entering. Butter churns were made of rowan wood
to keep the butter from being magically stolen, and a rowan whip was used
to control bewitched horses. The most magically effective was "flying

rowan," one growing with its roots in a cleft in the rock or the branches or stump of another tree rather than in the ground. Rowan trees were planted in churchyards to keep evil spirits away from the bodies of the dead.

Safety Issues: None.

Parts Used: Whole tree, leaves, wood, and berries.

How Used: Living plants, amulets, baths, washes, and working tools.

Magical Uses: A valuable resource for protective magic, rowan can be used to banish, protect, and purify. It is particularly useful for chasing off the more disruptive forms of faery and spirit activity, and for putting an end to hostile magical workings.

Ruby

Description: Like sapphire, ruby is a precious variety of corundum (aluminum oxide), which in its less spectacular forms is most often used as an abrasive in sandpaper. The brilliant red color of ruby comes from small amounts of chromium oxide.

Temperature: Fiery—warm and dry in the fourth degree.

Astrology: Sun in Leo; associated with the fixed star Regulus.

Lore: In many of the old texts of natural magic, ruby was seen as the most powerful of magical gems; it was held to bring strength, health, and vigor, to counteract melancholy, to curb uncontrolled desires and idle thoughts, and to banish unhappiness from the wearer's life. Its inner connection with Fire is so strong that some rubies were claimed to be able to boil the water in which they were placed. As an amulet, it should be worn on the left side of the body, preferably in a ring.

Safety Issues: None.

How Used: Amulets; water and oil infusions can be used in potions, baths, washes, oils, and scents.

Magical Uses: If you can afford one, ruby makes the best possible gem for working with the energies of Fire, and it can also help bring clarity and focus to the mind. A ruby set into a working tool of Fire, such as a wand, will amplify the elemental forces dramatically.

Rue

Rue (*Ruta graveolens*)

Description: An aromatic perennial native to southern Europe and northern Africa, rue has a pale green stem and leaves divided into oblong leaflets. Its flowers appear in clusters during the summer months.

Temperature: Fiery—warm and dry in the third degree.

Astrology: Saturn in Leo.

Lore: This bitter herb has an ancient link with sorrow, remorse, and divine grace; its name comes from the Greek word *ruta*, "repentance." Aristotle mentions that it was a common protective herb against hostile magic in his time, and the same belief is still active in many parts of Europe today.

Rue has also been used for love and fertility charms since ancient times, in large part because of its medicinal virtues, but it also has a reputation as an anaphrodisiac.

Hunters' lore claims that if you rub an arrow with rue, it will always find its mark.

Safety Issues: Rue is somewhat poisonous in large doses, and it should never be used in any form during pregnancy. It can cause skin rashes in sensitive people. It should also not be used by people taking blood-thinning agents.

Parts Used: Leaves.

How Used: Amulets, incense, baths, and washes.

Magical Uses: Rue is a powerful protective herb, especially against hostile magic and disease, and can also be put to work in exorcisms and purifications. Like asafoetida, it will banish spirits at need, and may be burnt as incense when a ceremonial working goes awry.

Saffron (*Crocus sativus*)

Description: Saffron is the pollen of the autumn crocus, a perennial that grows from an onionlike bulb. Its leaves are long and pointed, and wrapped with a grayish sheath at the bottom; its flowers, funnel-shaped and reddish, appear in late summer or early fall. The pollen-bearing parts of the flower are gathered and dried to produce saffron.

Temperature: Fiery—hot and dry in the third degree.

Astrology: Sun in Leo; associated with the fixed star Antares.

Lore: Known as the "blood of Hercules" in ancient Greece, saffron has a long history as a protective herb. It was a common ingredient in amulets to protect the wearer against disease. It also has been credited with aphrodisiac effects, particularly for women.

Safety Issues: In the very small amounts used in ordinary cooking, saffron is perfectly safe, but large doses (more than a gram or so) can cause fatal poisoning.

Part Used: Powdered pollen.

How Used: Amulets, seasoning for food, baths, and washes.

Magical Uses: Another potent solar herb, saffron may be used in communion meals for rituals of the Sun, and may be put to use in any other application where solar force is wanted.

Sage (*Salvia officinalis*)

Description: A low perennial shrub native to dry, rocky soils in southern Europe and the Mediterranean, sage has oblong, downy, richly scented gray-green leaves with prominent veins and a distinctive "crinkly" texture. Its flowers, purple, blue, or white, appear in long clusters in June or July; the leaves should be gathered before the first flowers appear. An essential oil is extracted from the leaves, but this is somewhat toxic and the non-

Sage

toxic oil of clary sage may be substituted for it in all magical uses (see *Clary Sage*).

Temperature: Fiery—warm in the first degree, dry in the second.

Astrology: Jupiter in Taurus. It is associated with the fixed star Spica.

Lore: A herb associated with longevity, sage was also held to mark the fortunes of the owner of any garden where it grew, flourishing in good times and withering in bad. The Romans called it *herba sacra*, "holy herb," and used it in their religious rites.

Safety Issues: Large doses of sage taken internally will produce a mild but unpleasant form of intoxication.

Parts Used: Leaves.

How Used: Living plants, amulets, sachets, incense, seasoning for food, potions, baths, washes, oils, and scents.

Magical Uses: An important herb of Jupiter, sage can be used in any working of that planet; it can season food or, in the form of a tea or potion made of the leaves, provide a suitable drink for a communion of Jupiter. Its broader uses, however, are as a purifying and cleansing herb, and it can be burnt as incense, used in amulets, or simply grown in the garden for these purposes. It is strongest for magical purposes if grown near rue.

St. John's Wort (*Hypericum perforatum*)

Description: St. John's Wort is a hardy perennial found over much of the world. It is fondest of sunny places and dry soils. Farmers in many Western states treat it as a noxious weed, which only goes to show how little attention most modern people pay to the treasures of the herbal realm! It has leaves set in pairs along the stems, and bright yellow, five-petaled flowers that bloom from June to September. The leaves are dotted with little, transparent glands that look like holes, and the petals are edged with black dots. The volatile oils that give it potent healing properties make the whole plant smell like turpentine.

Temperature: Fiery—warm and dry in the second degree.

Astrology: Sun in Leo.

Lore: In recent years, several herbalists have suggested that this herb was originally called St. Joan's Wort, because of its power to heal burns, and had its name and gender changed by sexist scribes later on. Unfortunately for this theory, the name St. John's Wort—*herba Sanctis Johannis* in Latin—first appeared in medieval herbals centuries before there ever was a St. Joan; since St. John the Baptist was beheaded, he makes a suitable patron for this herb as well, since it is also used by herbalists to treat cuts and open wounds.

The actual origin of the name has to do with the magical traditions surrounding the herb. St. John's Wort was the most common of several herbs that were put by the armload on bonfires on St. John's Eve, June 23; livestock were driven through the resulting clouds of smoke to given them protection against hostile magic and destructive spirits for the coming year, and sprigs of the herbs thus used were placed in houses and barns afterwards to protect them against ghosts and lightning. St. John's Wort was also used at need to keep faeries at bay. It is perhaps the most solar of all herbs, with a complex and potent relationship to the Sun on many different levels.

Safety Issues: St. John's Wort is somewhat phototoxic, and if you take it internally or apply it to the skin you should stay out of direct sunlight for the next day or so.

Parts Used: Flowers.

St. John's Wort

How Used: Amulets, incense, potions, baths, washes, and oils.

Magical Uses: St. John's Wort can be used for banishing, protection, and blessing in nearly any magical preparation, although its turpentine smell makes it a somewhat disagreeable incense (use frankincense to get the same effects in a more pleasant way). Amulets of the herb or simply bunches of flowers hung over doors and windows will protect a house against hostile magic or destructive spirits.

Salt

Description: Common table salt, sodium chloride, is found in high concentrations in sea water and in mineral deposits laid down by ancient oceans.

Temperature: Earthy—cold in the second degree and dry in the fourth.

Astrology: Saturn in Aquarius.

Lore: One of the most ancient and sacred of purifying substances, salt was often used in earlier times to banish hostile influences, and still plays a central role in protective rituals in North American folk magic. Many American children still learn to toss some over their left shoulder whenever salt is spilled; this custom was once meant to drive off the evil spirit who threatened whenever the holy substance was wasted or profaned.

Safety Issues: Too much salt taken internally can act as a poison, but it takes a good deal of work to manage this.

How Used: Amulets, seasoning for food; dissolved in water, it may be used in baths and washes.

Magical Uses: Salt is one of the standard tools of the working natural magician. Either naturally dried sea salt or kosher salt will give the best results; many other kinds are contaminated with chemicals that will interfere with salt's effects. Salt crystals will absorb magical energy and hold it in a fixed, inactive form; this makes salt particularly useful in dealing with hostile magic. Salt may also be used for blessings, banishings, purifications and any form of protective magic.

    For the strongest possible effect, heat salt at low heat in an oven for half an hour to dry it out completely, and keep it in an airtight container.

Sandalwood (*Santalum album*)

Description: The sandalwood tree is a tropical parasitic plant that grows on the roots of other trees, and often reaches a height of more than forty feet. Native to most of south and southeast Asia, it is grown commercially in Indonesia. An essential oil is extracted from the powdered wood.

Temperature: Airy—warm and moist in the third degree.

Astrology: Venus in Virgo.

Alternative Correspondence: Mercury.

Lore: The classical incense of India, sandalwood has been used in southern Asia as far back as records reach, and is referred to in the oldest parts of the Vedas. Temples in tropical areas were often made of sandalwood logs, both because of the scent and because the oil repels termites and other wood-eating insects.

Safety Issues: Not for use by people with diseases of the parenchyma of the kidney.

Parts Used: Powdered wood, essential oil.

How Used: Amulets, sachets, incense, baths, washes, oils, and scents.

Magical Uses: Sandalwood has protective, purifying, and visionary properties, and makes a good general base for incense blends. Use it in ritual workings to invoke the element of Air.

Sapphire

Description: Like ruby, sapphire is a precious variety of corundum, its blue color coming from very small amounts of titanium salts. The purer the blue, the more magically powerful the stone is held to be.

Temperature: Watery—cold and moist in the fourth degree.

Astrology: Jupiter in Pisces.

Lore: The sapphire is one of the most important stones in traditional natural magic, and relates to ruby in precisely the same way that water relates to fire. It was held to bring wisdom, peace, and spiritual insight, and was also used to banish diseases. In Christian magical lore, it was associated with the seventh order of angels, the Virtues.

Safety Issues: None.

How Used: Amulets; water and oil infusions may be used in potions, baths, washes, oils, and scents.

Magical Uses: Sapphire can be used, if you can afford one, to work with the magical energies of water. It amplifies the physical and nonphysical senses alike and brings mental balance. Placed in a working tool of water, such as a cup, it will amplify the elemental energies sharply.

Sard (see Carnelian)

Sardonyx

Description: Formed from parallel layers of sard and onyx, this striped stone combines the virtues of these two very different gems into a balanced and powerful whole.

Temperature: Watery—cold in the second degree and moist in the first.

Astrology: Mercury in Virgo.

Lore: Sardonyx has a very old reputation in magic. Among its more interesting traditional uses is as a talisman of invisibility. It was also used as a source of magical protection, and—at least in part because of its union of two very different stones—was held to bring about a happy marriage if one or both members of a couple wore it.

It was also used to strengthen the intellect and amplify the senses, and banish anger, folly, and uncontrolled passions. It should be worn in contact with the skin as much as possible, and may be placed under the tongue to amplify its effect.

Safety Issues: None.

How Used: Amulets; water and oil infusions may be used in potions, baths, washes, oils, and scents.

Magical Uses: Sardonyx can be used for any of its traditional purposes. While it will not grant invisibility (or the magical equivalent, which is simply a matter of not being noticed) by itself, it can be used to amplify ritual workings of this kind. It may also be used to focus the mind and heighten the senses; water infusions are a particularly effective way of putting this property to use.

Savory (*Satureja hortensis, S. montana*)

Description: The two species of savory, summer (*S. hortensis*) and winter (*S. montana*), differ in their growing habits but not at all in their magical uses. Summer savory is an annual, winter savory a perennial, but both are small plants with narrow leaves and a strongly aromatic scent. Both produce small pink or white flowers in summer and early fall. Essential oils are extracted from both kinds of savory.

Temperature: Fiery—hot and dry in the third degree.

Astrology: Mercury in Gemini.

Lore: Associated with the satyrs of Greek and Roman legend, savory was said to stimulate sexual desires.

Safety Issues: The essential oils of both kinds of savory are somewhat toxic and should never be used in contact with the skin.

Part Used: Leaves.

How Used: Amulets, sachets, seasoning for food, baths, washes, oils, and scents.

Magical Uses: Savory will help chase away glum moods and bring happiness. It also has a useful role in sexual magic.

Summer Savory

Seashell

Seashells

Description: The shells of a wide range of sea-dwelling animals can be found on many beaches, cast off by their former owners and washed up by the waves. They are made of calcium carbonate, the same substance as limestone, and can be treated as stones in most contexts.

Temperature: Watery—cold and moist in the third degree.

Astrology: Moon in Cancer.

Lore: Seashells have seen little use in traditional Western natural magic, but they play a role in some branches of sea magic.

Safety Issues: None.

How Used: Amulets, working tools; water infusions can be used in potions, baths, and washes.

Magical Uses: Seashells are, sensibly enough, among the best substances to use in natural magic relating to the sea or its ruler, the Moon. If at all possible, they should be gathered from the seashore by the magician at night, when the Moon is visible and waxing. They should be thoroughly dried and then washed in several changes of clean water before use, to clear away the energy patterns of their former owners.

Silver

Description: This soft, relatively heavy, white metal has been used for jewelry and other purposes for thousands of years.

Temperature: Watery—cold and moist in the third degree.

Astrology: Moon.

Lore: Nearly everyone knows that a silver bullet is the one thing that will stop a werewolf; this is one of the few scraps of Western natural magic that has been preserved in popular culture. More generally, silver has long been the sacred metal of the Moon, and in alchemy was the product of the White Stone, the first product of the Great Work.

Safety Issues: None.

How Used: Amulets, working tools; water infusions can be used in potions, baths, and washes.

Magical Uses: Silver is the standard metal to use in any amulet or tool meant to invoke lunar forces. Its high conductivity to etheric energy—the same quality that allows it to disrupt the projected etheric animal-forms that are the reality behind werewolf legends—makes it valuable in almost any working tool that needs to bear high levels of energy. It is also congenial to the faery, and amulets made for working with nature spirits will benefit from having a small amount of silver included.

Solomon's Seal (*Polygonatum multiflorum*)

Description: A perennial found over much of the Northern Hemisphere, Solomon's seal has a thick, horizontal rootstock that bears one or two stems that can grow up to three feet tall. Its heart-shaped, ridged leaves are green above and white beneath, and it produces pale, bell-shaped flowers in spring and summer.

Temperature: Earthy—cold and dry in the first degree.

Astrology: Saturn in Capricorn.

Lore: Traditionally, Solomon's seal was used by those in search of buried treasure. It also was credited with power to banish hostile spirits. It is magically most potent when gathered on midsummer's eve, although only plants in flower on that day should be harvested.

A section through the root will show a pattern similar to the Seal of Solomon used in ritual magic, whence the name of the plant.

Safety Issues: None.

Part Used: Root.

How Used: Amulets, incense, baths, washes, and oils.

Magical Uses: Solomon's seal is an important tool for rituals of consecration, as its Saturnian energies help fix magical charges in objects. If you wish to make a promise or an oath permanently binding, the same fixative qualities make Solomon's seal a good choice for related workings. I haven't had an opportunity to look for buried treasure with it, but this might be worth investigating if you live in an area where such things are likely to exist!

South Wind

Description: There are three south winds in the traditional weather lore: Auster blowing from due south, Notus from the southeast, and Affricus from the southwest.

Temperature: Airy—warm and moist.

Astrology: Auster is Venus in Libra, Notus Mercury in Gemini, and Affricus Saturn in Aquarius.

Lore: These airy winds were seen as bringers of warm, wet weather. Accordingly, traditional imagery normally pictured them with soggy hair and gray garments, wrapped in clouds and mists.

Safety Issues: None, barring the risks that follow getting thoroughly wet.

How Used: Wind may be used as a source or a carrier of magical energies. See *Wind*.

Magical Uses: See *Wind*.

Southernwood

Southernwood (*Artemisia abrotanum*)

Description: A close but much safer relative of the somewhat toxic worm-wood, southernwood has divided leaves with an almost threadlike appearance and pale yellow flower heads. Native to Europe, it has found a home in some parts of eastern North America.

Temperature: Fiery—warm and dry in the third degree.

Astrology: Mercury in Gemini.

Lore: A traditional aphrodisiac, southernwood is also called "lad's love" and "maiden's ruin," which may give some idea of its role in the old lore.

Safety Issues: Do not use during pregnancy.

Part Used: Leaves, flowers.

How Used: Amulets, sachets, incense, potions, baths, washes, and oils.

Magical Uses: Southernwood's primary use in natural magic is as an ingredient in various kinds of sexual workings.

Strawberry (*Fragaria spp.*)

Description: The sweet red fruit of the domesticated strawberry is familiar to most people, but surprisingly few realize that wild strawberries can be found over much of North America. The leaves are divided into three-toothed leaflets, and the flowers, small and white, bloom in late spring.

Temperature: The plant is earthy—cold and dry in the second degree; the fruit is watery—cold and moist in the second degree.

Astrology: Venus in Libra.

Lore: Strawberries have deep connections with sexuality and love, and are used as a symbol of desire in medieval art.

Safety Issues: None.

Part Used: Leaves, fruit.

How Used: The leaves can be used in amulets, sachets, potions, baths, and washes; the berry is best used in food and potions.

Magical Uses: Strawberries can be used, especially as food, to invoke the energies of Venus.

Strawberry

Styrax (*Liquidambar orientalis*)

Description: Styrax is a resin collected from a tree native to Asia Minor. The styrax tree has purplish bark, leaves divided into three-lobed leaflets, and white flowers. Harvesters collect the resin by pounding on the living bark, which causes the resin to seep out and harden in the air. An essential oil is extracted from the resin.

Temperature: Airy—warm and moist in the second degree.

Astrology: Sun in Sagittarius.

Lore: Styrax is commonly called "amber" in the incense trade, but its magical qualities are rather different. Both botanically and magically, it is closely related to benzoin (see *Benzoin*), and functions principally as a protective and purifying incense.

Safety Issues: None.

Parts Used: Resin, essential oil.

How Used: Amulets, sachets, incense, baths, washes, oils, and scents.

Magical Uses: Use styrax for purification and protection, or to invoke the element of Air.

Sunlight

Description: Magically as well as physically, the Sun is the primary source of energy for all things on Earth. Its power is so great, however, that it will overwhelm most other energies, especially those that have to do with the etheric level of experience. (This is why, for example, ghosts and other etheric phenomena rarely appear when the Sun is above the horizon.)

Temperature: Fiery—warm and dry in the second degree.

Astrology: Sun, in whatever sign of the zodiac the Sun happens to be in at the time.

Lore: The magical effects of sunlight are remembered dimly in all those folktales in which a giant, ogre, ghost, or goblin is vanquished by the Sun's first rays.

How Used: Source (but also dispeller) of magical energies; oil and water charged with sunlight may be used in potions, baths, washes, oils, and scents.

Magical Uses: Any working using solar energies specifically can be charged by exposing it to the direct rays of the Sun, especially during the two months after the spring equinox, when the Sun's magical energies are at their height. Workings of any other planet, however, should be shielded from sunlight, for the solar force will tend to deconsecrate them. This is particularly true of lunar workings.

Tansy (*Tanacetum vulgare*)

Description: Tansy is another "weed" with important healing qualities. Found on roadsides and in vacant lots over much of North America, it has somewhat ferny leaves made of many-toothed leaflets, and flowers that look like little yellow buttons.

Temperature: Fiery—warm in the second degree, dry in the third.

Astrology: Saturn in Libra.

Lore: In tradition, tansy is associated with immortality, and was used in Easter rituals in many Christian cultures. It was held to be sacred to many goddesses, as well as to the Virgin Mary (their Christian equivalent).

Safety Issues: Tansy is somewhat toxic and should be used internally only in very small amounts, if at all, and never while pregnant.

Parts Used: Leaves, flowers.

How Used: Amulets, sachets, incense, baths, washes, oils, and scents.

Magical Uses: Tansy's association with immortality makes it a useful herb in workings meant to help the recently dead with their transition.

Tansy

*Serpyllum
Thyme*

Thyme (*Thymus vulgaris, T. serpyllum*)

Description: This familiar kitchen herb grows native in the Mediterranean lands, but is cultivated all over Europe and North America for culinary uses. Small and shrubby, with tiny paired leaves and woody stems, it bears clusters of bluish two-lipped flowers through late spring and summer and is a favorite of bees. An essential oil is extracted from the leaves and flowers; this comes in a less purified "red" and a more purified "white" form.

Temperature: Fiery—warm and dry in the third degree.

Astrology: Venus in Aries.

Lore: Thyme is named as an elf plant in the old lore, and was traditionally among the flowers not to be brought inside the house.

Safety Issues: Thyme is toxic in large doses when taken internally. Both red and white essential oils must be used in moderation, and should be avoided during pregnancy.

Parts Used: Leaves, whole plant.

How Used: Living plants, amulets, sachets, incense, seasoning for food, potions, baths, washes, oils, and scents.

Magical Uses: An effective herb in protective magic, thyme will also attract the attention of the faery, especially when planted in a garden. It makes a good purifying incense.

Tin

Description: This brittle, shiny metal is relatively rare in nature, and has become rarer still through several thousand years of systematic mining.

Temperature: Watery—cold in the second degree and moist in the third.

Astrology: Jupiter.

Lore: Except for its role as the planetary metal of Jupiter and a certain amount of use in summoning rain and thunder, tin has been given little attention by natural magicians in the West.

Safety Issues: Tin is quite toxic and should not be used in any form that will be taken internally or come into prolonged contact with bare skin.

How Used: Amulets, working tools.

Magical Uses: Tin may be used for any working of Jupiter. Brittle and hard to work, it is difficult to fashion into objects in its pure form, but tin sheet can be incorporated into a range of tools meant to work with Jovian energies. It may also be used for weather magic.

Tobacco (*Nicotiana tabacum*)

Description: This much-maligned and much-abused plant was sacred all over the Americas and grown by native tribes who cultivated no other crop. There are several species, all native to different parts of the New World; the one listed here is the one commonly domesticated. It grows two to three feet tall, with large oblong leaves and clusters of large reddish flowers.

Temperature: Fiery—warm and dry in the second degree.

Astrology: Mars in Libra.

Lore: Tobacco was not much used in traditional Western natural magic, but its role in the native magics of North America is important enough that magicians practicing on this continent should keep it in mind. Tobacco is the traditional offering to the spirits of the North American land, playing

Tobacco

the same role played by wine, for example, as an offering to the gods in ancient Greece. It was either placed, unburnt, as an offering in a sacred place, or smoked in a consecrated pipe.

Safety Issues: TOXIC. Tobacco is poisonous, and should never be taken internally. If the smoke is inhaled to excess, as most people know nowadays, it can cause a range of serious and potentially fatal lung and circulatory problems.

Part Used: Leaves.

How Used: Amulets, sachets, and incense.

Magical Uses: Use tobacco to perform Earth magic in North America, as an offering or (in small quantities) as an incense. It also has strong Martial energies and may be used effectively to invoke the energies of the red planet. Good pipe tobacco or unprocessed leaves should be used wherever possible, as the tobacco used in many cigarettes has been adulterated with a range of chemicals, some of them toxic and few of them harmonious with the plant's magical energies.

Topaz

Description: An aluminum silicate, topaz ranges in color from pale yellow to brown and in transparency from nearly clear to opaque. The clear yellow variety is the most useful for magical workings.

Temperature: Fiery—warm and dry in the third degree.

Astrology: Sun in Gemini.

Lore: An important healing stone, topaz was used magically to dispel lust, greed, and anger, to treat insanity, and to banish insomnia. It was also held to protect the wearer from hostile magic and the envy of others, and to grant friendship and fidelity. In Christian magical lore, topaz is associated with the second order of angels, the Cherubim.

Safety Issues: None.

How Used: Amulets; water and oil infusions may be used in potions, baths, washes, oils, and scents.

Magical Uses: One of the most well-omened of magical stones, topaz brings happiness and should always be considered when depression or low spirits are an issue. Its protective powers are also worth using when this is a desired quality.

Turquoise

Description: The name of this stone, technically a copper aluminum phosphate, is a garbling of the old French word for "Turkish," because the deposits known to medieval Europe are found in parts of Asia once controlled by the Ottoman Empire. Most Americans, by contrast, think of it in the context of native jewelry from the Southwest, where it occurs in large amounts. The sky blue variety is the most magically potent.

Temperature: Watery—cold and moist in the second degree.

Astrology: Moon in Pisces.

Lore: Turquoise, in the old lore, has the very specific power of protecting the wearer from falls, especially falls from horseback. More generally, it was held to protect against hostile magic, to bring success, and to banish melancholy.

Safety Issues: None.

How Used: Amulets; water and oil infusions may be used in potions, baths, washes, oils, and scents.

Magical Uses: Use turquoise for protective magic, especially for those who run the risk of falling from heights.

Valerian (*Valeriana officinalis*)

Description: Valerian is a perennial native to Europe but found over much of the eastern half of North America, having escaped from cultivation. It grows two to four feet tall, with a ridged stem and leaves divided into narrow, saw-toothed leaflets. Its flowers, white or reddish, bloom in clusters at the top of the stem in early summer. An essential oil is extracted from the root.

Temperature: Leaves airy—warm in the first degree and moist in the second; root fiery—warm in the first degree and dry in the second.

Astrology: Mercury in Scorpio.

Lore: Valerian was mostly used in natural magic as a protective amulet, although its healing virtues have a long and honorable history in herbal medicine.

Safety Issues: Valerian is mildly toxic and should be taken internally only in small doses. The essential oil lacks the toxic components and is relatively safe.

Parts Used: Leaves, root.

How Used: Amulets, sachets, incense, potions, baths, washes, oils, and scents.

Magical Uses: A potent herb of purification and protection, valerian is particularly useful for cleansing a space prior to magical work, and a little valerian infusion or tincture can be added to consecrated water to enhance the power of blessings and purifications.

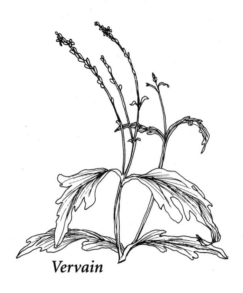

Vervain

Vervain (*Verbena officinalis*)

Description: Native to the Mediterranean countries, like so many of the important herbs in Western natural magic, vervain has escaped from cultivation and can be found in disturbed ground and on roadsides in much of North America. A stiff stem branching toward the top supports its paired, lobed leaves and its small white or purple flowers, which bloom all through summer and early autumn.

Temperature: Fiery—hot and dry in the second degree.

Astrology: Venus in Gemini.

Lore: Vervain was one of the two most sacred plants of the ancient Druids—the other being mistletoe—and also went by such telltale names as "Druid's weed," "enchanter's plant," and "holy herb." The traditions surrounding it point equally to its magical importance. It was grown in the garden to bring wealth, placed near infants to make them grow up to be quick learners, and hung in the house to keep evil spirits away. Blacksmiths quenched iron blades in an infusion of vervain leaves to give them magical sharpness. Vervain also had a reputation as an aphrodisiac, and was used in many traditional love charms.

For best results, it should be gathered with the left hand at midsummer, when the star Sirius is rising and neither the Sun nor the Moon is visible in the sky.

Safety Issues: None.

Part Used: Whole plant.

How Used: Living plants, amulets, sachets, incense, potions, baths, washes, and oils.

Magical Uses: Vervain is among the best herbs for magical work, as it can be put to use in nearly any kind of magic. It has particular power in visionary work and as a protective herb, and may be used by poets and musicians who seek a deeper contact with the sources of inspiration. It may also be added to any natural magic preparation for increased effect.

Vinegar

Description: Chemically, vinegar is a solution of acetic acid in water; less technically, it's what happens when a fermented liquid is allowed to sit too long. White vinegar, the kind most generally sold in grocery stores, is manufactured from various kinds of grain, but wine vinegar and apple cider vinegar are also readily available in many places and are more useful for most magical purposes.

Temperature: Fiery—warm in the second degree and dry in the first.

Astrology: The astrological correspondence depends on the source. See *Apple* and *Grape* for the correspondences of these two varieties of vinegar. Since ordinary white vinegar may be made from any number of different grains, which are rarely named on the label, its astrological correspondence is usually impossible to determine.

Lore: Various ways of using vinegar to banish spirits have been practiced in folk magic for centuries. Infusions of herbs in vinegar also have a significant role in folk magic, especially in North America.

Safety Issues: None.

How Used: Vinegar may be evaporated to banish spirits, or used in baths and washes.

Magical Uses: Vinegar may be used as a base for infusions, but its most important use in Western natural magic is as a means of banishing magical energies, particularly in the context of a magical attack or haunting. A dish of white vinegar left uncovered on the mantle will slowly evaporate, and the vapor keeps energy patterns from taking definite shape in the area. This will keep most kinds of hostile magic from functioning, and make it impossible for ghosts and spirits to take on any coherent form. (Any acid will do the same thing, but vinegar is much safer than most of the alternatives.) The same effect may be used to exorcise a haunted building or to cleanse a place where destructive magic has been worked.

Water

Description: Water is the most important substance on earth, at least from the perspective of living things. According to modern science as well as many more ancient myths, life began in the sea, and each of us carries around our own private "sea" of blood and other body fluids as one of the basic requirements of survival. Water is equally important in natural magic, with a dizzyingly wide range of uses.

Temperature: Watery—cold and moist in the second degree.

Astrology: Moon in Pisces.

Lore: Different kinds of water have different magical powers in traditional lore. Rain and dew water, especially at certain seasons of the year, are charged with the subtle life-energy of the world and are especially useful for magical and alchemical work; see *Dew* and *Rain*.

Running water is a magical eraser; any magically charged object immersed in running water will lose its powers, while crossing a stream is an old way to throw hostile spirits and spells off one's track. Baron Karl von Reichenbach, a nineteenth-century scientist (famous in his time as the discoverer of paraffin) who was not afraid to experiment with the magical side of existence, determined that this erasing effect becomes stronger with cold, reaching a maximum when the water is at a temperature of 39 degrees Fahrenheit.

The ocean and all connected with it have links to the otherworld, the Moon, and to faeries. It is a profound source of power for those that dare to call on it. In Western tradition, sea magic is generally considered the most unpredictable kind of magical work, with substantial dangers to the unprepared or the arrogant.

Safety Issues: None, barring the risk of drowning in any sufficiently large amount of it.

How Used: Water is used magically as a source or vehicle of energies, as a magical eraser, and as a base for potions, baths, and washes.

Magical Uses: The effects of water depend substantially on the water's source, temperature, and level of purity. If you have access to a pure spring or well, this is far and away the best source of water to use. If not, distilled or carbon-filtered water is useable, much more so than the chlorinated and (usually) contaminated product of most public water systems.

West Wind

Description: There are three west winds that blow everywhere on the Earth, according to the traditional lore of natural magic: Favonius blowing from due west, Zephyrus from the southwest, and Circius from the northwest.

Temperature: Watery—cold and moist.

Astrology: Favonius is Moon in Cancer, Zephyrus is Jupiter in Pisces, and Circius is Mars in Scorpio.

Lore: These moist winds were seen as the bringers of springtime and fertility. In the traditional imagery, accordingly, they were portrayed as young and laughing, with blue and white garments and wreaths of flowers about their heads.

Safety Issues: None.

How Used: Wind can be used as a source or carrier of magical energies. See *Wind*.

Magical Uses: See *Wind*.

Wind

Description: The ocean of air that surrounds our planet has its own waves and currents, the winds. See *East Wind*, *North Wind*, *South Wind*, and *West Wind* for details of the four major winds, each of which has its own special character. Different localities also have their own local winds, determined by details of the area's climate and topography. In earlier times, these had names and personalities assigned to them as well.

Temperature: The temperature of any given wind depends on direction, season of the year, and other factors.

Astrology: The planet and zodiacal sign of each wind depends on its direction. See specific winds for details.

Lore: Many old methods of divination rely on winds to predict the future.

Safety Issues: None.

How Used: Wind can serve as a source or a vehicle for magical energies. See below.

Magical Uses: The winds can be used magically in two ways: one based on where they are coming from, the other based on where they are going. First, a wind carrying the energies of a given element can be used to charge an object with the energies of that element simply by allowing the wind to blow onto or over the object during the ritual of consecration. (This, as already mentioned, is why it's traditional not to allow the wind to blow on an herb when you are harvesting it—the elemental balance of the plant will be changed by allowing the wind's energies to intrude during this critical time.) Second, a working meant to have its effect in a distant place, or over a wide area, can use the wind as a vehicle. This works particularly well if the working involves incense, smoke, or the evaporation of an essential oil or potion, and if the wind is blowing toward the place or places where the working is meant to have its effect.

Wormwood (*Artemisia absinthium*)

Description: Wormwood is native to northern Europe and was introduced early to North America, where it now grows wild through much of Canada and the northern U.S. Many stems grow two to four feet high from a single rootstock, bearing deeply lobed leaves and tiny greenish-yellow flowers that bloom in late summer and early fall.

Temperature: Fiery—warm in the first degree and dry in the second.

Astrology: Mars in Cancer.

Lore: A salve made of wormwood is said to drive away goblins.

Safety Issues: Wormwood is somewhat toxic and should be taken internally only in very small doses, if at all. Other plants of the same genus, such as southernwood and mugwort, can be substituted for it in internal uses. Avoid excessive or long-term use, and do not use during pregnancy.

Part Used: Whole plant.

How Used: Amulets, sachets, incense, baths, washes, oils, and scents.

Magical Uses: The energies of wormwood have purifying and protective effects, and are particularly useful when it is necessary to hinder hostile magic or to banish negative forces. Wormwood also has powers over visionary work, and it may be used by those seeking prophetic visions of the future.

Yarrow (*Achillea millefolium*)

Description: Another common weed with uncommon healing powers, yarrow can be found almost everywhere in the world in fields and pastures, along roads and pathways, and in disturbed ground. It has a stiff, round stem branched near the top, finely divided leaves that look a little like fern fronds, and clusters of small white or yellow flowers atop the stems that bloom all though summer and fall. An essential oil is extracted from the dried herb.

Yarrow

Temperature: Earthy—cold in the first degree and dry in the third.

Astrology: Venus in Leo.

Lore: In East Asia, yarrow stalks are put to use in divining with the Book of Changes. In the West, by contrast, yarrow is mostly a medicinal herb but has also been used as a charm to bless marriages.

Safety Issues: Yarrow is mildly poisonous in large doses, and should be avoided during pregnancy.

Parts Used: Flowers, essential oil.

How Used: Amulets, sachets, potions, baths, washes, oils, and scents.

Magical Uses: Yarrow may be included to good effect in love workings directed toward permanent relationships and marriages.

Yew (*Taxus spp.*)

Description: This sturdy evergreen tree, found over much of the northern hemisphere, grows up to sixty feet tall. Its bark is scaly and reddish, its needles short, and it tends toward a rounded, broad profile rather than

Yew

the conical shape of most evergreens. Instead of a cone, it produces a red, fleshy berry.

Temperature: Earthy—cold and dry in the third degree.

Astrology: Saturn in Capricorn.

Lore: The primary death-tree of European tradition, yew was commonly planted in and around cemeteries, partly so that its evergreen foliage would symbolize eternal life and partly so that its special powers would keep the dead safely in their graves.

Safety Issues: TOXIC. All parts of yew are poisonous, except the flesh of the ripe berry, and should not be taken internally in any form.

Parts Used: Whole tree, wood, boughs, and needles.

How Used: Live trees, amulets, sachets, incense, baths, washes, oils, scents, and working tools.

Magical Uses: Use yew for protection against spirits, especially spirits of the dead. It is particularly useful in exorcism and in laying a ghost to rest.

Tables of Correspondences and Uses

Type of Substance

Animal
Cattle, chicken, deer, fish, pig

Herb
Agrimony, angelica, anise, asphodel, barley, basil, bean, belladonna, betony, blessed thistle, borage, bracken fern, bryony, burdock, caraway, catnip, celandine, centaury, chamomile, chicory, cinquefoil, clary sage, coltsfoot, comfrey, coriander, cumin, daffodil, daisy, dandelion, dill, dittany of Crete, elecampane, eyebright, fennel, foxglove, fumitory, garlic, ginger, grape, hazel, hellebore, hemlock, hemp, henbane, High John the Conqueror, hops, horehound, horsetail, houndstongue, houseleek, hyssop, iris, ivy, jasmine, lady's mantle, lavender, leek, lemon balm, lettuce, lily, lovage, maidenhair fern, mandrake, marigold, marjoram, mistletoe, motherwort, mouse-ear, mugwort, mullein, nettle, nightshade, onion, oregano, parsley, patchouli, pennyroyal, plantain, rose, rosemary, rue, saffron, sage, St. John's Wort, savory, Solomon's seal, southernwood, strawberry, tansy, thyme, tobacco, valerian, vervain, wormwood, yarrow

Gum or Resin
Angelica, asafoetida, benzoin, camphor, frankincense, hemp, lettuce, myrrh, styrax

Metal
Copper, gold, iron, lead, silver, tin

Oil
Almond, angelica, anise, asafoetida, basil, bay laurel, benzoin, camphor, caraway, cedar, chamomile, cinnamon, clary sage, coriander, cumin, dill, elecampane, fennel, frankin-

cense, ginger, grape, hops, hyssop, iris, jasmine, juniper, lavender, lignum aloe, linden, lovage, marigold, marjoram, mugwort, myrrh, nutmeg, olive, orange, oregano, parsley, patchouli, pennyroyal, rose, rosemary, sage, sandalwood, savory, styrax, thyme, valerian, yarrow

Stone or Gem
Agate, amber, amethyst, beryl, bloodstone, carnelian, chalcedony, chrysolite, diamond, emerald, garnet, hyacinth, jade, jasper, jet, lapis lazuli, magnetite, malachite, moonstone, obsidian, onyx, quartz, ruby, sapphire, sardonyx, topaz, turquoise

Tree or Tree Product
Acorn, almond, apple, ash, bay laurel, birch, camphor, cedar, cinnamon, elder, elm, frankincense, hawthorn, holly, juniper, lignum aloe, linden, mace, myrrh, nutmeg, oak, olive, orange, rowan, sandalwood, styrax, yew

Other
Dew, east wind, Epsom salt, honey, moonlight, north wind, rain, salt, seashells, south wind, sunlight, vinegar, water, west wind, wind

Temperature

Fiery
Agrimony, almond, amber, amethyst, angelica, anise, asafoetida, ash, asphodel, bay laurel, betony, birch, blessed thistle, bloodstone, bryony, burdock, caraway, carnelian, catnip, cedar, celandine, centaury, chamomile, chicken, chrysolite, cinnamon, clary sage, coriander, cumin, daffodil, deer, dill, dittany of Crete, east wind, elder, elm, eyebright, fennel, fish (salted), foxglove, frankincense, fumitory, garlic, garnet, ginger, hellebore, hemp, High John the Conqueror, holly, honey, hops, horehound, hyssop, iris (root), ivy, jasper (red), juniper, lady's mantle, lavender, leek, lemon balm, lignum aloe, lily (bulb), linden, lovage, mace, magnetite, malachite, marjoram, mistletoe, motherwort, mouse-ear, mugwort, myrrh, nettle, nutmeg, onyx, oregano, pennyroyal, rosemary, rowan, ruby, rue, saffron, sage, St. John's Wort, savory, southernwood, sunlight, tansy, thyme, topaz, tobacco, valerian (root), vervain, vinegar, wormwood

Airy

Agate, apple (sweet), basil, bean, benzoin, borage, bracken fern, cattle, chalcedony, elecampane, grape, jasmine, lapis lazuli, marigold, olive (fruit and oil), onion, opal, parsley, pig, south wind (Affricus), sandalwood, styrax, valerian (leaf)

Watery

Beryl, camphor, daisy, dew, Epsom salt, fish, iris (flower), iron, jasper (green), lettuce, lily (flower), moonlight, moonstone, obsidian, orange, quartz, rain, sapphire, sardonyx, seashells, silver, strawberry (fruit), tin, turquoise, water, west wind (Zephyrus)

Earthy

Acorn, apple (sour), barley, belladonna, chicory, cinquefoil, coltsfoot, comfrey, copper, dandelion, diamond, emerald, hazel, hemlock, henbane, horsetail, houndstongue, houseleek, hyacinth, jade, jet, lead, maidenhair fern, mandrake, mullein, nightshade, north wind (Boreas), oak, olive (leaves, branches and bark), patchouli, plantain, rose, salt, Solomon's seal, strawberry (plant), yarrow, yew

Planetary Correspondences

Saturn

Asafoetida, asphodel, barley, belladonna, comfrey, elm, Epsom salt, fumitory, hellebore, hemlock, hemp, henbane, holly, horsetail, ivy, jet, lead, mandrake, mullein, myrrh, north wind (Boreas), obsidian, onyx, patchouli, pig, rue, salt, Solomon's seal, south wind (Affricus), tansy, yew

Jupiter

Acorn, agrimony, almond, amethyst, betony, borage, cedar, chicory, clary sage, dandelion, east wind (Caecias), houseleek, hyacinth, hyssop, jasper, lapis lazuli, leek, lemon balm, lignum aloe, mace, oak, olive, sage, sapphire, styrax, tin, west wind (Zephyrus)

Mars

Anise, basil, beryl, blessed thistle, bloodstone, bryony, coriander, cumin, diamond, east wind (Subsolanus), garlic, garnet, ginger, hawthorn, hops, iron, juniper, magnetite, nettle, onion, plantain, tobacco, west wind (Circius), wormwood

Sun

Amber, angelica, ash, bay laurel, benzoin, carnelian, celandine, centaury, chamomile, chicken, chrysolite, cinnamon, daffodil, daisy (English), deer, dittany of Crete, east wind (Eurus), eyebright, fish (red), frankincense, gold, grape, honey, High John the Conqueror, lovage, malachite, marigold, mistletoe, orange, rosemary, rowan, ruby, saffron, St. John's Wort, sunlight, topaz

Venus

Apple, bean, birch, burdock, catnip, copper, daisy (oxeye), emerald, foxglove, jade, lady's mantle, motherwort, mugwort, north wind (Aquilo), pennyroyal, rose, sandalwood, south wind (Auster), strawberry, thyme, vervain, yarrow

Mercury

Agate, bracken fern, caraway, chalcedony, cinquefoil, coltsfoot, dill, elder, elecampane, fennel, hazel, horehound, houndstongue, jasmine, lavender, linden, maidenhair fern, marjoram, nightshade, north wind (Corus), oregano, parsley, sardonyx, savory, southernwood, south wind (Notus), valerian

Moon

Camphor, cattle, dew, fish, iris, lettuce, lily, moonlight, moonstone, mouse-ear, nutmeg, opal, quartz, rain, seashells, silver, turquoise, water, west wind (Favonius)

Zodiacal Correspondences

Aries

Betony, blessed thistle, bloodstone, chicken, cinnamon, coriander, cumin, east wind (Subsolanus), garlic, ginger, hemp, hops, juniper, magnetite, marjoram, mouse-ear, myrrh, nettle, rosemary, thyme

Taurus

Bracken fern, cattle, cinquefoil, clary sage, coltsfoot, diamond, linden, lovage, mandrake, north wind (Aquilo), onion, sage

Gemini

Agate, asafoetida, bryony, leek, maidenhair fern, mullein, oregano, savory, southernwood, south wind (Notus), topaz, vervain

Cancer

Agrimony, camphor, caraway, chalcedony, daisy, dill, emerald, honey, hyssop, jasmine, lemon balm, moonstone, mugwort, olive, orange, quartz, seashells, west wind (Favonius), wormwood

Leo

Almond, amber, angelica, asphodel, bay laurel, borage, burdock, celandine, chamomile, chrysolite, daffodil, east wind (Eurus), eyebright, holly, High John the Conqueror, lavender, lettuce, marigold, mistletoe, motherwort, onyx, ruby, rue, saffron, St. John's Wort, yarrow

Virgo

Barley, bean, carnelian, catnip, chicory, elecampane, fennel, hazel, houndstongue, north wind (Corus), patchouli, sandalwood, sardonyx

Libra

Apple, belladonna, dandelion, foxglove, hellebore, jade, nightshade, opal, parsley, rose, south wind (Auster), strawberry, tansy, tobacco

Scorpio

Anise, basil, beryl, hemlock, horehound, ivy, jasper, lady's mantle, lily (white), pennyroyal, pig, valerian, west wind (Circius)

Sagittarius

Acorn, amethyst, ash, birch, cedar, centaury, deer, east wind (Caecias), elder, hawthorn, houseleek, hyacinth, lapis lazuli, lignum aloe, mace, malachite, nutmeg, oak, rowan, styrax

Capricorn

Benzoin, cassia (see *Cinnamon*), comfrey, dittany of Crete, elm, fumitory, north wind (Boreas), plantain, Solomon's seal, yew

Aquarius

Frankincense, garnet, henbane, iris, jet, obsidian, salt, south wind (Affricus)

Pisces

Epsom salt, fish, grape, horsetail, lily (yellow), rain, sapphire, turquoise, water, west wind (Zephyrus)

Methods of Use

Living Plants

Angelica, ash, asphodel, basil, bay laurel, betony, birch, bryony, caraway, chamomile, coriander, daisy, elder, elm, foxglove, hawthorn, hazel, holly, houseleek, lady's mantle, lavender, leek, mullein, oak, oregano, rosemary, rowan, sage, thyme, vervain, yew

Amulets

Acorn, agate, agrimony, almond, amber, amethyst, angelica, anise, apple, ash, asphodel, barley, basil, bay laurel, bean, belladonna, benzoin, beryl, betony, birch, blessed thistle, bloodstone, borage, bracken fern, bryony, burdock, camphor, caraway, carnelian, catnip, cedar, celandine, centaury, chalcedony, chamomile, chicken, chicory, chrysolite, cinnamon, cinquefoil, clary sage, coltsfoot, comfrey, copper, coriander, cumin, daffodil, daisy, dandelion, deer, diamond, dill, dittany of Crete, elder, elecampane, elm, emerald, eyebright, fennel, fish, frankincense, fumitory, garlic, garnet, ginger, gold, grape, hawthorn, hazel, hellebore, hemlock, hemp, henbane, High John the Conqueror, holly, honey, hops, horehound, horsetail, houndstongue, houseleek, hyacinth, hyssop, iris, iron, ivy, jade, jasmine, jasper, jet, juniper, lady's mantle, lapis lazuli, lavender, lead, lemon balm, lettuce, lily, linden, lovage, mace, magnetite, maidenhair fern, malachite, mandrake, marigold, marjoram, mistletoe, moonstone, motherwort, mouse-ear, mugwort, mullein, myrrh, nettle, nightshade, nutmeg, oak, obsidian, onion, onyx, opal, orange, oregano, parsley, patchouli, pennyroyal, plantain, quartz, rose, rosemary, rowan, ruby, rue, saffron, sage, St. John's Wort, salt, sandalwood, sapphire, sardonyx, savory, seashells, silver, Solomon's seal, southernwood, strawberry, styrax, tansy, thyme, tin, topaz, tobacco, turquoise, valerian, vervain, wormwood, yarrow, yew

Sachets

Agrimony, angelica, anise, basil, bay laurel, bean, benzoin, betony, camphor, caraway, catnip, cedar, celandine, chamomile, chicory, cinnamon, clary sage, coltsfoot, coriander, daffodil, daisy, dandelion, dill, dittany of Crete, elecampane, elm, fennel, frankincense, fumitory, ginger, grape, hawthorn, High John the Conqueror, hops, hyssop, iris, jasmine, juniper, lavender, lemon balm, lily, lignum aloe, linden, mace, marigold, marjoram, mistletoe, motherwort, mouse-ear, mugwort, mullein, myrrh, nutmeg, orange, oregano, patchouli, pennyroyal, rose, rosemary, sage, sandalwood, savory, southernwood, strawberry, styrax, tansy, thyme, tobacco, valerian, vervain, wormwood, yarrow, yew

Incense
Almond, angelica, asafoetida, basil, bay laurel, benzoin, birch, blessed thistle, borage, camphor, cedar, cinnamon, coltsfoot, dittany of Crete, elecampane, frankincense, fumitory, ginger, hazel, hemp, iris, jasmine, jet, juniper, lady's mantle, lavender, lettuce, lignum aloe, mace, marigold, marjoram, mugwort, mullein, myrrh, nutmeg, oregano, patchouli, rose, rosemary, rue, sage, St. John's Wort, sandalwood, Solomon's seal, southernwood, styrax, tansy, thyme, tobacco, valerian, vervain, wormwood, yew

Food (or seasoning for food)
Almond, angelica, anise, apple, barley, basil, bay laurel, bean, borage, burdock, caraway, cattle, chicken, cinnamon, coriander, cumin, dandelion, deer, dill, elder, elecampane, fennel, fish, garlic, ginger, grape, hemp, honey, leek, lettuce, lovage, mace, marjoram, nutmeg, olive, onion, orange, oregano, parsley, pig, rose, rosemary, saffron, sage, salt, savory, strawberry, thyme

Potions
Agate, agrimony, amber, amethyst, angelica, anise, apple, barley, basil, beryl, betony, blessed thistle, bloodstone, borage, burdock, carnelian, catnip, celandine, chalcedony, chamomile, chicory, chrysolite, clary sage, coltsfoot, comfrey, dandelion, dew, diamond, dittany of Crete, elecampane, emerald, eyebright, fennel, garnet, ginger, gold, grape, hawthorn, hemp, honey, hops, horehound, horsetail, hyacinth, hyssop, jade, jasper, jet, lady's mantle, lapis lazuli, lavender, lemon balm, lettuce, linden, lovage, magnetite, malachite, marigold, marjoram, moonlight, moonstone, mugwort, mullein, nettle, obsidian, onyx, opal, orange, oregano, parsley, plantain, quartz, rain, rose, ruby, sage, St. John's Wort, sapphire, sardonyx, seashells, silver, southernwood, strawberry, sunlight, thyme, topaz, turquoise, valerian, vervain, yarrow

Baths and Washes

Agate, agrimony, almond, amber, amethyst, angelica, anise, asphodel, basil, bay laurel, beryl, betony, birch, blessed thistle, bloodstone, borage, burdock, camphor, caraway, carnelian, catnip, cedar, celandine, centaury, chalcedony, chamomile, chicory, chrysolite, cinnamon, cinquefoil, clary sage, coltsfoot, comfrey, coriander, cumin, daffodil, daisy, dandelion, dew, diamond, dill, dittany of Crete, elecampane, elm, emerald, eyebright, fennel, frankincense, fumitory, garnet, ginger, gold, grape, hawthorn, hazel, High John the Conqueror, holly, hops, horehound, horsetail, houndstongue, hyacinth, hyssop, iris, jade, jasmine, jasper, jet, juniper, lady's mantle, lapis lazuli, lavender, lemon balm, lettuce, lignum aloe, lily, linden, lovage, mace, magnetite, malachite, marigold, marjoram, mistletoe, moonlight, moonstone, motherwort, mouse-ear, mugwort, mullein, myrrh, nettle, nutmeg, obsidian, onyx, opal, orange, oregano, parsley, patchouli, pennyroyal, plantain, quartz, rain, rose, rosemary, rowan, ruby, rue, saffron, sage, St. John's Wort, salt, sandalwood, sapphire, sardonyx, savory, seashells, silver, Solomon's seal, southernwood, strawberry, styrax, sunlight, tansy, thyme, topaz, turquoise, valerian, vervain, vinegar, wormwood, yarrow, yew

Oils

Agate, agrimony, almond, amber, amethyst, angelica, anise, asafoetida, asphodel, basil, bay laurel, benzoin, beryl, betony, birch, bloodstone, camphor, caraway, carnelian, cedar, chalcedony, chamomile, chicory, chrysolite, cinnamon, clary sage, coltsfoot, coriander, cumin, daffodil, diamond, dill, elecampane, emerald, fennel, frankincense, garnet, ginger, gold, grape, hazel, hemlock, hemp, holly, hops, horehound, houndstongue, hyacinth, hyssop, iris, jade, jasmine, jasper, jet, juniper, High John the Conqueror, lady's mantle, lapis lazuli, lavender, lemon balm, lettuce, lignum aloe, lily, linden, lovage, mace, magnetite, malachite, marigold, marjoram, mistletoe, moonlight, moonstone, motherwort, mouse-ear, mugwort, mullein, myrrh, nutmeg, obsidian, olive, onyx, opal, orange, oregano, parsley, patchouli, pennyroyal, quartz, rose, rosemary, ruby, sage, St. John's Wort, sandalwood, sapphire, sardonyx, savory, Solomon's seal, southernwood, styrax, sunlight, tansy, thyme, topaz, turquoise, valerian, vervain, wormwood, yarrow, yew

Scents

Agate, agrimony, almond, amber, amethyst, angelica, anise, basil, bay laurel, benzoin, beryl, birch, bloodstone, camphor, caraway, carnelian, cedar, chalcedony, chamomile, chrysolite, cinnamon, clary sage, coltsfoot, coriander, cumin, daffodil, diamond, dill, elecampane, emerald, fennel, frankincense, garnet, ginger, gold, hemp, honey, hops, hyacinth, hyssop, iris, jade, jasmine, jasper, jet, juniper, lady's mantle, lapis lazuli, lavender, lemon balm, lignum aloe, linden, lovage, mace, magnetite, malachite, marigold, marjoram, moonlight, moonstone, mugwort, myrrh, nutmeg, obsidian, onyx, opal, orange, oregano, parsley, patchouli, pennyroyal, quartz, rose, rosemary, ruby, sage, sandalwood, sapphire, sardonyx, savory, styrax, sunlight, tansy, thyme, topaz, turquoise, valerian, wormwood, yarrow, yew

Working Tools

Agate, almond, amber, amethyst, ash, beryl, birch, bloodstone, carnelian, cattle, chalcedony, chicken, chrysolite, copper, deer, diamond, emerald, garnet, gold, hawthorn, hazel, hemlock (for consecration), holly, hyacinth, iron, jade, jasper, jet, lapis lazuli, lead, magnetite, malachite, moonstone, mouse-ear (for tempering), oak, obsidian, onyx, pig, quartz, rowan, ruby, sapphire, sardonyx, seashells, silver, Solomon's seal (for consecration), tin, topaz, turquoise, yew

Magical Uses

Amplifies Other Workings

Amber, bryony, centaury, cinquefoil, dew, dittany of Crete, frankincense, gold, grape, hazel, High John the Conqueror, lady's mantle, magnetite, mandrake, mistletoe, moonlight, quartz, rain, Solomon's seal, sunlight, vervain

Anaphrodisiac

Camphor, lavender, lettuce, lily, onyx, rue

Aphrodisiac

Garlic, ginger, grape, hemp, jasmine, lettuce, patchouli, rose, saffron, savory, southernwood, strawberry

Banishing

Angelica, anise, asafoetida, asphodel, basil, bay laurel, bean, benzoin, betony, cedar, centaury, chalcedony, daffodil, diamond, dill, emerald, fumitory, garlic, hawthorn, High John the Conqueror, holly, hyssop, iron, jasper, jet, mistletoe, mouse-ear, mugwort, myrrh, plantain, rosemary, rowan, rue, St. John's Wort, salt, sunlight, vinegar, wormwood, yew

Blessing

Angelica, blessed thistle, chamomile, coriander, cumin, daffodil, dandelion, dill, fennel, frankincense, gold, hellebore, lignum aloe, mugwort, myrrh, St. John's Wort, salt, silver, sunlight, valerian, vervain

Consecration

Gold, hemlock, lignum aloe, marigold, mouse-ear, myrrh, quartz, sage, silver, Solomon's seal, sunlight, vervain

Divination

Almond, bay laurel, clary sage, dandelion, emerald, hemp, lavender, opal, sandalwood

Earth Magic

Fumitory, henbane, ivy, lead, oak, patchouli, pig, Solomon's seal, tobacco, vervain

Faery/Nature Spirit Work

Ash, barley, beryl, birch, daisy, elecampane, elm, foxglove, hawthorn, honey, rowan, silver, thyme, tobacco, vervain

Fertility

Acorn, agate (green), barley, catnip, fennel, horsetail, jade, High John the Conqueror, lovage, mistletoe, moonstone, rain, rue, strawberry

Fluid Condensers

Chamomile, dew, eyebright, gold, quartz, salt, silver

Funerals, Ghosts, and Underworld Workings

Asphodel, betony, cedar, elder, marjoram, oregano, parsley, pennyroyal, pig, tansy, vinegar, yew

Garden Magic
Agate (moss), comfrey, jade, lovage, moonstone

Healing
Amber, angelica, ash, chalcedony, fennel, ginger, gold, jasmine, lavender, mistletoe, motherwort, quartz, ruby, rue, saffron, sapphire, vervain

Hunting Magic
Rue

Invisibility
Bracken fern, chicory, hellebore, houndstongue, maidenhair fern, sardonyx

Love
Amethyst, apple, belladonna, daisy, emerald, hemp, iris, jasmine, High John the Conqueror, lemon balm, lovage, marjoram, moonstone, oregano, rose, strawberry, yarrow

Luck
Angelica, cumin, garlic, High John the Conqueror, moonstone, mugwort, opal (black only), ruby, topaz, vervain

Personal Transformation

Charisma
Chrysolite, cinquefoil, High John the Conqueror

Courage
Agate (tawny), basil, beryl, bloodstone, borage, carnelian, diamond, garlic, garnet, nettle, pennyroyal

Emotional Balance
Anise, benzoin, carnelian, emerald, eyebright, jasmine, lemon balm, magnetite, motherwort, mouse-ear, ruby, sage, sapphire, sardonyx, savory, topaz, turquoise

Energy
Diamond, lemon balm, nettle, ruby

Happiness
Savory, topaz

Insight
Agate (green), clary sage, eyebright, obsidian, sapphire, sardonyx

Intuition
Bloodstone, dandelion, horehound, silver, vervain

Magical States of Consciousness
Centaury, dandelion, frankincense, lignum aloe, vervain

Memory
Magnetite, rosemary, vervain

Mental Clarity
Amber, amethyst, beryl, chalcedony, dill, eyebright, horehound, lily, moonstone, obsidian, ruby, sardonyx

Prudence
Agate (tawny), comfrey

Relaxation
Chamomile, coltsfoot, hemp, hops, lavender, lettuce, linden, sage, valerian

Stability
Dittany of Crete, fumitory, garnet, Solomon's seal

Strength of Will
Garnet, nettle, ruby

Wisdom
Hazel, sage, sapphire

Prosperity and Success
Ash, frankincense, garlic, jade, High John the Conqueror, mistletoe, ruby, turquoise, vervain

Protection

Agate, agrimony, angelica, anise, basil, bay laurel, benzoin, beryl, betony, birch, blessed thistle, bryony, caraway, carnelian, catnip, cedar, centaury, chalcedony, chamomile, cinnamon, cinquefoil, coriander, cumin, daffodil, daisy, dandelion, dill, elder, emerald, fennel, frankincense, garlic, garnet, ginger, hawthorn, hellebore, High John the Conqueror, holly, hyacinth, hyssop, iris, iron, jade, jasmine, jasper, jet, lapis lazuli, magnetite, malachite, mandrake, marigold, mistletoe, motherwort, mugwort, mullein, myrrh, nightshade, onion, orange, plantain, rosemary, rowan, rue, saffron, sage, St. John's Wort, salt, sandalwood, silver, styrax, sunlight, thyme, topaz, turquoise, valerian, vervain, vinegar, wormwood, yew

Purification

Angelica, asafoetida, basil, bay laurel, benzoin, frankincense, fumitory, lily, myrrh, onyx, rosemary, rowan, rue, sage, salt, sandalwood, styrax, sunlight, thyme, valerian, vervain, vinegar, wormwood

Sea Magic

Fish, moonlight, nutmeg, rosemary, sapphire, seashells, silver

Sleep and Dreams

Agrimony, amethyst, anise, elm, hyacinth, lavender, linden, moonlight, opal, plantain, silver

Spiritual Development

Frankincense, gold, lignum aloe, myrrh, rue, sage

Visionary Work

Agate (green), almond, bean, bloodstone, catnip, celandine, chamomile, clary sage, coltsfoot, dandelion, elm, eyebright, hemp, hops, hyacinth, lavender, linden, moonlight, mugwort, nutmeg, quartz, sandalwood, silver, valerian, vervain, wormwood

Weather Magic

Beryl, bloodstone, bryony, houseleek, hyacinth, jade, jasper (green), leek, oak, quartz, tin

Weddings and Handfastings

Anise, caraway, marjoram, oregano, rose, sardonyx, strawberry, yarrow

PART 3

THE
NATURAL
MAGIC
WORKBOOK

Using the Natural Magic Workbook

The first two parts of this book have explored the basic concepts, philosophical and practical, of natural magic, and provided a collection of traditional lore about the magical properties of herbs, stones, oils, and other substances. The rest of the book covers the practical applications of all this information. Here our focus shifts to the ways in which it's possible to work with the magical powers hidden within material things.

It needs to be stressed, though, that what follows is meant primarily as a source of ideas to set you on the road to your own personal style of natural magic. Granted, it's entirely possible to take the information in this book as given, as though using recipes from a cookbook, and turn out effective amulets, potions, oils, and other natural magic preparations. Still, this is a limited approach at best. Once you've grasped the principles behind natural magic and gained some experience with the practice, you'll find it much more rewarding to begin developing new formulations and new approaches on your own.

For this reason, among others, the information that follows is much less comprehensive than it might have been. I haven't included, for example, every possible way to make an amulet, to brew a floor wash, or to compound a scent, nor have I provided pages of recipes for every conceivable magical purpose. Instead, I've covered practical methods that work well and can be used easily and safely by beginners, and provided examples of how these various methods can be adapted to accomplish a wide range of different magical purposes. For reasons covered in the chapter on magical ethics, too, I've left out techniques and information that can readily be used to hurt other people; there's no valid reason to make such information any more widely available than it has to be.

The following pages, then, are by way of an introduction to the practice of natural magic. My hope is that your own explorations in the art will take you far beyond what is covered here.

A Note on Measurements

In some of the following recipes, amounts of herbs and other substances are given in parts—e.g., "use equal parts rosemary leaves and lavender flowers," "take three parts angelica root and one part chamomile flower," and so on. Unless otherwise stated, parts are determined by weight, not by volume. (A good kitchen scale is thus a useful piece of equipment for the natural magician.) In other recipes, I've given measurements in standard American units (cups, teaspoons, and the like). In all cases, feel free to experiment—although it's wise to pay attention to the safety issues covered in the Encyclopedia and elsewhere in this book.

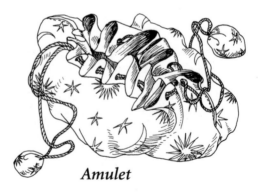

Amulet

Amulets

Of the many different ways to put natural magic to work, amulets are at once the simplest and one of the most useful. An amulet is simply a small amount of some substance with magical powers, put someplace where its energies will have a desired effect. The most common and most useful way to make an amulet, one used all over the world, is to make a little bag of cloth or leather, fill it with the appropriate materials, and put it to use. In North American folk magic, amulets of this sort are often called "hands," "tobies," or "mojo bags;" their names in other traditions are beyond count.

It's common to bless or consecrate an amulet of this kind with a ceremony of some kind, simple or complex, and in this way combine the powers of ritual and natural magic; still, this isn't required. As explained in the first chapter of this book, an amulet made from magically potent substances will have an effect even if it's not consecrated by ritual means. (That is, after all, the whole point of natural magic.)

What You'll Need

To make a bag amulet of the sort just described, you'll need a circular piece of flannel between two and four inches across, a sewing needle, heavy thread or embroidery cotton of the same color as the flannel, and the substances you intend to put into the amulet. The bag can be of any color you prefer, but it's very common (and effective) to put amulets for protection or healing in red bags, and those for blessing and other positive purposes in white ones. The entry on Colors in Part Two of this book can be used as a resource if you decide to work with a more complex scheme; alternatively, any of the standard systems of magical color correspondences can be used to good effect for bag amulets.

How It's Done

Thread the needle with a length of thread or embroidery floss at least four times as long as the flannel circle is wide. With the flannel laid out flat, sew a circle of plain running stitches about half an inch in from the edge all the way around, as shown in Diagram 4. When you have finished the circle, pull the thread through until the two ends

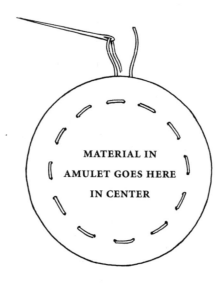

Diagram 4

are roughly the same length. Put the herbs, stones, or other magical substances into the center, and then pull on both ends of the thread to draw the bag closed. Knot the thread, wrap the thread all the way around the bag to help hold it shut, and tie another knot. If the amulet is meant to be worn around the neck, the two ends can then be tied to a longer cord, or alternatively the original length of cord can be cut long enough to reach around the neck and tie in back. If the amulet will be used in some other way, trim the ends of the thread to a convenient length.

Classic Amulet of Protection

There are many different ways to make an amulet of protection, drawing on the lore of different traditions and the different hostile forces against which one might need protection. For defense against hostile magic, though, one of the best amulets is also one of the simplest.

To make this, you'll need the materials for a standard bag amulet, as given above. You'll also need a tablespoon or so of salt—kosher salt or natural sea salt are the best kinds for this and all other forms of natural magic—and a single small nail, which should be of bright metal (not painted) and sharp. Prepare the bag as above, using red cloth. Using two pairs of pliers, or one pair and a bench vise, bend the nail; put half the salt onto the cloth, add the nail, and then add the rest of the salt. Pull the bag closed and tie it. This amulet is most effective when worn around the neck of the person who needs to be protected, with the cord measured to let the bag hang at the level of his or her heart.

Amulets for a Handfasting

An amulet is an effective way for a natural magician to pass on blessings to other people, and occasions such as weddings or handfastings are a traditional time for such magical gifts to be given. The following amulets of Venus are meant to bring the gift of lasting love to a couple.

You'll need the materials for two bag amulets, as described above, and a mix of equal parts of rose petals, strawberry leaves, and yarrow flowers, enough to fill both. Both amulets should be made precisely the same. The two people being married or handfasted should each be given one of the amulets, and should put it in a private place in the home.

Sea Magic Amulet

Another worthwhile use for natural magic is to help attune the wearer's energies and awareness to some aspect of the magical cosmos. A magician who wishes to make contact with a particular realm of energies—whether in ritual, meditation, or visionary work—can draw on the powers of natural magic to help make the link strong and form an anchor for the energies to be contacted. For those realms farther from the human, in particular, this can be a significant source of help. An amulet of this sort, for example, could be made to assist with sea magic.

For this purpose, a bag amulet is made from blue or sea-green cloth. Into it should be put equal parts of lady's mantle and rosemary, a pinch of ground nutmeg, and a piece of a seashell. Finally, before closing the bag, a single drop of seawater should be added to the mix. The amulet can then be worn during any operation of sea magic.

Sachets and Potpourris

Many of the substances used in natural magic have scents, pleasant or otherwise, and the magical energies in the substances are present in the scents as well. For thousands of years, at least, magicians have made use of this secret in a variety of ways. Most people with any background in magic at all are familiar with the use of incense, but there are other approaches to the use of scent in magic that are worth learning.

The simplest of these involves nothing more than mixing together fragrant herbs, barks, and other substances, and allowing them to release their scents of their own accord. Sachets, which are bags of sweet-smelling substances, and potpourris, which are open containers, are two of the most common ways of using such mixtures. Up until the first few decades of the twentieth century, the art of making such mixtures was common in most households, and even today many people have grandmothers and older relatives who know how to mix their own sachets and potpourris. The magical dimensions of the art, though, are less well known, although some of the old texts of natural magic provide recipes of various kinds.

All work with scent reaches deep into the personal dimension and touches on aspects of consciousness that cannot be communicated in words. The messages of scent touch the deepest and most primal levels of awareness, levels we share with other animals and—on a broader scale—with all forms of life. In a culture that has long had a great deal of trouble dealing with nature in any form, these are levels of consciousness most of us have never learned to contact directly, but they still have potent effects on every aspect of the self.

The potential uses of scented substances in natural magic, then, are limited only by the imagination of the magician who uses them. The following are only a few of the possibilities.

Sachets

A sachet is a cloth bag filled with something fragrant, and typically used to scent clothing or other objects in storage. It can be made in the same way as a bag amulet, although a thinner fabric—for example, muslin—and a larger bag normally make for a more effective sachet. Other shapes can be made by those with basic sewing skills.

Anything with a scent and a magical effect can be used in a sachet. As with any other use of scent in magic, blends of different fragrances in sachets are very much a personal matter, and you'll want to experiment with different blends to develop your own personal style.

What You'll Need

A muslin bag that will hold at least several tablespoons of herbs, and the scented substances you wish to use, are the basic requirements. Alternatively, you'll need enough cloth to make a bag to suit your purposes.

How It's Done

To make a bag, use the description above, under Amulets, or make a flat bag by taking a piece of cloth of any convenient size, folding it in half, and stitching up the three sides, as shown in Diagram 5. Make sure to fill up the bag *before* you stitch it shut!

If you already have the bag, simply fill it with the substances you've chosen and put it in the place you wish to scent.

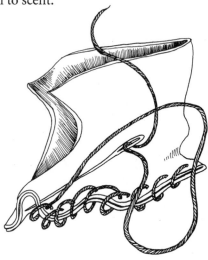

Diagram 5

Consecrating Sachet for Magical Tools

Magical working tools are typically consecrated by way of ritual magic, but natural magic can also be used to strengthen the energies placed in a tool and to keep them at high intensity. One way to do this is to use a sachet in the container where you store your working tools. If you have separate, airtight containers for different tools, you can make different sachets to harmonize with the specific energies that have been invoked into each tool; if not, a single sachet filled with herbs of consecration and magical amplification will do the trick.

For the latter, take equal parts of vervain leaf and Solomon's seal root, and fill a muslin bag loosely until it is half full. Drop in a small quartz crystal, and fill the bag the rest of the way with the herbs, making sure not to pack them (this would interfere with the diffusion of the scent). Tie or sew up the bag, place it next to your magical tools, and leave it there. Once every year or so, replace with a new sachet; the herbs will have lost their virtue and should be composted or thrown out, but the quartz crystal can be rinsed in cold water, left in direct sunlight for several hours, and then used again.

Potpourris

The only difference between a potpourri and a sachet is that a potpourri goes into an open container, and is used to scent the air in a room. Small pottery bowls are often used for potpourris, and it's not hard to find bowls with pierced lids that have been specially made for this purpose. Magically, potpourris can be put to use any time an indoor space needs to be charged with some particular magical energy.

What You'll Need

The scented materials you intend to use and a ceramic container that will allow the scent to diffuse are all that's required.

How It's Done

Put the scented material in the container and set it in the space you intend to scent. That's all there is to it.

Bedroom Potpourri

The following potpourri will help add spice to your love life. It works best if you have a steady partner or spouse, as the effects will tend to build over time.

Take equal parts of patchouli leaves and jasmine blossoms, and twice the same amount of rose petals. Mix thoroughly, put in a potpourri bowl or some other open container, and place in your bedroom close to the bed.

Herbal Pillows

Another way of using fragrant herbs and other substances is more specialized. A flat sachet can be inserted into a pillow and used to affect anyone who sleeps with his or her head resting on it. This is especially useful when learning or performing magical dreamwork.

What You'll Need

A flat bag, made as described above under Sachets, and the scented materials you wish to use.

How It's Done

Put the sachet into your pillowcase several hours before you intend to go to sleep, to allow the scents to diffuse throughout the pillow. If you're comfortable having the sachet right beneath the place where your head will rest, this is most effective.

Magical Dream Pillow

Make a flat sachet of muslin, or some other soft and relatively thin fabric, and fill loosely with equal parts of lavender, hops, and mugwort. If you can find a small and relatively flat quartz crystal, add this to the mix. Put this into your pillow when you intend to do magical dreamwork. Make sure that you have your dream journal by your bedside, and breathe in deeply, smelling the herbs, as you begin whatever method of dreamwork induction you prefer to use. On nights when you simply want a good night's sleep—something that it's wise to do regularly—take the dream pillow out and put it into a tightly sealed container, such as a resealable plastic bag.

Food

All food is magical, at least potentially. That extraordinary man of the Renaissance, the alchemist and doctor Paracelsus—Philippus Aureolus Theophrastus Bombastus Paracelsus von Hohenheim, to allow him the full glory of his improbable name—taught that digestion was pure alchemy, with the subtle energies of the stomach playing the alchemist's part and the body serving as furnace and alchemical glassware alike. The everyday miracle that turns corn flakes, hamburgers, bean burritos, and tempura shrimp into living energy and human flesh is as magical as anything that takes place in a ritually cast circle or the temple room of a magical lodge.

This everyday alchemy is only one side of the magic of food, for food can also be used as a way of working magic on the self. To eat something is to take it into your body, to make it part of yourself. This represents a source of power, but also a potential danger, since the effects of eating magical food are likely to be lasting ones. It's for this reason, for example, that consecrated food is an important part of the rituals of many religions; the cakes and wine of many Wiccan sabbat rituals and the bread, salt, and wine of the Golden Dawn elemental communion are only two of many examples.

In working natural magic with food, the seasonings are generally the easiest factor to shape according to your magical purpose. It's difficult to vary the main ingredients of many foods beyond a certain point; a cake needs to contain flour, milk, eggs, baking powder, and so on, for example, or it's probably going to turn into an inedible mess when it's baked. These basic ingredients, though, can be used as a foundation on which you can build the structure of your magical purpose using herbs, spices, and other optional ingredients. Since most herbs and spices used in cooking also have magical uses, this isn't difficult to manage.

What You'll Need

The requirements here are simply your favorite recipes, the ingredients they require, and the magical additions you'll be using.

How It's Done

Every recipe has its own tricks and requirements and, for the most part, the only way to learn these is by actually trying it out and tasting the results. If you're planning on preparing something magical for a group ritual, or for some important personal ritual, make it a few times first to be sure the result will be what you want!

Solar Broiled Chicken

Despite the title, this dish isn't necessarily made in a solar oven—although this might be worth trying if you live in a sunny climate. The Sun's more important role here is symbolic and magical; this dish may be used as the center of a magical feast for a solar ceremony—a summer solstice ritual, for example—or for any other magical working involving the subtle energies of the Sun.

Take a cut-up fryer chicken, thawed, and rub each piece all over with oil (sunflower oil is best, but olive oil will do). Rub each piece of oiled chicken heavily with a mix of salt, rosemary, and just a little saffron. Line a broiler pan with foil to simplify the cleanup, put the chicken in, and broil 10–12 minutes on each side. There you have it.

Universal Magical Bread

The following bread recipe deserves wider circulation in the magical community, as it a) is the simplest and easiest one I've ever encountered, b) produces the best home-made French bread you're ever likely to find, c) can have almost any imaginable combination of extra ingredients and seasonings added to it, and d) has provided tasty loaves of bread for more communion rituals, after-the-ceremony feasts, and magical lodge potlucks than I can count without referring to my magical journals. (It also makes good dinner rolls and pizza dough, in case you're curious.)

To make a loaf of Universal Magical Bread, you'll need two-and-a-half cups of unbleached white flour, one cup of water, a teaspoon of salt, a tablespoon of yeast, and three hours of time, of which perhaps twenty minutes will actually be taken up in preparing and baking the bread.

Start by warming the water until a finger dipped into it feels neither hot nor cold. Take the water off the heat and stir the yeast into the water, adding a little at a time so that it doesn't clump. Let it sit for five to ten minutes, or until it starts to foam. In the meantime, stir the salt into the flour.

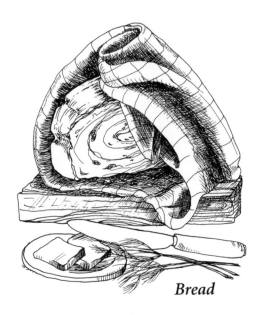

Bread

When the yeast is ready, mix yeast and water into the flour and salt. Work all the flour into the fluid, trying to get an even consistency. Sooner or later, you'll have to start using your hands, which you should flour lightly first. Once you have a dough of more or less even consistency, turn it out of the bowl onto a lightly floured board and knead the dough gently for 5 minutes or so—just enough to get some spring into the dough.

Return the dough to the bowl, cover it with a cotton cloth, and leave it in a warm place to rise. When it has doubled in size (which will take around 30–45 minutes, depending on the temperature), punch it down gently and let it rise a second time. When it doubles again, turn it out onto the board and shape it into a French loaf; put it on a greased baking sheet, cover it, and let it rise a third time while the oven heats up. Before putting the loaf into the oven, cut three or four shallow diagonal cuts in the top to allow for expansion.

Handling the oven requires a little subtlety. The oven should be preheated to 450 degrees, but once it reaches this temperature and the bread goes in, the temperature should be turned down to 375 degrees. This "falling oven," as it's called, is crucial to getting the right texture. Baking time will vary slightly depending on a dizzying array of factors; 25 minutes is around average, but it's best to watch the color—the crust should be golden brown—and to apply the traditional baker's test: if you turn the loaf over and tap the bottom with a finger when it first comes out, you should hear a good hollow "thump" rather than a muffled, doughy sound.

Variations on this basic recipe can be made by adding magically appropriate herbs, spices, dried fruit, nuts, or seeds to the dry ingredients, replacing up to a half cup of the flour with some other grain or flour, or replacing some of the water with honey. One variation that works especially well is called Druid Bread.

Druid Bread

Celtic Traditionalists should take note that there is no evidence whatsoever that ancient Druids made or ate this bread. On the other hand, I know for a fact that at least one modern Druid has made many loaves of it, and half a dozen others have eaten it with gusto; as with so many Druidical matters, this is as close to authenticity as anyone is ever likely to get. (For the record, it's called "Druid Bread" because I came up with the recipe for the summer solstice ritual of a Druid grove, and the other Druids present liked it.)

To make Druid Bread, follow the recipe for Universal Magical Bread, replacing half a cup of the flour with Scottish style (steel cut) dry oatmeal, and a quarter of a cup of the water with a third of a cup of honey—thistle honey is symbolically best if you can find it. The honey will make the bread brown faster, and you'll want to take this into account when timing the baking.

As a final note to the subject of magical food, Solar Broiled Chicken and a loaf of Universal Magical Bread make a great dinner with fresh seasonal vegetables and your choice of white wine.

Potions, Baths, and Washes

Legends from nearly every human culture tell of the hidden powers of magical wells, springs, lakes, and rivers, and coastal peoples around the world have their tales of the magic of the sea. In most of the ancient legends, particular magical powers dwell in particular sources or bodies of water, and water from elsewhere has different powers or none at all. This is still an important feature of some traditions of folk magic, but it has its limitations—if the nearest magical spring that has the power you need is a hundred miles away, after all, your ability to use that power in a hurry will be rather limited!

No doubt it was thousands of years ago that some clever mage or wise woman first realized how to get around this problem by soaking herbs, stones, or other magical substances in a container of ordinary water and producing magically charged water as needed without the hundred-mile hike. The result was an approach to natural magic that still has many uses today.

According to the traditional philosophy of magic, water has certain properties that make it a superb magical tool. The most important of these properties is that water

Infusion

picks up and holds onto etheric charges with great effectiveness. This can be used in either of two ways—to take energies away or to put them in place. Something that has an unwanted etheric charge, on the one hand, can be cleansed by using water to pick the charge up and carry it away. On the other, something that needs to be charged in a particular way, if it's exposed to highly charged water, can be made to pick up the charge itself.

Another important magical property of water is that, when it's relatively pure, it has no particular magical influence of its own. Magically passive, it will accept nearly any force that might be needed for a working, no matter what planet, sign or element is involved. Strange as it may sound, water can even be charged with the energies of elemental Fire. (The elements aren't identical with the physical substances of the same names, remember.) This makes water a superbly flexible tool for natural magic.

Finally, water has one other property that makes it valuable in natural magic: it's used everywhere, all the time, in a nearly infinite number of ways in everyday life. We drink water, cook with water, bathe with water, scrub floors with water, wash cars with water, and on and on—and anything that can be done with ordinary water can also be done with magically charged water and directed toward magical effects.

Potions

A potion is a magically charged drink. Potions in earlier times were routinely made from a range of bizarre and noxious ingredients—powdered mummy, mashed centipedes, dried viper meat, and so on. Fortunately, the potions used in modern natural magic are more along the lines of herbal teas; this may be less exotic, but it's just as effective, and the results are generally much better tasting.

Since potions, like food, enter your body and become part of it, they offer an effective way of working magic on yourself—of focusing your awareness in particular ways, for example, or of helping you to acquire useful personal qualities and get rid of unproductive ones. Equally, though, since they become part of your body, they require more care than other preparations. Aside from the risk of poisoning if you choose the wrong ingredients, they can lead to imbalance if the same sort of potion is overused.

There are two standard ways of making a potion for magical work: infusion and maceration. Both these processes also have a role in every other kind of water magic, and so they are well worth learning early on in your training.

Infusion

If you've ever made a cup of tea, you know all you need to know about making an infusion, because that's exactly what tea is—an infusion of leaves in hot water. Any herb that's safe to take internally can be used for an infusion.

What You'll Need

The one special tool you'll need to prepare herbal infusions is a tea ball or strainer of the sort used for loose tea. You'll also need a kettle for boiling water, and a heatproof container—a ceramic coffee cup or mug is as good as anything—for the infusion to steep in.

How It's Done

Again, it's just like making tea. Bring water to a full boil on the stove. Put the herb or herbs into the strainer or tea ball, filling it no more than half full, and put it in your coffee cup or other steeping container. When the water boils, fill the cup with water and leave the herbs to steep for at least five minutes. Take the strainer or tea ball out of the water, and let the infusion cool as much as needed before use.

Infused Potion for Magical Dreamwork

Take equal parts of lavender flowers, chamomile flowers, and clary sage leaves, and make an infusion as above. Drink one cup half an hour before going to bed. As you go to sleep, hold in your mind the intention of dreaming about a particular subject, or use any other method of dreamwork induction you prefer; keep paper and a pen, or a tape recorder, by your bedside to record your dreams when you first wake from them.

Maceration

Macerations are used for the most delicate herbs and flowers, which lose much of their effect if exposed to boiling water, and for stones, which can be damaged by being heated. It's also useful when you are using water that has already been charged—for example, when you have collected dew water in the spring and want to make an herbal potion with it. Heating the water will dispel most of the charge, and so a cold maceration is a much more useful approach.

What You'll Need

All you need to prepare a maceration is a clear glass jar with a tight lid—canning jars work very well for this purpose—a sunny or moonlit windowsill, and a strainer.

How It's Done

If you've ever made sun tea, you already know how to make a magical maceration. Put the substance to be macerated into the jar, and add the water. Seal the jar and put it on the windowsill. How long you let it sit there will depend on what you're macerating—three to six hours for herbs, up to three days for stones. At the end of that time, pour the maceration through the strainer into another container. Stones lose nothing by the process—the only thing they impart to the water is a magical charge—and should be saved and used again.

Most macerations should be used within a day or so of making, as they tend to sour when kept for a longer time. If you need something to last longer, consider making an essence, as described below.

Macerated Potion for Courage

Take a piece of carnelian and prepare a water maceration as above, leaving it to steep for at least twenty-four hours; the more direct sunlight it receives, the better. Then add four borage flowers or one teaspoon of dried borage leaf, and continue to macerate in sunlight for at least three hours. Strain, and drink one cup to help banish shyness and provide courage.

Essences

Related to macerations, but even more effective as a way of handling delicate magical energies, are essences. Many people in the magical community nowadays are familiar with flower essences as a healing tool; the Bach flower remedies, first developed by Dr. Edward Bach in England in the 1920s, have become a common and useful approach to gentle healing, especially for conditions rooted in the emotional and mental spheres. What many people don't know is that the procedure used to make flower essences is essentially magical in nature, and can be used quite effectively to make potions and other water preparations for magical use.

Essences

Essences are made by using the etheric effects of sunlight or moonlight to charge water with the subtle energies of flowers, gemstones, and other magical materials. The process is a simple, one, and well worth learning. The one limitation is that any plant material you use for an essence has to be as fresh as possible—in fact, it works best to harvest them directly into the bowl you'll use to make the essence. A delay of as little as fifteen minutes between the harvesting of the flowers and the making of the essence can cause most or all of the plant's etheric energy to leak away.

Essences are especially sensitive to the emotional state and consciousness of the person who makes them, and it's wise to attune yourself to the planetary energy of the flower or stone you're using before making the essence.

What You'll Need
The basic ingredients for an essence are the flowers, stones, or other materials to be made into the essence, pure water, and either good brandy or apple cider vinegar as a preservative. The tools and equipment you'll need include a clear glass bowl, a bottle into which the essence is to go, and a funnel.

How It's Done
Make sure all your equipment is as clean as possible before you begin, and choose a sunny day or a clear moonlit night, depending on the energy you want to use to charge

the essence. If it's to contain flowers, you'll need to choose a time when the flowers are in full bloom. Stones may be put into the bowl before you add the water; flowers and other plant material should be cut or harvested from the plant and allowed to fall directly into the water. The total amount of water in the bowl should be half the volume of the bottle you'll use for the finished essence. The bowl should then be set in full sunlight or moonlight on the bare soil or grass—not on concrete or any other nonliving surface—and allowed to soak up the light for around three hours. (If you have pets, they should be kept away from the bowl during this time, as they're likely to drink the water.)

When the three hours are up, take the stones, flowers, or other material out of the water, straining it if necessary, and use the funnel to pour it into the bottle, which will then be half full. Fill up the other half with brandy or apple cider vinegar as a preservative; most flower essences will start to spoil within about six hours if this step is neglected. Cap the bottle tightly and store in a cool dark place. To use the essence, take two to four drops with an eyedropper and add it to a half glass of water, and drink the result.

Essence Potion for Clairvoyance

Make an essence following the procedure given above, using quartz crystal as the material and moonlight on the night of the full moon to accomplish the charging. Add four drops to a glass of water and drink before attempting any form of clairvoyant work.

Baths

Magical baths have a very long history. From ancient times, shamans and magical practitioners in many different cultures have bathed as part of their preparation for ritual work, in plain water or in water magically charged in various ways.

Bathing in plain cold water is actually one of the best preparations for magical work, and many magicians make it a habit to do this every morning. The full process, as I was taught it, has three steps. First of all, with a soft-bristled bath brush, brush your skin all over to open the pores and increase circulation. Next, wash your whole body with a washcloth and the coldest water you can stand; finally, dry off briskly with a towel. This sort of magical bath is good for physical health, and it also cleans away the etheric traces that build up on the aura, especially in urban areas or where destructive magic has been practiced. For those under magical attack, this practice is an important source of strength and should never be omitted.

Not all magical baths are so Spartan, though! Hot water also has its place in this branch of water magic, and there are a range of techniques for charging a hot bath with magical energies. Like potions, magical baths can be used to bring about changes in the self, and they also have a valuable place in magic meant to affect the way other people perceive the magician.

The methods generally used for magical baths include the two we've already covered—infusion and maceration—and several others: bag infusion, bath salts, and bath oils (which are covered in the section on Oils, pp. 256–260).

Bag Infusion

This is another very simple method of water magic; like ordinary infusion, it's something many people have done without ever knowing they were practicing something with magical possibilities. It can be used with any herb.

What You'll Need

The important tool here is a small bag of muslin with a drawstring close, of the sort that can be found at most herbal supply shops or made in five minutes with needle and thread. Failing that, a piece of plain cotton muslin three or four inches square and a piece of string will do. A bathtub and herbs complete the kit.

How It's Done

Stuff the herbs in the bag, pull the drawstring shut and tie it in a knot you'll be able to open later; alternatively, put the herbs in the center of the square of muslin, bring the sides up around so that the herbs are kept in a pocket of cloth, and tie the string around the ends of the cloth, close up against the herbs, to hold them in. As soon as you start the bath filling, put the bag in the water and let it start steeping. By the time you get in, your bath water will have turned into weak herbal tea, which is basically the idea.

Bath for Attracting Love

Take one ounce each of rose petals, lemon balm, and lovage, and make a bag infusion as described above. If you wish, an incense of Venus can be burnt to further scent the space. Bathe, concentrating the whole time on the idea of love and your goal of attracting a lover. To finish, dry yourself off with a rose-red towel.

Bath Salts

Bath salts are one of the true luxuries of natural magic, and compounding them is an art, not merely a procedure. The best bath salts are made by combining mineral salts— a mix of equal parts Epsom salt and ordinary table salt is the standard blend—with essential oils extracted from herbs, flowers, trees, and spices. It's important to use real essential oils, rather than blended perfume oils. These latter are usually cut with solvents and other artificial ingredients; this sharply weakens their magical potential and may have health risks as well.

The process of making bath salts is easy enough; it's in the choosing and mixing of the scents that the art comes in. Aromatherapy books can be used as a resource, and some of the better ones are listed in the Bibliography.

What You'll Need

Beyond the essential oils and salts you'll be using, and a bathtub, the equipment is minimal. You'll need a spoon for mixing, and a jar with an airtight lid. None of these should be made of metal or of a porous material that will pick up scents. (If you can't find a jar without a metal lid, put a piece of plastic wrap over the mouth before screwing the lid on.) You may also need an eyedropper, although many brands of essential oil come with droppers already in place.

As far as salts, you'll need Epsom salt, which is available at drugstores and many supermarkets, and either kosher salt or naturally dried sea salt, both of which you'll find at supermarkets or specialty groceries.

How It's Done

Measure out ¼ cup each of epsom salt and table salt into the jar, and stir until they are thoroughly mixed together. Then, using an eyedropper if necessary, drop the essential oil or oils into the salts. The number of drops to use depends on the number and potency of the oils you use, but more than 12–16 drops of all oils combined is probably overkill. As soon as you've added the oils, cover the jar and shake the mixture to help the oils disperse. Wait at least half an hour before using the salts, to give the oils time to blend and permeate the salts. Put into the bathwater just before you climb in.

Bath Salts for a Solar Ritual

A bath before a major magical working can be a valuable preparation, and many of the old books of magic require it. To prepare for an invocation of the Sun, make bath salts using the method above, using four drops each of bay laurel oil, cinnamon leaf oil (not cinnamon bark oil, which can burn your skin), and orange oil. Let stand for an hour, then add to the bathwater and bathe, concentrating on the purpose of your ritual. When you finish, dry yourself, anoint yourself with a solar oil, don your magical robes, and start the ritual.

Washes

A wash is magically charged water used to rinse or cleanse an object or an area. Washes have some place in Old World traditions of natural magic, but it's in the New World that they have become a major tool of the practicing magician. In North American folk magic, washes can be used to bring magical energies to bear on anything that can handle contact with water. Floor washes (which are exactly what the term suggests, washes mopped onto the floor and left to dry) form one of the standard ways to magically charge an indoor space for any desired purpose.

All of the techniques listed above for potions and baths can also be used to make magical washes. An infusion or maceration can simply be used by itself, a bag of herbs can be put in a clean mop bucket and used to create a floor wash, and scented salts can also be added to hot water and used for a wash (although this last approach should not be used on wood, which can be discolored by the salts as they dry).

Floor Wash for Blessing a House

Take 1 ounce of angelica and make a strong infusion, steeping the root in freshly boiled water for at least 10 minutes. Wash out your mop bucket, fill it with clean water, and add the infusion. Then, using a mop that has never been used for any purpose before, mop the floors all through the house, starting at the front door and finishing in the kitchen. Let the wash dry.

Consecrating Wash for a Shewstone

"Shewstone" is the old term for a crystal ball. A common tool for clairvoyant work in Western magical traditions, it can be made more effective by cleaning it regularly with a wash. Take ¼ ounce each of clary sage, eyebright, and valerian root and make an infusion. Allow it to cool, and then use it, along with a clean white cloth, to wash the shewstone before each use. The wash should be made in small batches, and bottled and refrigerated between uses to keep it from spoiling.

Another method of making a wash draws on the magical effects of vinegar, which disperses etheric patterns. This is especially useful for banishing disruptive spirits or keeping hostile magic at bay. There are two different ways of making a magical vinegar: slowly, by maceration, or fast, by infusion. Just as with water, vinegar macerations can be made with any substance, including stones and substances already charged, while vinegar infusions only work well with herbs.

Vinegar Maceration

If you've ever made an herbal vinegar for salad dressing, you already know all there is to know about this process. If not, you're about to learn what is probably the only magical technique that can also be used to jazz up green salads. (There are good reasons why many natural magic techniques are also known as "kitchen magic.")

What You'll Need

All that's needed to make macerated vinegars is the vinegar itself—any kind will do, although wine vinegar is traditional and seems to have a stronger effect—a bottle or jar with an airtight lid, and the substances you'll use to charge the vinegar. An ounce or so of most herbs will do the job.

How It's Done

Put the substances into the bottle, pour in the vinegar until the bottle is nearly full, seal the bottle, put it away in a cupboard and leave it there for at least one month. Strain and use when you're ready. That's all there is to it.

Vinegar Infusion

Like water infusions, vinegar infusions are made by soaking herbs in hot liquid. Infused vinegars are generally not as strong magically as the macerated kind, but can be made much more quickly—a significant point when a banishing or an exorcism needs to be done as soon as possible.

What You'll Need

The requirements for infused vinegars are the same as those for macerated vinegars, with the addition of a saucepan for heating the vinegar. The bottle or jar used for the infusion needs to strong enough to hold boiling liquid without shattering; a canning jar works well.

How It's Done

Measure out enough vinegar to fill the jar to within an inch or so of the top; pour into the saucepan and heat, covered, to a steady boil. Meanwhile, crumple the herbs and put them into the jar. When the vinegar has boiled, pour it into the jar, cover, and leave to cool. A few days is normally enough to bring it to full strength.

Banishing Vinegar for Floor Washes

Take ½ ounce each of angelica, cinquefoil, St. John's Wort, and vervain, and make either a maceration or an infusion with vinegar, using one of the recipes above. When needed for a floor wash, add half a cup to a mop pail of clean water and, with a new mop, wash the entire floor of the house or apartment to be protected, starting with the kitchen and finishing at the front door.

Fluid Condensers

Potions, baths, and washes are among the oldest applications of natural magic. Fluid condensers, by contrast, are a recent addition to the natural magician's toolkit. Their origins lie in the traditions of Renaissance alchemy, and their full development took place in central European magical schools in the last few centuries. So far, there are only a very few books in English that discuss fluid condensers and their uses, and only one—Franz Bardon's excellent *Initiation into Hermetics*—that does so in any detail.

What is a fluid condenser? In simplest terms, it's a substance that is better than most at holding onto etheric energies, the densest and most material of the energies used in Western magic. As discussed in the first section of this book, etheric energy is deeply linked to life and breath, and forms the link between the two levels of human experience that we in the modern West label "mind" and "matter."

Nearly all the substances that are used in natural magic are fluid condensers to one degree or another. Most things that will hold an etheric charge, though, put a very specific and focused pattern into the energies they contain. This is an advantage if the pattern is exactly the one you want—in fact, it's fundamental to natural magic—but it doesn't allow for much flexibility. In ritual work, particularly, the ability to place different charges in the same kind of substance is a necessity for many branches of magical practice, including the making and consecration of talismans and magical working tools.

This is what fluid condensers will do. An object—say, a piece of heavy watercolor paper—can be painted with a coat or two of an appropriate fluid condenser, allowed to dry, and then used as the basis for a magically consecrated talisman. Another object— say, a concave glass disk with the back painted flat black—can be treated in the same way, and will then be much more receptive to the energies it will wield as a magic mirror.

Making a Gold Solution

The essential material for fluid condensers is a small amount of dissolved gold. There are several ways to go about getting this. If you have access to a specialty photo supply

Fluid Condenser

store, gold chloride can be bought there; one part of this dissolved in twenty parts of distilled water makes an excellent gold tincture. For those with access to alternative health care supplies, several homeopathic medicines containing gold—aurum chloratum, aurum metallicum, or aurum muriaticum—can also be dissolved in water; you should use a 1x, 2x, or 3x potency, as the more extreme dilutions have too little actual gold to do the job.

If you can't manage one of these, there's a fairly easy way to make a gold solution yourself, which is given below.

What You'll Need

To make a gold solution, you'll need a piece of solid gold jewelry, 14 carat or better, that won't make anyone upset if it's damaged; a pair of pliers; a heatproof glove or oven mitt; a glass or enamel-coated saucepan; a cup of distilled water; and a heat source, such as an alcohol lamp or a gas stove burner. A pair of chemist's safety goggles is a good idea as well.

How It's Done

Holding the piece of gold by the pliers, and the pliers by the heatproof glove, heat the gold as hot as possible. Then drop it into the water. The water will spit and hiss as it cools down the hot gold; if you don't have the safety goggles, turn your face away and protect your eyes. Let the gold cool. Once it and the water are both at room temperature, fish the gold out of the water with the pliers and repeat the process. The gold should be doused in the water at least seven times to get a good solution. Once it cools, the solution should be strained through filter paper or fine linen, bottled, and kept in a cool place. If you intend to use the gold again to make more gold solution, you should polish it thoroughly first.

Making a Fluid Condenser

However you prepare your gold solution, it can then be combined with an appropriate potion, bath, or wash to make a fluid condenser ready for magical use.

What You'll Need
The ingredients for a fluid condenser are an infusion or decoction made by any of the methods covered above, and ten drops of your gold solution per cup of liquid. If you intend to keep the fluid condenser stored for more than a day or two, you'll also need an amount of strong alcohol—pure distilled spirits are best, but strong vodka or brandy will do nearly as well—equal to the amount of liquid, as a preservative to keep mold at bay.

How It's Done
Simply add the gold solution to the liquid, stir or shake well, and use. If you need to add alcohol, add it at the same time.

Fluid Condenser Eyebath for Clairvoyance
Just before the night of the full moon, take a small amount of fluid condenser using an infusion of eyebright in distilled water; do not add alcohol to this particular condenser, since you will be putting it directly in your eyes! (For the same reason, it's a good idea to filter the infusion carefully before adding the gold solution.) Once it's made, magically charge it with the intention that it will amplify the power of clairvoyance—the ability to see into magical realms of experience. You can use whatever method of charging or consecration you wish for this part of the process.

Once the condenser is made and charged, put three drops into each eye on the night of the full moon, preferably at moonrise. If at all possible, let the rising moon be the first thing you look at after the drops go in; if the moon is hidden by clouds, look toward the part of the sky where it would otherwise be visible. Do this nine times on nine successive full moons to attain strong clairvoyant abilities.

Condenser Paper for Talismans

Talismans are among the more useful devices in traditional Western ritual magic. On the most basic level, a talisman is an object—usually a disk of metal, wax, or parchment—which is marked with carefully chosen symbols and then consecrated with magical energies corresponding to those symbols, in order to accomplish a specific task. On a somewhat deeper level, a talisman is a living thing created by magic; the material object is its physical body, while the energies brought into it at its consecration form its other, subtler bodies. In place of a soul, however, it has a purpose—the purpose for which it was created and consecrated—and it will direct all its energies to that purpose, night and day, until the purpose is accomplished or the talisman is deconsecrated. Like the bunny in the advertisement, it just keeps on going.

The art of making and consecrating talismans belongs properly to ritual magic, not natural magic, and information about it can be found in any good book on the subject. Still, one detail that has not often been understood in recent years is that natural magic can be used to amplify and strengthen a talisman. The standard way to do this is by making the talisman out of a substance that resonates well with the energies that will be summoned into it.

In earlier times, this was usually done by making the talisman out of one of the seven planetary metals, with brass filling in for mercury—it's a little hard to carve symbols in quicksilver, after all! On the other hand, the cost of a disk of solid gold six inches across and a quarter of an inch thick—good dimensions for a metal talisman—is enough to make a talisman of the Sun unavailable to all but the richest modern magicians.

Fortunately, there are other options, and perhaps the best makes use of fluid condensers.

What You'll Need

Prepare a fluid condenser from gold tincture and a potion corresponding to the planet, element, or sign of the zodiac you wish to use as the energy basis for the talisman. The only other things you'll need are a small paintbrush (preferably with natural bristles) and a piece of heavy watercolor paper; both of these can be bought at any art supply store.

How It's Done

Cut out a piece of the watercolor paper in the shape of the finished talisman (in most branches of the tradition, a disk 3–4 inches across is standard). Now paint the paper with the fluid condenser, just as though you were painting it with water color paint. Let the paper dry thoroughly, then repeat the process twice more.

If the talisman is to be charged with the energies of the Sun, Venus, or Mars, or any of the zodiacal signs these rule, it should be left out to dry each time in direct sunlight, if at all possible; if you intend to invoke the Moon, Jupiter, or Saturn, or any of their signs, it should be dried each time in moonlight if this can be arranged. Elemental talismans may be dried in places corresponding to the element in question—those of Air, beneath the open sky; those of Fire, in direct sunlight or near (but not too near) a fire; those of Water, in a cool place with a glass or bowl of water nearby; those of Earth, in a basement or other dry place underground.

Once the paper has dried the third time, keep it wrapped in silk or linen to prevent it from picking up unwanted energies. As soon as possible, draw or paint the symbols on the paper and consecrate the talisman.

Oils and Scents

Since ancient Egyptian times, if not before, sacred oils, ointments, and perfumes have been used to consecrate and bless, and they have a dizzying range of roles in magic, religion, and mythology. It's worth remembering, for example, that the title "Christ" and its Hebrew equivalent, "Messiah," both literally mean "anointed with oil."

Oils and scents have many of the same magical qualities as potions. Like potions, they are made of one or more magically effective substances dissolved in a liquid—a menstruum, to use the traditional term—that serves as carrier and basis. Oil, alcohol, and water all have different capacities to dissolve the various scented substances, and these differences have potent effects on the ways in which each carrier can be put to work. In particular, many strongly scented compounds dissolve much more effectively in oil or alcohol than in water. In ancient times, accordingly, most perfumes had an oil base; nowadays, alcohol and various artificial compounds fill the same role. The recipes covered here include oil and alcohol preparations, since the ingredients needed for both are relatively easy to obtain.

Scents can range from the simple to the wildly complex, and perfumery is among the most subtle and personal of all magical arts. For ordinary magical use, a palette of readily available essential oils or herbal extracts can provide all the tools you need, but if the art of magical perfumery interests you there are many more possibilities. Just to start with, there are some 4,000 natural plant-based scents currently used in perfumery, and according to the theory of natural magic every one of them should have some magical effect to offer.

Oil or Alcohol Maceration

Maceration, one of the simplest way to make your own magical oils and scents, is also one of the best. The technique is the same as that for water macerations, which was given under Potions above; only the liquid involved is different.

Maceration

What You'll Need

The requirements are simply a glass jar with an airtight lid, a piece of cheesecloth or a fine mesh strainer, the herbs or other substances you intend to use, and enough of the menstruum to fill the jar mostly full. The lid of the jar should have no bare metal exposed to the inside; if it does, put a layer of plastic wrap over the mouth of the jar before you put on the lid, so that the metal does not react with the menstruum.

If you intend to use oil, extra-virgin olive oil, sweet almond oil, or any other natural oil with a mild scent can be used. If you plan on making an alcohol maceration, pure grain alcohol is best if you can get it, and strong vodka is almost as good; denatured alcohol, which is mixed with small amounts of various poisonous substances, should be avoided in any natural magic application.

How It's Done

Put the herbs or other substances into the jar, pour in the menstruum, cover, and leave in a cool dark place for anywhere from a few hours to a month or more, depending on the strength of the substance and the intensity of the fragrance you want. Shake up the maceration at intervals to help the fragrance diffuse throughout the oil. Once the maceration has reached the strength desired, strain the herbs or other substances out using the cheesecloth or mesh strainer, and put the result to use.

If you're making an oil maceration and the herbs you're using are fresh, take vodka or pure grain alcohol with an eyedropper and put a shallow layer on top of the oil; this helps to prevent mold, which can be a problem with oil macerations. (Macerating the oil in the refrigerator will also help, but this slows up the maceration process somewhat.) Oil macerations with dried herbs don't seem to have the same problem, at least in my experience.

Essential Oil Blends

Far and away the easiest way to make oils and scents for magical use is to use pure essential oils. With some exceptions, these can be bought inexpensively, and a small bottle goes a very long way; the better grade of essential oils on the market are very pure, which maximizes their magical effectiveness. Essential oil-based oils and scents can also be made up fresh as needed, which can be helpful if you don't have time to allow a maceration to work.

The one thing that always must be remembered when working with essential oils is that you should never use them on your body undiluted. (The one exception to this rule is lavender oil, which is mild enough that it can be applied directly to bare skin.) Used straight, many essential oils can cause skin burns, rashes, and (in some cases) serious poisoning. If you intend to use an essential oil in a preparation that will go on your body, dilute a few drops of the oil in a carrier oil such as sweet almond oil or extra-virgin olive oil, mix thoroughly, and then use the results. You can also make an old-fashioned solid perfume by heating up a quarter cup or so of beeswax until it melts, stirring in essential oils, pouring the result into a shallow, wide-mouthed jar and letting it cool and harden.

Macerated Anointing Oil

One of the classic uses for oils in the natural magic tradition is for anointing oneself or others. Many initiation rituals involve anointment, and anointing oils can also be used for many kinds of practical magic—for example, workings of protection, blessing, and empowerment can be greatly strengthened by including anointment in the rite. There are many different recipes for anointing oils; this one will be found effective for general use.

Take equal parts of angelica, mugwort, and vervain and macerate in olive oil for at least one month. Strain and store in a cool, dark place.

Essential Oil-Based Anointing Oil

Another oil that will be found effective for general anointing use can be made by adding 6 drops of essential oil of bay laurel and 2 drops of essential oil of chamomile to ¼ cup of olive oil.

Aleister Crowley's Oil of Consecration

This recipe is based on the one given in Crowley's useful volume *Book 4*, a general survey of ritual magic. It is a good blend for most magical purposes. Into ¼ cup of olive oil, mix 12 drops each of the essential oils of galangal, myrrh, and cinnamon leaf (not cinnamon bark oil, which can cause skin burns even in dilution). It can be stored in a small glass bottle or phial.

St. John's Wort Oil

This powerful oil may be used to good effect in banishings and exorcisms. Interestingly, it also has a long history in herbal medicine; knights riding to the Crusades took it with them to treat wounds, as it banishes bacteria and infections just as effectively as hostile spirits.

Fill your jar with St. John's Wort flowers, and add olive oil to macerate. Unlike most other macerations, this one should be left in a place where it will get direct sunlight for as long as possible each day; St. John's Wort is the most solar of herbs, and it gathers both magical and medicinal strength from exposure to the Sun. The oil will turn blood red as it macerates, and should be left until the color is quite intense. Strain, store, and use as needed.

Ritual Scent for a Venus Working

Scents, as mentioned above, are an intensely personal matter, and a scent that will appeal to one person may well make another wrinkle their nose and back away. With this caution, the following recipe is offered for a scent to use as a magical invocation to the energies of Venus.

Take ¼ cup of rose petals, as fresh and strongly scented as possible. Add a pinch each of dried mugwort and vervain leaves, and macerate in alcohol for at least a month, until the scent of roses is strong in the fluid. Strain, bottle, and store in a cool, dark place.

Diffusing Essential Oils

Essential oil diffuser lamps are devices that hold a small bowl of essential oil over a candle flame, heating the oil and diffusing it into the air. These devices are one of the most important advances in magical technology in many years. They allow most of the effect of incense to be produced without generating smoke, which is often a serious problem for those magicians with asthma or other respiratory troubles. Since the blend of essential oils in the diffuser can be changed at will, too, they allow enormous flexibility in the use of scents.

What You'll Need

The sheer simplicity of the process is one of its best features. All you'll need is the diffuser lamp (available at New Age and alternative health shops and import markets), a small candle (the little low ones in metal cups, usually sold under the name of "tea lights," are best), a little water, and your choice of essential oils. The diffuser itself should be made of pottery or soapstone if at all possible; the kind made of metal tend, predictably, to smell like hot metal rather than essential oil when used.

How It's Done

Fill the little bowl on top of the diffuser about one-third full of water, and add a few drops of essential oil. Light the candle and put it in its place. As the bowl and the water heat up, the scent of the oil will spread throughout the space. You can add more oil to the bowl at any point, either to renew the scent or to bring in different fragrances.

Soaps

Soap may not seem like a likely vehicle for magical work, but magical soaps have been used in some traditions and could well be used in others. (Can you think of anything else in our culture that would do a better job of symbolizing purification and cleansing?) In the last few decades, too, the art and craft of soapmaking has undergone a renaissance of its own.

There are at least two ways to prepare a magical soap—one simple, one a good deal more complex. The simple one starts off with plain, unscented soap and then adds magical ingredients, primarily essential oils, to produce a liquid soap or shampoo with magical qualities. The more complex one starts with raw materials—oils, soapmaker's lye, water, and whatever else you decide to add—and produces homemade soap bars from scratch. While this latter is a relatively simple process, it does require a certain amount of background information and some detailed instructions, and will not be covered here. If this ancient craft interests you, you'll want to read one or more of the books on soapmaking listed in the Bibliography.

Soapmaking

Making Magical Soap

The simpler approach, which will be covered here in detail, is a matter of mixing magical ingredients into soap that someone else has already made.

What You'll Need

The ingredients you'll need for magical soap include a pint or so of plain, unscented liquid soap, of the sort you can buy in bulk at most natural foods stores; a mixing bowl; a funnel; a spoon; and the essential oils and any other ingredients you intend to use. In place of liquid soap, you can use unscented shampoo to make a soap product for personal use, or you can simmer one ounce of plain, unscented bar soap, cut into shavings with a knife, in two cups of water until all the shavings dissolve. In place of essential oils, you can also use a strong infusion, decoction, or maceration of herbs in water; any other sort of water-based potion can also be used. For a magical shampoo, one quarter of the water can be replaced with apple cider vinegar, which is good for your hair and scalp; the vinegar, of course, can also be used to macerate or infuse herbs beforehand.

How It's Done

Put the liquid soap in the mixing bowl, add the essential oils or potion, mix thoroughly, and pour back into the soap bottle through the funnel. That's all there is to it. Don't hesitate to add a lot of essential oil; many soapmakers use around 1% essential oil by volume in their homemade soaps. (This works out to approximately one teaspoon of essential oil per pint of liquid soap.) If you want to make several different blends for different purposes at the same time, you'll need an assortment of clean soap bottles, and of course you'll need to wash the mixing bowl, funnel, and spoon thoroughly between batches.

Purifying Soap

This soap would be a good choice for cleaning up a space where the energies have been contaminated—for example, an apartment whose previous tenant was an alcoholic or drug addict—or for general household use during a magical attack. Add ½ teaspoon each of essential oils of bay laurel and rosemary to a pint of liquid soap. For personal purification and protection, replace the soap with unscented shampoo and use only a quarter teaspoon of rosemary.

Incense

There are few things more definitely connected with magic than incense, and for good reason. For thousands of years people have been burning various substances in the fire to scent the air and open up the path to magical states of experience. Some of the materials that have been used for this purpose are drugs, pure and simple, but there are better ways to shape consciousness than the brute-force methods of drug use. Here, as elsewhere in the magical arts, subtlety is the key.

There are several different forms of incense in common use these days, and all of them have their value to the practitioner of natural magic. The oldest, and still the most important for the practicing magician, is loose incense, which is simply dried plant material of various kinds. Unlike most other varieties, loose incense has to be put on lit charcoal in order to burn. This may be an inconvenience, but it also allows precise control of how much incense is burning at any given point, and it's also far and away the easiest of all incenses to make.

Pebble incense is one of those Victorian crafts that has been very nearly forgotten at present, but is well worth reviving in magical circles. As the name implies, this takes the form of small, hard balls of incense, and must be burnt on charcoal like the loose variety.

Stick incense is the kind most people think of first when incense is mentioned. It's usually made of a paste of herbs, wood powder, glue, and water, formed around thin pieces of bamboo into long slender sticks. A simpler kind of stick incense can be made by taking unscented sticks and "painting" them with essential oils.

Cone incense and cylinder incense are made of the same kind of mixture as stick incense, but are shaped into different forms. These are harder to find unless you live in an area with good import shops or herb stores.

Making stick, cone, or cylinder incense is well within the abilities of most people, but—as with making your own soap—it requires a good deal of information and detailed instructions, and will not be covered here. (Those who want to explore the art of making these kinds of incense will find references on the subject in the Bibliography.) Loose incense, pebble incense, and the kind of stick incense made by applying essential oils to unscented wood-powder sticks are another matter, as these are much less complex to make.

Loose Incense

This is simply a collection of herbs and other scented substances that is put on glowing charcoal to burn and give off smoke. It's often a good idea to try any incense blend first as loose incense in small batches, since this allows you to adjust proportions and experiment freely.

What You'll Need

A censer or heatproof bowl; some self-starting charcoal (available wherever bulk incense is sold, or from mail order houses); a mixing bowl; a mortar and pestle for grinding; and airtight jars for the final results are the only pieces of equipment needed. The ingredients are entirely a matter of your preferences and purposes.

How It's Done

Start by testing the ingredients you have in mind to make sure they will work together (or at all!) as incense. The scent of fresh or dried plant material is not necessarily a guide here; mint, for example, smells awful when burnt. The only effective way is to light your charcoal, put it in the censer or heatproof bowl, wait until it's hot, and drop a small amount of the ingredient you have in mind right on the charcoal. Wait until it has stopped giving off smoke, and then try a pinch of the next ingredient on the list. Once you've made sure that all of them work well as incenses (or have set aside the ones that don't), try mixing together a pinch of each ingredient into a blend and burning that. Adjust the ingredients, testing each mix, until you've found one that works for you. Then note down the proportions, make a slightly larger batch in the mixing bowl, stir up thoroughly, and try a pinch on the charcoal. (Most self-lighting charcoal will burn for an hour or more, so you can afford to take your time.) When you've finally got the blend right, mix it up. Large pieces of bark, leaf, and so on should be ground up in the mortar and pestle, and if you prefer incense with a relatively smooth, even texture and scent it may be a good idea to grind all of it to powder. Once you've finished, put the incense in an airtight jar and leave it someplace where it will not be exposed to direct sunlight or temperature extremes.

Pebble Incense

Once upon a time, pebble incense was one of the things that nearly every young woman in the English-speaking world knew how to make before she left her parents' home. Like many of the forgotten crafts of our great-grandparents' time, it's well worth reviving.

What You'll Need

A mortar and pestle, a mixing bowl and spoon, and a flat surface covered with wax paper are all the equipment that you'll need. Ingredients consist of the herbs, flowers, and other scented material you intend to use in the incense, the essential oil or oils, and the whites of one or more eggs, depending on the quantity you want to make.

How It's Done

Grind up the solid ingredients thoroughly in the mortar, then pour the powder into the mixing bowl and add the essential oil a drop at a time, stirring between drops to disperse the oil. When the mixture smells right, begin stirring in the egg white a little at a time until the mixture is moistened all the way through, but not yet sloppy. On the wax paper, roll small amounts of the mixture into little balls one-third to one-half inch across. Dry these until hard; if you live in a humid climate, drying them in an oven set on "warm" may be a good idea. Put one or two of the resulting pebbles on hot charcoal to release the scent.

Stick Incense from Essential Oils

This is another form of incense that is simple to make and very useful for the practicing magician.

What You'll Need

The requirements here are plain, unscented incense-style sticks, which can be purchased from aromatherapy supply shops and a surprising number of other stores; a small paintbrush with natural bristles, which can be found in any art supply store; and the essential oils you intend to use. A large lump of modeling clay or a piece of wood with several very small holes drilled into it, a small wide-mouthed jar for mixing essential oils, and a collection of airtight jars for the finished product will also be needed.

Stick Incense

How It's Done

Take the essential oils and make a blend that fits your purpose and your esthetic sense, using the little jar as a mixing container. When the blend is right, stick the bamboo ends of several of the incense sticks into the modeling clay or the holes in the wood, so the sticks stand upright. Using the brush, "paint" the incense sticks with the essential oil blend, just as though you were coating them with a layer of paint. As soon as the sticks look relatively dry—depending on the dryness of the wood powder, this may happen immediately—put them into the airtight bottle or jar where they will be stored; this will minimize the amount of essential oil that is lost. Set up more sticks, paint them, and continue until you've done as many as you wish. If there's any essential oil blend left over afterwards, take an eyedropper and put a drop or two into the jar with the freshly made incense sticks.

Purification Incense

For works of cleansing, purification, and banishing, take equal parts angelica root and myrrh and burn over charcoal; alternatively, grind up the angelica root, mix with powdered myrrh and a few drops of bay laurel essential oil, and make into pebble incense.

Love Incense

For the more erotic kinds of love magic, make stick incense with an essential oil blend of six parts rose and one part each of ginger, jasmine, and patchouli. For the more spiritual kinds, replace the last three ingredients with lily and yarrow.

Visionary Incense

A good blend to burn when scrying, crystal gazing, or performing other kinds of visionary work may be made by taking equal parts of mugwort, hops, and vervain and adding a pinch of nutmeg. Use sparingly; a little of this mix goes a long way.

Church Incense

This is the classic blend used in Roman Catholic churches, and borrowed (with good reason) by many practitioners of ceremonial magic for general ritual use. Take ten parts of frankincense, four parts of benzoin, and one part of styrax; grind up finely and mix thoroughly.

Kyphi Incense

Finally, for traditionalists, here is the most famous of all incenses, the classic blend of ancient Egypt. There are many different recipes for kyphi, even in documents dating from the time of the pharaohs. The following version is based on two of the surviving accounts from Egyptian papyri.

Take two parts each of juniper berries, galangal root, calamus root, frankincense, and pine resin; one part each of orris root, broom flowers, myrrh, and styrax; three parts each honey and raisins; and enough red wine to moisten the final result. Pound the raisins into a paste, and mix with the honey; grind all the other ingredients (except the wine, of course) together in a mortar, and mix the result into the honey and raisin mixture, moistening with the wine as needed to produce a paste. Roll the result into little balls, and let dry thoroughly before storing.

Candles

Each of the four traditional elements has its special tools in natural magic. Amulets and magical foods correspond to Earth, potions, baths and washes to Water, and sachets and scents to Air. Fire, in turn, has incense—although this overlaps in important ways with Air—and, centrally, candles.

Candles are standard equipment in all kinds of Western magical practice, and not just because they were the most common portable light source in the days before flashlights. The actual presence of fire has magical effects that a light bulb simply cannot duplicate. Magicians of many traditions, paying attention to these effects, have found a dizzying number of ways to use them in practice. As a result, it's a rare altar that doesn't have at least one candle burning on or near it, and a rare ceremony that doesn't make at least some use of the magical powers of living flame.

As with several other things in this Workbook, it's entirely possible for you to make your own candles from scratch, and—again, as with some of the other things we've explored—this opens up possibilities that relying on storebought candles doesn't allow. On the other hand, candlemaking is another relatively specialized craft, and should be studied in books devoted to the subject.

On a simpler level, there are at least two things that can be done with candles in natural magic. The first has to do with symbolism. Different colors and numbers, as mentioned under those headings in the Encyclopedia, relate to different energies and magical purposes. To light a red candle is to call on primal energy; to light five red candles is a simple but functional way of summoning the magical forces associated with the planet Mars in astrology.

The second approach to candle magic is to use the candle as a vehicle for oils and other scented material. In traditional North American hoodoo or conjure magic, that amazing and unfairly neglected hybrid of African, European, and Native American occult lore, a colored candle is often lit and "dressed"—that is, rubbed with a magical oil, always starting from the middle and working toward both ends—to perform a magical working. The color of the candle and the composition of the oil depend on the purpose of the working. While the specific recipes used by hoodoo doctors differ somewhat from those of Western natural magic, the technique seems to work equally well either way. Any oil you like can be used in this way.

Wax-Dressed Candles

A slightly more complex version of this process uses melted wax to give a candle a solid coat of scented material. The wax dressing can also be colored with candle pigments, allowing you to combine color and scent.

What You'll Need

To make wax-dressed candles, you'll need a saucepan and spoon that you can devote to noncooking uses; a new candle, preferably one with an inch or so of wick above the wax; enough spare candle wax to make a good coating for the candle; your choice of essential oils; an empty coffee can or some other container large enough to hang the candle inside, and something—a knitting needle, a wooden chopstick, or what have you—long enough to reach across the coffee can's mouth and narrow enough that you can tie the wick of your candle to it. If you want to color the dressing, you'll need some wax pigments, which you'll need to get from a craft store or a candlemakers' supply.

How It's Done

First tie the wick of the candle to the knitting needle (or whatever you're using) and set the latter across the mouth of the coffee can, so that the candle hangs freely in the middle. Melt the spare wax in the saucepan over a medium heat until the wax is liquid and runny. (This doesn't take long; don't leave the wax on the stove unattended or you may have a stove fire to deal with.) Add the color, if any, and the essential oils, and then gradually pour the liquid wax over the candle. Do this several times, pausing between coats to allow each coat of wax to dry and harden a little. When the whole candle has an even coating of wax, you're done; leave the candle hanging for half an hour or so to allow the dressing to finish hardening.

The Natural
Magic Kit

Many of the different preparations we've just covered can be prepared in advance for future use, and this is generally a good idea—after all, if you find yourself suddenly needing to do a magical working on little or no notice, having to take time to make an herbal vinegar or a wax-dressed candle may be the last thing you want to do. Even with preparations that lose their magical potency over long storage, or that can be made up so quickly that there's no need to ready them in advance, it's often a good idea to set aside some of the raw materials so that you don't run out of the wrong thing at the wrong time. For any serious student or practitioner of natural magic, some sort of natural magic kit is a necessity.

What should such a kit contain? To a great extent this depends on the kind of magic you tend to do most often, and on the tradition of ritual magic (if any) that you combine with natural magic. A healer who uses natural magic to supplement herbal medicine and other natural healing arts will need one sort of kit; a high priest or high priestess who devotes his or her time to teaching, counseling, and ceremony will need a different one; a Hermetic magician seeking the transformation of the self through the disciplines of Golden Dawn magic will need one different still. Much also depends on what natural magic techniques you have mastered and prefer to use; it won't do you much good to collect the materials for bath salts, for example, if you haven't learned how to combine them or don't like the results when you use them.

It's usually best, therefore, to set aside the very common temptation to run out and get a complete kit at the very beginning, and take a more gradual approach. The key to assembling a useful kit is to start working with natural magic, see what preparations you find most congenial, and then collect the tools and materials you need to make use of them. In all likelihood, your kit will evolve over time as different procedures cycle in and out of your repertoire, and this is all to the good; after all, anything that has stopped evolving is probably dead.

As an example of one natural magician's kit, the following tools, supplies, and materials can usually be found in or near the cupboard where I keep my natural magic gear:

- 2 ounces each angelica root, asafoetida, frankincense resin, hops, St. John's Wort

- 1 ounce each cedarwood shavings, dittany of Crete, mugwort, rosemary, vervain, yarrow

- 1 head fresh garlic

- 1 bottle each essential oils of bay laurel, chamomile, cinnamon leaf, clary sage, lavender, patchouli, rosemary

- 1 pound kosher salt

- 1 pound Epsom salt

- 1 bottle mixed Abramelin incense (frankincense, benzoin, lignum aloe, rose)

- 2 bottles prepared magical vinegars, one for banishing and protection (angelica, rosemary, St. John's Wort) and one for blessing and healing (angelica, lavender, vervain)

- Commercially manufactured incense sticks, one packet each of frankincense, styrax ("amber"), rose, cedar, pine

- 2–3 packets self-lighting charcoal for incense

- 1 dozen muslin drawstring bags for baths, washes, etc.

- Censer for burning loose incense over charcoal

- Incense stick holder for burning stick incense

- Wooden kitchen matches

- Medium and small glass bowls for mixing herbs, salts, etc.

- Soapstone essential oil diffuser lamp

- Porcelain mortar and pestle

- One yard each red, white, and black cotton broadcloth (for amulet bags)

- Needles and matching heavy thread

- Red, white, and black cord for amulets

1 packet small paneling nails, sealed in a resealable plastic bag with a packet of moisture-absorbent compound to prevent rust

Assorted small bottles and jars for preparations

Herbs, stones, and other materials currently under study

This, it bears repeating, is one example drawn from a world of possibilities, and it should be used as an example of what can be done rather than a shopping list or set of specifications. The selection of materials and equipment is based partly on my preferences, partly on the requirements of the particular traditions of magic I follow and the specific situations that tend to come up most often in my life just now. A few years ago the selection would have been a good deal different; a few years from now it will no doubt be different again.

If you travel a good deal, or if you are often called to go somewhere far from home for magical purposes, you may also find it useful to put together a traveling natural magic kit. A shoulderbag or fabric briefcase makes a good container for such a kit, which should be able to hold what you will need where you are going, as well as a selection of generally useful materials and equipment. Leave room also for an amulet of protection for travelers.

The Magician's Garden

An important application of natural magic in everyday life is the magical garden. In reality, just as in legend, the cottages of medieval wise women and the country houses of Renaissance mages had their gardens, in which mandrake, yarrow, lady's mantle, dittany of Crete, and many other magical plants flourished alongside the ordinary household herbs that everyone grew in those times. It's a tradition that is still very much worth following today, both for practical reasons—there's no better way to supply yourself with fresh herbs for magical uses—and for the sake of learning the subtle lessons only personal contact with the living Earth can bring.

The Windowbox Garden

It's not necessary to own acres of real estate to grow a magical garden. One sunny windowsill facing south can provide room for a half-dozen clay pots or a wooden window box, and this can become the home for an assortment of magical herbs, including some of the most powerful and useful. If you have access to a balcony or a corner of a backyard, you can do a great deal more, but even so a windowsill garden or two may be a good way to start exploring the possibilities of the magical side of gardening.

Plants grown in containers have the same basic needs as those grown outside in the ground—light, water, and soil—but the special environment of a windowsill places a few extra demands on the gardener. Ordinary soil tends to pack down and hold water poorly in containers; it's thus a good idea to use a mix of equal parts commercial potting mix, compost (homemade or commercial), and ordinary garden soil. If you live in an area where invasive weeds or plant diseases are a problem, the garden soil should be spread thin on a baking tray, wetted thoroughly, and then baked for an hour in an oven at 275 degrees. Water is a simpler matter, although you should be careful not to overwater—wait until the soil is dry to a depth of one inch or so before watering your plants—and light should not be a problem so long as the location you choose is fairly sunny.

Windowbox Garden

Some of the herbs that can easily be grown in windowboxes or small containers are these:

Basil—an annual, basil can be planted in eight-inch pots or any larger containers, and will grow one to two feet high. Plant after the last frost if it's to be outdoors, anytime if it's to be an indoor plant. Cut leaves from the stems regularly; the more you cut, the more will grow.

Chamomile—either the annual or the perennial species can be grown in containers, and will grow up to six inches high. It prefers plenty of sun and should not be overwatered.

Dittany of Crete—a relative of oregano, dittany of Crete prefers sunny and dry conditions. Plant in eight-inch pots.

Ginger—this tropical herb can be grown with surprising ease as an indoor potted plant. Simply take a fresh ginger root, plant it in a pot with the bud side up, and water frequently. The larger the container you use, the more root you'll be able to harvest.

Oregano—good as a cooking and medicinal herb as well as a magical one, oregano is a perennial that will grow easily in pots and other containers. Pick the leaves as you need them.

Rosemary—you'll need to grow one of the dwarf varieties in a window-box garden, since ordinary rosemary routinely grows four to six feet tall. It can be grown outside on a patio or balcony, or in a smaller container indoors if you're willing to keep it well trimmed. Rosemary prefers dry and sunny areas, and will suffer if it's overwatered.

Thyme—there are many different varieties of thyme, and most of them will grow well indoors, even in small pots. Many varieties are no more than a few inches high at maturity, and it often works well to plant thyme beneath other, taller herbs in large containers.

Depending on the size of containers you're able to use, the range of possible plants that can be grown in this way can be expanded almost indefinitely. The warmth of an indoor locations also makes it possible to grow plants that won't normally flourish in temperate areas; I've seen banana trees flourishing indoors in far-from-tropical Seattle, and while bananas aren't especially important in Western natural magic, there are other tropical plants that are.

The Backyard Garden

If you have access to something more than a windowsill or a patio, the possibilities are even greater. Exactly what you can do depends on your local climate and soil, but most parts of North America will grow most of the standard herbs, shrubs, and trees used in Western natural magic.

In establishing an outdoor garden, the most important step is learning to pay attention to the fine details of your backyard environment. Different plants have different needs and preferences, and a plant that will flourish in one part of a garden may struggle or die a few feet away. Just as with a container garden, light, water, and soil make up the crucial set of environmental factors for plants in an outdoor garden, but these are much more dependent on what's actually there in the place where you put your plants. Since the plants themselves can't pull up their roots and walk to a better site, you'll need to learn to think like a plant—to notice where sun and shade gather, where water puddles when it rains, and so on—so that you can plant in the right place to start with.

Most seed packets and nursery plants come labeled with information about the plant's needs, and this can be used as a basic guide. There are also a number of very good books on growing herbs, some of which are included in the Bibliography; one or

Backyard Garden

more of these ought to be somewhere on your bookshelves if you intend to do any serious gardening.

You should certainly plan on using organic methods in growing plants for magical purposes. This is partly a matter of keeping residues and contaminants out of your magical potions and amulets, but also has much to do with establishing good relations with the visible and the hidden aspects of the natural world alike—relations that have everything to do with the successful practice of natural magic. Use compost to build up the fertility of your garden's soil rather than using chemical fertilizers that impoverish and unbalance the soil; deal with insects and diseases by keeping your plants well nourished and your garden clean rather than by spraying with toxic pesticides. In general, in this as in any other branch of natural magic, it's best to work with Nature in your garden, rather than against her—after all, she has a much better idea of how things work than you do.

The Planetary Garden

Another dimension of the magical garden relates to the way different arrangements of plants can be used as a means of magical symbolism and action. One common habit in the herb gardens of the Middle Ages and Renaissance, especially those devoted to healing or magical herbs, was to set out plants in an arrangement based on the symbolism of the elements, planets, or signs of the zodiac. Some of the most beautiful Renaissance gardens copy the whole magical image of the world—reaching from the world of the four elements, up through the realms of the planets, to the timeless sphere of the stars—all reflected and reproduced in a skillful arrangement of symbolically appropriate flowers, herbs, shrubs, and trees.

While the grand scale of these classic gardens is out of reach of most modern magicians, the same thing can be done in a smaller way. A planetary garden, for example, can be made from a circle of ground four to six feet across. Divide the circle into seven parts, using stones or a single line of paving bricks between each segment to mark the divisions. In a temperate region, you might then plant rue and hellebore in Saturn's section, borage and sage in Jupiter's, basil and garlic in Mars', dwarf rosemary and chamomile in the Sun's, mugwort and lady's mantle in Venus', lavender and oregano in Mercury's, and lily and mouse-ear in the Moon's. In each segment, the first herb named should be planted closer to the center, the second further out. At the center of such a circle it was once traditional to put a statue of Pan, whose seven-toned reed pipe symbolized the "music of the spheres," the natural harmony of the seven planetary energies in the cosmos.

Similar things can be done with the elements and the signs of the zodiac, following the correspondences covered in the Encyclopedia section of this book. If you have the space and the inclination, you may find it best to follow one of these patterns, or do something else that harmonizes with your own preferred magical system. The important point is that you should think of your garden not simply as a place to grow plants that you can then use in magic, but as a magical work in its own right. To plant a garden—over and above its many other values—is an act of magic, one that can be used to shape experienced reality in any way you decide.

Harvesting Magical Herbs

When you have the freedom to grow your own magical herbs, it becomes possible to incorporate magic into the harvesting process. In earlier times, it was held that herbs had to be harvested in particular ways or at particular times to have any magical efficacy at all. My own experience, as well as that of most other modern natural magicians, is that things aren't quite so rigid; even commercially grown and harvested herbs retain magical powers that can be put to work. In order to have magical herbs at the peak of their powers, though, the process of harvesting should be done with the magical dimension in mind.

There are two aspects to doing this. The first is a matter of timing. Different plants, and different parts of the same plant, may be best harvested at different times of year. As a rule, leaves, and entire herbs should be gathered just before the plant first flowers in the spring. Roots of annuals and all fruits, nuts, and seeds should be harvested in the autumn; roots of perennials should be harvested in late fall or winter, when the whole life force of the plant has returned to the root to weather out the barren half of the year. Whatever the season, the standard time to harvest magical plants is at dawn, before the first rays of the Sun touch the plant; if there is any significant amount of dew, allow it to evaporate off naturally before harvesting.

All this represents only the first stage of timing, though. The second comes from the point that harvesting a plant for magical purposes is itself a magical operation, subject to the same rules of timing discussed earlier in this book. Any of the three methods of magical timing already given—the patterns of Sun and Moon, the use of electional astrology, or the system of planetary hours and elements—can be used to time the harvest; in the latter two cases, use the planetary or elemental correspondence of the plant to be harvested to work out which planet or sign should be strong, or which planetary hour or tattwa should be in course, at the time of harvest.

Beyond timing, there are also a set of traditional rules for harvesting magical herbs which work well in practice.

1. Before you harvest a plant—if at all possible, several days before—locate the plant, sit down on the ground in front of it, and silently tell it what you have in mind. Explain why you need to harvest part or all of it, and what you will be doing with it once you have done so. Listen inwardly for a response. If you work within a magical tradition that teaches scrying in the spirit vision or other kinds of visionary work, communicate with the plant through that mode. In effect, you are asking the plant's permission to harvest it; if you get a strong "no," listen to it.

2. On the morning when you intend to harvest, go out before sunrise. With a wooden staff or wand—metal must never be used for this—draw a circle in the earth around the plant.

3. Place yourself so that you are facing the plant and the wind is at your back. If the wind shifts, change position accordingly. The wind must never be in your face while you are harvesting for magical purposes.

4. During and after the harvesting process, the plant must not touch your bare hands (or any other part of your skin) or the ground. If you are harvesting in a way that will leave most of the plant intact, spread a silk or linen cloth on the ground and cut the parts you need so that they fall on the cloth. If you are harvesting the whole plant, grasp the plant through silk or linen and uproot it, or hold it through a layer of cloth while digging it up. Either way, put the plant into a silk or linen bag as soon as it has been harvested.

5. Never use iron or steel implements to harvest magical plants, and never allow magical plants to come into contact with iron or steel at any time, as any such contact will discharge some of the plants' magical virtues. Trowels and other garden tools of hard plastic are fairly easy to come by these days, and are a definite help to the natural magician. If you can obtain a bronze knife, sickle, or bolline—a much rarer piece of equipment nowadays—treasure it, and use it to cut leaves and stems. If you can't find one, a piece of broken pottery, an obsidian or flint blade, or (at worst) a sturdy plastic table knife will do the job.

6. If you uproot a plant completely, leave a small offering behind in the hole. A little grain and honey is a common form of offering; in North America, a small twist of tobacco is the standard offering to Earth spirits and other supernatural beings. The offering is made to appease the elementals and Earth spirits, and keep them from trying to harm you or interfere in the magical working you have in mind. If at all possible, sow seed or put in another plant in the same place as soon as seasonal and lunar cycles permit.

The keynotes to all magical harvesting are respect and forbearance. In taking plants for your use, you are asking another living thing to surrender part or all of its body for your purposes, and the process of harvesting should be done with that in mind.

Planting by the Moon

Another branch of natural magic that is highly relevant here is the traditional lore of planting by the Moon. Every natural magician who can plant a garden—even if this comes to no more than a few herbs in pots in a sunny window—should consider exploring this branch of the tradition. The Moon, as mentioned more than once in this book, is the celestial power that rules natural magic; over and above its positive effects on plant growth, planting by the Moon teaches an awareness of lunar cycles and an attentiveness to the dance of celestial energies that shapes all magical work.

There are two main aspects to the art of planting by the Moon. The first of these involves attention to the Moon's phases as it waxes and wanes through its own cycle relative to the Sun; the second involves attention to the constellations of the zodiac through which the Moon moves.

The Moon and Its Phases

A lunar month is the period from New Moon to New Moon, and comes to a little over twenty-nine days. The traditional lore divides the lunar cycle into two halves—the waxing or growing half, when the Moon is growing from its first thin crescent to the full, and the waning or shrinking half, when it dwindles from the full to its last thin crescent and then to invisibility. The first quarter, halfway along the Moon's journey from new to full, and the third quarter, halfway along the return journey from full back to new, are the dividing points within these halves. Most calendars give the dates of New Moon, first quarter, Full Moon, and third quarter, and any decent almanac, ephemeris, or astrological calendar will give the exact time when the Moon passes through these stations of its cycle.

The basic rules for using the phases are these:

New Moon to First Quarter

This is the best time for planting crops that are grown for their leaves or flowers, or for any part that does not contain seeds—for example, lettuce, cabbage, and most herbs—and are annuals, finishing their complete growth cycle in a single season.

First Quarter to Full Moon

This is the best phase to plant annuals grown for some part that contains seeds—for example, peas and beans, fruits, grain crops, and herbs grown for seed.

Full Moon to Third Quarter

Any crop that bears below the ground—that is, anything grown for its roots or bulbs—should be planted in this phase, and this is also the best time for pruning. Crops, especially moist ones like fruit, should be harvested at this time if they will be stored for more than a few days.

Third Quarter to New Moon

This phase, once called the "eld of the moon," should never be used for planting or transplanting, only for weeding and harvesting crops, for canning, drying, and all kinds of preserving.

The Moon and the Signs

In every lunar month, the Moon passes once through each of the twelve signs of the zodiac. According to the traditions of astrology, the passage through each sign colors the Moon's energy, just as a colored filter changes a light shining through it. The qualities of the signs thus affect the *anima mundi*, the soul of the Earth, and living things respond to these changes in energy.

Each of the signs has its particular character, part of which has to do with the element and planet governing it and part of which is a function of its own unique energy. In terms of their effects on the Moon (and thus on plants and other living things), the characters of the signs are as follows:

♈ Aries, the Ram

> **Planet:** Mars
> **Element:** Fire

Aries is a barren sign, hot and dry because of its fiery nature. Onions and other fiery plants can be planted or transplanted during this time, but most others do poorly. This is a good time to clear away weeds, to dig beds, and to plow fields. Canning, drying, and preserving do well during this sign, as do baking and cooking. Aries is also a good sign for hunting, and medium for fishing.

♉ Taurus, the Bull

Planet: Venus

Element: Earth

Taurus is a fertile sign, the best sign for planting and transplanting all crops that bear below the ground. It is also good, though not quite so good, for planting crops that bear above the ground, and seems to be especially good for leafy green vegetables. Canning, drying, and preserving do well during this sign. Plants put in the ground during this sign will be hardy and withstand drought well. Moon in Taurus is also a good time for fishing.

♊ Gemini, the Twins

Planet: Mercury

Element: Air

Gemini is a medium sign, fair for planting and transplanting all crops. It is the best of all signs for beans; all legumes will grow and bear fruit abundantly if planted or transplanted during this time. This sign is also very favorable for canning, drying, and preserving, and relatively favorable for killing weeds and digging garden beds.

♋ Cancer, the Crab

Planet: Moon

Element: Water

Cancer is a fertile sign, the best of all signs for planting crops that will bear above the ground, and very good for root crops as well. Crops planted during this sign will withstand drought well, although paradoxically this is also one of the best signs for irrigation and watering. Cutting hair during this sign is said to stimulate hair growth.

♌ Leo, the Lion

Planet: Sun

Element: Fire

Leo is a barren sign, and plants planted or transplanted during this sign will do poorly; it is the best of all signs, though, for weeding. When the Moon is in Leo, pull weeds and clear away brush. This is also a good sign to dig garden beds.

♍ Virgo, the Virgin

Planet: Mercury

Element: Earth

Virgo, despite its earthy qualities, is a barren sign, and anything planted or transplanted during this time is likely to do poorly. Seeds planted during this sign, according to traditional lore, will rot in the ground rather than sprouting. Correspondingly, this is an excellent sign to turn compost or apply it to your garden.

♎ Libra, the Scales

Planet: Venus

Element: Air

Libra is a fertile sign, especially favorable for plants that are grown for their flowers. It is moderately good for roots and plants grown for their pulp. This is also a good sign to cut hair, as it will grow back stronger and thicker.

♏ Scorpio, the Scorpion

Planet: Mars

Element: Water

Scorpio is the most fertile sign for plants that bear above ground, and also favorable to a lesser degree for root crops. It is the best sign for transplanting. Fruit trees, shrubs, and vines should be planted in this sign if at all possible, as they will bear abundantly. This is also one of the best signs for hunting and fishing.

♐ Sagittarius, the Archer

Planet: Jupiter

Element: Fire

Sagittarius is a barren sign because of its fiery energy. Onions and other fiery plants can be planted at this time with fair to good results, but most other crops do poorly. Never transplant when the Moon is in Sagittarius. This is a good sign for hunting, however, and for canning, drying, and preserving. Moon in Sagittarius is also a good time to cut hair.

♑ Capricorn, the Goat

Planet: Saturn

Element: Earth

This is a fertile sign, especially good for root crops but also good for crops that bear above the ground. Trees, shrubs and vines should be pruned during this sign. This is also a good sign for canning, and a fair one for fishing. Moon in Capricorn is the best sign for laying foundations.

♒ Aquarius, the Water Bearer

Planet: Saturn

Element: Earth

Aquarius is a medium sign, relatively good for crops that bear above the ground, although if the weather is wet seeds will tend to rot in the ground.

♓ Pisces, the Fishes

Planet: Jupiter

Element: Water

This sign is very favorable for all crops that bear above the ground, particularly flowers, and also good for root crops. Trees, bushes, and vines do well when transplanted or pruned during Pisces, and irrigation and watering are favored by this sign as well. Pisces is also said to be the best sign for fishing, sensibly enough, and it is a good sign to cut hair.

For best results, pay attention to both the phase and sign of the Moon when selecting a day and time to do garden work. Since fertile and barren signs are fairly evenly
distributed around the Moon's cycle, it shouldn't be difficult to find a fertile sign
between the New Moon and the first quarter, for example, in which to plant flowers, or
a barren sign in the eld of the Moon to pull weeds. If you practice a magical tradition
in which this is appropriate, invoke the Moon or an appropriate lunar deity before
doing your garden work to strengthen your connection with its energies.

Natural Magic and Alchemy

Beyond natural magic, but bordering it in many ways, is the art and science of alchemy. To work with natural magic is often to stray close to the edges of alchemy, and not infrequently to stray over those edges into the first steps of the Great Work. While this book is not the place for a complete introduction to alchemy—that is a subject for a book all its own—it's a good idea to be aware of the basic ideas of alchemy, and to have some experience of the simplest kind of alchemical operations, in order to get the most out of natural magic.

So what is alchemy? According to the version of history most of us learned in the public schools, alchemy was a primitive ancestor of chemistry, a system of thought that wasted centuries trying to turn lead into gold using hopelessly inadequate methods. According to a newer interpretation, one based on the ideas of the psychologist Carl Jung, alchemy was a primitive form of depth psychology expressed in a cumbersome symbolic language borrowed from primitive chemistry. Neither of these definitions, though, is used by people who actually practice traditional laboratory alchemy, and both of them are founded squarely on the highly arrogant modern habit of assuming that no one in the past could possibly have known something we don't.

The definitions used by actual alchemists are quite different. Albert Reidel, one of the most respected figures in modern alchemical studies, defined alchemy as "the raising of vibrations." Though the terminology he used was modern, the basic idea dates back thousands of years. In an older way of speaking, the purpose of alchemy was often described as "helping Nature to achieve her perfections."

The alchemy of metals, the only kind most people have heard of these days, was only one of the parts of nature in which this quest for greater perfection could be carried out. In most modern alchemical schools, in fact, it's standard to start work with an entirely different branch of the alchemical tree, the alchemy of herbs. There are many other branches beyond these: alchemies of mind and spirit, alchemies of sex, alchemies of agriculture, alchemies that cover much of the ground of our present sciences—but from a very different perspective. All these are potential fields for modern alchemical work, and many of them are currently being explored by present-day alchemists.

In every kind of alchemy, the basic processes are the same in broad outline, although any one process may be expressed in an infinity of different practical forms. The most important of all alchemical processes—in fact, one that has been used to define the whole work of alchemy—is divided into two stages. *Solve* and *coagula*, their traditional Latin names, are still the most common words used for these steps. "Dissolve" and "coagulate," "separate" and "unite," "analyze" and "synthesize": each of these pairs express some part of the meaning of this fundamental pattern of alchemical practice.

Whenever an alchemist goes to work—whether with metals, herbs, sexual energies, or anything else—some unity will be separated out into its component parts, and then those parts will be brought together into a new unity. In the process, typically, the separate parts are purified and potentized, so that the new unity born from the coagula phase is not simply a repetition of the old unity before the solve; in Dr. Reidel's phrase, its vibrations have been raised, while in the older language of alchemy, the substance has been brought closer to the perfection intended for it by Nature.

Making an Alchemical Magistery

As with most of the procedures covered in this book, this process can best be seen by putting it into action. The following elementary method of herbal alchemy is a standard first exercise in modern alchemical schools; it produces an alchemical magistery—the Vegetable Stone—with powerful effects in healing as well as in practical magic.

A quick pass through basic alchemical theory will help make some basic sense of the procedure that follows. In alchemical teaching, everything is made up of "sulfur," "mercury," and "salt." These are not, however, the chemical substances that bear these names nowadays; rather, sulfur represents the energetic, volatile principle in any material; mercury represents the fluid, interactive principle; and salt represents the stable, solid principle. In plants, the sulfur consists of volatile essential oils, fats, and some vegetable waxes. The mercury in a living plant is sap, but sap—a mixture of water and sugars—becomes alcohol when fermented, and so alcohol is considered the pure or perfected form of plant mercury. The salt of a plant is the solid material left when all the oils and fluids are extracted. What we'll be doing in the following process is separating the sulfur and mercury of a plant from the salt, purifying the salt, and then bringing the three aspects back together.

Alchemy

What You'll Need

Many of the basic processes of alchemy can be done with simple kitchen equipment—another connection between alchemy and natural magic—and this is one of them. For your alchemical tools, you'll need two glass canning jars with lids, a small piece of plastic wrap, a funnel, a piece of cheesecloth, a metal spoon, a heatproof glass baking dish with a lid, heatproof oven mitts, a mortar and pestle, and a jar with an airtight lid for the final product. A warm place like the top of a hot water heater and a well-ventilated kitchen with a good oven complete the list. The materials you'll need are enough of some suitable herb to fill one of the canning jars about a third full—it's traditional to use lemon balm for one's first tincture, but this isn't required—and a few cups of very pure alcohol, at least 175 proof; good brandy or vodka will do the job, and so will a pure grain alcohol such as Everclear. (Never use denatured alcohol for any alchemical or natural magic preparation; it contains small amounts of poisonous chemicals, and can make you sick or kill you if you take it internally.)

How It's Done

Alchemical processes are even more strongly affected by astrological factors and planetary hours than are the other processes covered in this book. The state of consciousness of the alchemist also has a powerful effect. For best results, every step of an alchemical working should be timed by astrology, by planetary hours, or (when possible) by some combination of the two, and you should use whatever means work best for you—ritual, meditation, prayer—to attune yourself to the planetary energy with which·you intend to work.

Start the physical side of the procedure by grinding up the herb to a very fine powder with the mortar and pestle. Then, taking one of the canning jars, put the powdered herb inside, and add alcohol until the jar is about half full. Put the plastic wrap over the opening of the jar, and then put on the lid; this keeps the alcohol vapors from coming into contact with metal, which can spoil the result. Put the jar in a warm place—right around 100 degrees is best—and leave it there for several hours at the very least. (There is effectively no maximum; the longer the herb macerates, the stronger the resulting tincture will be.) You'll know that the extraction is well under way as the alcohol takes on an increasingly dark green color.

When you decide the maceration is ready, pour the alcohol out of the first canning jar, through the cheesecloth and funnel, into the second. Once again, seal it with the plastic wrap, put on the lid, and put it away in a closet. Scoop out the herb, spread it on the bottom of the baking pan, and take the whole thing outside. Set it on a fireproof surface, and drop a lit match onto the alcohol-soaked herb. The alcohol will burn with a cool bluish flame and there will be a good deal of smoke. Stir the herb with a metal spoon at intervals, to make sure that all the alcohol has burned away. If there's any significant amount of wind, you may need to shield the pan or use a screen; it's important that the fine ash not be lost.

When the flame has gone out and the herb no longer smells of alcohol at all, take the baking pan into the kitchen, cover it, put it in the oven, and begin baking at 500 degrees or more. This step is also going to produce a good deal of smoke, so you'll want to disconnect smoke alarms and open windows beforehand. The goal is to calcine the herb—that is, to reduce it to a white or grayish-white ash. All through this process, keep a careful eye on the oven and check it at regular intervals.

When the herb has been calcined, turn off the oven and let everything cool down to room temperature. Put the ash—the alchemical salt of the herb—into the mortar and grind it up into fine powder with the pestle. Pour it carefully into the jar you've chosen for the final product. Then, using the eyedropper, add the alcohol extract you made from the original herb, a little at a time, until the ash has absorbed as much liquid as it can. The result will be a Vegetable Stone, a waxy whitish substance that contains all the magical virtue of the original plant, multiplied many times over. It should be stored in a cool, dark place, and examined at intervals; it will tend to change slowly in color and other characteristics as it matures.

Other alchemists prefer to keep the alchemical salt and the tincture separate, and to combine a teaspoon of the tincture with a few grains of the salt for each use. In either case, a very small quantity of either the Stone or the salt-tincture mixture can be added to water to produce a powerful potion. This can be used for ordinary magical purposes, but alchemical processes have a spiritualizing effect; this means, among other things, that an alchemical potion will tend to have potent transformative effects on the person who takes it, no matter what the intended purpose; it also means that misuse of alchemical magisteries for selfish or destructive purposes tends to bring an especially heavy backlash. Here as elsewhere in this art, a word to the wise is sufficient.

Bibliography

Albertus, Frater (Albert Reidel), *The Alchemist's Handbook* (NY: Weiser, 1974).

Anonymous, *An Herbal* [1525] (NY: New York Botanical Garden, 1941).

Anonymous, *The Kalendar & Compost of Shepherds* (London: Peter Davies, 1930).

Arano, Luisa Cogliati, *The Medieval Health Handbook: Tacuinum Sanitatis* (NY: Braziller, 1976).

Best, Michael R. and Frank H. Brightman, eds., *The Book of Secrets of Albertus Magnus* (NY: Oxford UP, 1973).

Beyerl, Paul, *The Master Book of Herbalism* (Custer, WA: Phoenix, 1984).

Bramson, Anne, *Soap: Making It, Enjoying It* (NY: Workman, 1975).

Budge, E. A. Wallis, *Amulets and Talismans* (New Hyde Park: University Books, 1968).

Cavitch, Susan Miller, *The Natural Soap Book* (Pownal, VT: Storey, 1995).

Culpeper, Nicholas, *Culpeper's Complete Herbal & English Physician* (Glenwood, IL: Meyerbooks, 1990).

Dodt, Colleen, *The Essential Oils Book* (Pownal, VT: Storey, 1996).

Evans, Joan, *Magical Jewels of the Middle Ages and Renaissance* (NY: Dover, 1976).

Ficino, Marsilio, ed. and tr. Carol V. Kaske and John R. Clark, *Three Books on Life* (Binghamton: Renaissance Society of America, 1989).

Freeman, Margaret B., *Herbs for the Medieval Household* (NY: Metropolitan Museum of Art, 1943).

Frisk, Gosta, ed., *A Middle English Translation of Macer Floridus De Viribus Herbarum* (Uppsala: Almqvist & Wiksells, 1949).

Gerard, John, *The Herbal, or General History of Plants* (NY: Dover, 1953).

Gordon, Lesley, *Green Magic: Flowers, Plants and Herbs in Lore and Legend* (Exeter: Ebury, 1977).

Greer, John Michael, *Circles of Power: Ritual Magic in the Western Tradition* (St. Paul: Llewellyn, 1997).

————, *Earth Divination, Earth Magic* (St. Paul: Llewellyn, 1999).

————, *Paths of Wisdom: Principles and Practice of the Magical Cabala in the Western Tradition* (St. Paul: Llewellyn, 1996).

Hansen, Albert, *Gem Lore* (Seattle: Ivy Press, 1903).

Heninger, S. K., *A Handbook of Renaissance Meteorology* (Durham, NC: Duke UP, 1960).

Huson, Paul, *Mastering Herbalism* (NY: Stein & Day, 1974).

Hyll, Thomas, *The Gardener's Labyrinth, or, A New Art of Gardening* (London: Jane Bell, 1652).

Johnson, Jerry Mack, *Down Home Ways* (NY: Greenwich, 1978).

Junius, Manfred, *Practical Handbook of Plant Alchemy* (NY: Inner Traditions, 1985).

Kunz, George Frederick, *The Curious Lore of Precious Stones* (NY: Lippincott, 1913).

Lawless, Julia, *The Encyclopaedia of Essential Oils* (Rockport: Element, 1992).

Lust, John, *The Herb Book* (NY: Bantam, 1974).

Miller, Richard Alan, and Iona Miller, *The Magical and Ritual Use of Perfumes* (Rochester, VT: Destiny, 1990).

Mohr, Merilyn, *The Art of Soapmaking* (NY: Camden House, 1979).

Porteous, Alexander, *Forest Folklore, Mythology and Romance* (London: George Allen & Unwin, 1928).

Raetsch, Christian, *The Dictionary of Sacred and Magical Plants* (Bridport, Dorset: Prism, 1992).

Seton, Ernest Thompson, *The Book of Woodcraft and Indian Lore* (Garden City, NY: Doubleday, 1926).

Smith, Steven R., *Wylundt's Book of Incense: A Magical Primer* (York Beach, ME: Weiser, 1989).

Stavish, Mark, *A Short Course of Plant Alchemy* (in preparation).

Wigginton, Eliot, ed., *The Foxfire Book* (NY: Anchor, 1972).

Worwood, Valerie Ann, *The Fragrant Mind: Aromatherapy for Personality, Mind, Mood, and Emotion* (Novato, CA: New World, 1996).

Zalewski, C. L., *Herbs in Magic and Alchemy* (Bridport, Dorset: Prism, 1990).

Index

REACH FOR THE MOON

Llewellyn publishes hundreds of books on your favorite subjects!
To get these exciting books, including the ones on the following pages,
check your local bookstore or order them directly from Llewellyn.

Order by Phone

- Call toll-free within the U.S. and Canada, 1–800–THE MOON
- In Minnesota, call (651) 291–1970
- We accept VISA, MasterCard, and American Express

Order by Mail

- Send the full price of your order (MN residents add 7% sales tax) in U.S. funds, plus postage & handling, to:

  Llewellyn Worldwide
  P.O. Box 64383, Dept. K295-X
  St. Paul, MN 55164–0383, U.S.A.

Postage & Handling

(For the U.S., Canada, and Mexico)

- $4.00 for orders $15.00 and under
- $5.00 for orders over $15.00
- No charge for orders over $100.00

We ship UPS in the continental United States. We ship standard mail to P.O. boxes. Orders shipped to Alaska, Hawaii, the Virgin Islands, and Puerto Rico are sent first-class mail. Orders shipped to Canada and Mexico are sent surface mail.

International orders: Airmail—add freight equal to price of each book to the total price of order, plus $5.00 for each non-book item (audio tapes, etc.).

Surface mail—Add $1.00 per item.

Allow 2 weeks for delivery on all orders.
Postage and handling rates subject to change.

Discounts

We offer a 20% discount to group leaders or agents. You must order a minimum of 5 copies of the same book to get our special quantity price.

Free Catalog

Get a free copy of our color catalog, *New Worlds of Mind and Spirit*. Subscribe for just $10.00 in the United States and Canada ($30.00 overseas, airmail). Many bookstores carry *New Worlds*—ask for it!

Visit our website at www.llewellyn.com for more information.

Earth Divination, Earth Magic
A Practical Guide to Geomancy

John Michael Greer

Here is a complete manual of the art of geomancy—one of the three major divination systems (including astrology and tarot) that are part of the Western magical tradition. Much of the material in this book has been completely out of print since the Renaissance.

The medieval and Renaissance traditions of geomancy made use of simple but powerful methods of interpretation that are easy to learn and use. *Earth Divination, Earth Magic* provides history and basic theory, a detailed guide to the symbolism and meaning of the sixteen geomantic figures, and a thorough set of instructions for casting a chart. You will also learn how to use the figures as focal symbols for meditation and clairvoyance, and as sigils for talismans and ritual magic.

- Discover long-forgotten methods of geomantic divination used in the Middle Ages and the Renaissance

- Explore methods of meditation, clairvoyance, and ritual magic connected to geomancy

- Read a complete fourteenth-century manual on the interpretation of geomantic figures, translated out of medieval Latin into English for the first time

1-56718-312-3
6 x 9, 264 pp., illus. $12.95

To order, call 1-800-THE MOON
Prices subject to change without notice

Circles of Power
Ritual Magic in the Western Tradition

John Michael Greer

Despite its popularity, the Golden Dawn system of magic has potentials that are all but untapped. Even the simplest Golden Dawn practices have aspects that have never been brought out in print. Hidden away in the Order's papers, those of its successor Orders, and in the older traditions on which the Golden Dawn was based, are little-known techniques and approaches that give the system much of its power and meaning.

Circles of Power is the definitive practical handbook on the Cabalistic magic of the Golden Dawn. It goes step-by-step through the entire body of Cabalistic ritual magic, from the basic building blocks of the system, through simple ceremonial workings, to powerful advanced techniques of energy work and personal transformation. Dozens of detailed rituals, most of them completely new, allow the power of Golden Dawn magic to be put to work in a wide range of applications.

1-56718-313-1
6 x 9, 384 pp., illus. $20.00

To order, call 1-800-THE MOON
Prices subject to change without notice

Paths of Wisdom

Principles and Practice of the Magical Cabala in the Western Tradition

John Michael Greer

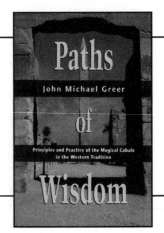

Unlock the hidden potentials of your self and the universe—of macrocosm and microcosm—with the key of the Cabala. *Paths of Wisdom* gives you complete instruction to perform Cabalistic magic. This general introduction to the magical Cabala in the Golden Dawn tradition will be used by the complete beginner, as well as by the more experienced magician or Cabalist. But *Paths of Wisdom* also contains practical material on the advanced levels of Cabalistic work, based on a perspective inherent in most of the Golden Dawn-derived approaches to magic. Originating as a secret mystical school within Judaism, Cabala was transmitted to the great magicians of the Renaissance and became the engine behind the body of Western magical methods. From Cornelius Agrippa to the adepts of the Golden Dawn, the magicians of the West have used the Cabala as the foundation of their work. Central to this tradition is an understanding of magic that sees esoteric practice as a spiritual Path, and an approach to practical work stressing visualization and the use of symbolic correspondences. Through meditation, Pathworking, magical rituals, and mystical contemplation you'll incorporate the insight of the Cabala into your daily life.

1-56718-315-8
6 x 9, 416 pp., illus. $20.00

To order, call 1-800-THE MOON
Prices subject to change without notice